To Sybil, my wife and friend

ACKNOWLEDGEMENTS

With many thanks to all the following for their help with this book:

Bill Allen (Gomark)
Ken Bell (Computer Aided Services)
Bob Campbell (Letraset)
Alan Coul (Amtech International Ltd.)
Martyn Day (CADdesk)
Sally Day (Techex)
Emma Freeman (Aptech)
Simon Hayes & Jo Epstein (KRCS)
Paul Holmes & Louise Stewart-Muir (Computers Unlimited)
Hilary Lambert (Digital Media Systems Ltd.)
Evelyn Ness (of Leading Edge, for Adobe)
Daphne Powers (Symbolics Ltd.)
Kanwal Sharma (Lewis Sharma Design & Apple UK)
Margaret Silk (Softline Distribution Ltd.)
Jonathan Stoppi (Cadonmac)
Tom Schlageter (AVA CAD/CAM)
Sabina Thompson (Apple Centres West)
Stephen Ward (AutoDesk)

Special thanks to Bill Allen and Paul Holmes for their time and
interest, and also to Mike Phillips for many helpful comments on the
first draft of the book.

TRADEMARKS
Throughout this book trademarked names occur. Rather than put a
trademark symbol in every occurrence of a trademarked name, we
state that the names are used only in an editorial fashion and to the
benefit of the trademark owner with no intention of infringement of
the trademark.

CONTENTS

CHAPTER 1

INTRODUCTION

There is a particular magic about creating and moving objects in three dimensional space of which I never tire and which I hope to share with the reader. Computer modelling is an exciting area in which to become involved. Computers have not only revolutionised traditional modelling in many cases but have allowed excursions into areas of complexity which have never before been possible and have made these journeys accessible to users without the previously required specialist skills.

This book looks at current modelling and rendering on the Apple Macintosh range of computers. It also deals with some aspects of the subject which are not yet implemented in applications for the Mac (in the confident expectation that they will be soon) and aims to give an overview of the background to computer modelling. Whilst it is not possible to write with total confidence about hardware and software that is not yet available, we can be sure that computers will grow faster and more powerful and that these improvements will broaden the range of people building computer models, and increase the sophistication of the models they can build.

I have tried to produce a book which can be useful not only to the novice but also to the experienced modeller who is new to the Mac and to the experienced Mac user who is new to modelling. As a result there will be chapters which readers in each of the last two categories can pass by.

The book deals, in some depth, with the principles involved in modelling and rendering, as this theoretical knowledge helps to make sense of the practical issues of building a model on a computer. Apart from anything else, when you appreciate how much work the machine is having to do to produce a full-colour, high resolution, photo-realistic rendering of your detailed model of the universe, you might begin to forgive the delay in bringing it to screen! I also wanted to suggest what is possible on the Mac in different modelling categories; architecture, for example, being likely to make very different demands from those of animated TV advertisements.

It would be ideal to be completely familiar with every modelling and rendering package available for the Mac, but this is not practical, even though it is very quick to start working with a new package on such a user-friendly machine as the Mac. Often it is possible to go a long way without any reference to the manual, but to appreciate each package's strengths and weaknesses, to learn each new paradigm that is offered, and to become fluent in working with any one piece of software takes weeks, or months, of continuous involvement. I have, therefore, looked at a large number of packages, worked briefly with most of them, worked seriously with some of them, read all the available reviews and asked the opinions of those who use them regularly.

Since many applications will be updated in the lifetime of this book, it is not appropriate to criticise features which might well be improved in future upgrades. It is intended, therefore, that the appendix which looks at current Mac applications should give the reader a sense of the variety of ways in which software for modelling and rendering can be implemented, as well as briefly listing the features of each specific package.

In particular I have tried to illustrate the main features of each modeller's interface, as this gives very strong clues about what the package is intended to do, and how it is intended to be used. In no case were those important first impressions given by the interface seriously contradicted by the later behaviour of the package. Whilst I am sure that anyone can learn to use any program, I believe that you can tell very quickly which is going to be the one for you (bearing in mind that each has been designed with a different type of person in mind). Are you, for instance, an artist or an engineer? Do you want to doodle your way to a final model or to describe it precisely by numerical input? Will you be plotting out the result or animating it on video?

A recent survey shows that 87% of designers work on Macs, but whatever your current discipline and whatever your background, the hardware and software to do the job you want are out there waiting for you now. There has never been a better time to go 3-D on a Mac.

CHAPTER 2

MODELLING & RENDERING

It would be easy to start writing about the 'How?' and the 'Why?' of computer modelling without stopping to mention the 'What?'. Consider briefly, therefore, the fundamental nature of the processes we are to look at and the new tools they provide.

2.1 WHAT IS MODELLING ?

Modelling might seem like an exciting thing to do, but what exactly is it and why is it so different from merely drawing ?

Since you are already reading this book you are likely to be sufficiently interested in the subject to have considered the question, but many people have an initial difficulty in making the conceptual jump from two dimensions to three and this, therefore, seems a good place to start. The world around us is three-dimensional, having height, width and depth. Although we can talk about a picture being two-dimensional, in the real world the drawn marks are wedded to a surface which has a measurable thickness and a locatable position in three dimensional space. It also has an existence in time, which is often termed the fourth dimension, and this temporal dimension is entered if we need to animate something (though it is not of primary interest to us here). In order to design for this world, to imitate parts of it, or to create some other imaginary world, we need to be able to work in all three spatial dimensions. This is unavoidable when working with real materials – sawing wood, building with bricks or moulding clay for instance, as we manipulate them with our hands, but if we need to develop our ideas using a two-dimensional medium, such as in a drawing or on a computer screen, then we need to adopt an appropriate visual language.

This might appear intuitively obvious, but we see the problem from a Western, post-renaissance viewpoint where perspective is understood and photographs are familiar. It does, however, require a degree of intellectual sophistication to interpret flat images which describe the three-dimensional world.

2.2 NAVIGATING A 3-D COMPUTER WORLD

How is it possible to navigate a three-dimensional environment when we are looking at a two-dimensional monitor screen ? Perspective gives us a lot of assistance and the overlapping of solid objects indicates their relative spatial positions although real world depth clues are often much more subtle. Spatial depth can be indicated by the diminution of scale of texture in a scene, though aerial perspective is more difficult to evoke. This change in the apparent colour and clarity of distant objects, due to atmospheric influences, can be simulated only at the expense of much computing time. We will look at the way objects can be represented on the screen in the section on viewing models.

Many 3-D modelling packages offer three or four different views of the current scene on the screen at once in separate windows. Top view (plan), front view (front elevation) and side view (side elevation) for example, offer three co-ordinated diagrams which allow spatial positions to be evaluated accurately though not intuitively. Each of these two dimensional views is parallel to the plane of the monitor screen and the cursor can, therefore, travel around it to access the contents in an understandable fashion. The choice of views can usually be set to determine whether the view is of top or bottom, front or back, left or right, and additionally a 'camera' view gives a perspectival view (as if looking through a camera viewfinder) from a defined point in space which corresponds

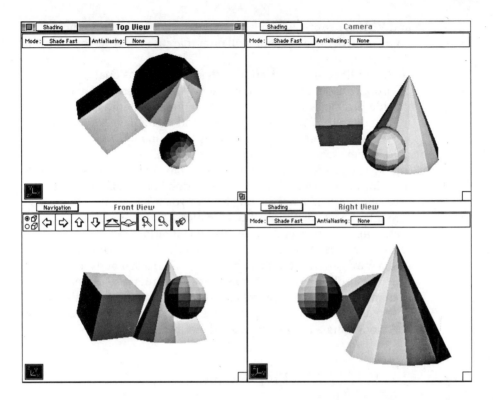

The 4 view windows in the modeller Infini-D

to the viewer's imagined position. These windows can be redrawn as close to simultaneously as the application will allow, though inevitable delays can make interactive navigation tedious and it is common to use abbreviated versions of the object(s), when possible, for the sake of speed. Some applications offer a single, perspectival view of the current scene which immediately raises the question of how movement in the extra dimension can be made clear.

The means of achieving this varies according to the application, but one solution is for the mouse alone to control movement in one plane (i.e. in two dimensions) and for the mouse, when used with a prescribed key held down, to allow movement through a plane at right angles to the first (i.e. the third dimension). This is only one of a number of solutions in use, and it tends to take a period of familiarisation before any method becomes comfortable to use. The ability to seem to enter into the scene itself would be very helpful and Virtual Reality, which is mentioned later but is currently at a crude state of development, will offer that possibility at some time in the near future.

An additional complication with a thre- dimensional environment is that you can only see all of the scene if you are outside it. Once you have moved your viewpoint into the scene you may find that objects lie behind you, and if you have stayed outside the scene but magnified your view by 'zooming in', your reduced field of view may have cut off your sight of all objects. Most interface tools are not expressive enough to deal with these problems in an intuitive way and since monitors don't have wing mirrors it becomes a little like negotiating a room you are in whilst looking through a cardboard tube. The Macintosh, however, has a reputation for offering best available interface in a given situation and is as good as any in the modelling field, although the spatial navigation solutions are not as standardised between different applications as other aspects of the interface. Indeed it has been instructive, in the course of researching this book, to discover how many different paradigms there are for satisfactorily describing and navigating a three-dimensional world on a computer screen.

2.3 WHAT IS RENDERING ?

Our first impression, or mental picture, of computer modelling might well be of transparent, line-drawn, geometrical objects in an endless grey vacuum, a world of mathematical scenes and algebraic surfaces. This description of the generation of computer models suggests a heavily diagrammatic representation of any real world, and in order to create a realistic image of the world our objects need more treatment than just having their hidden surfaces removed.

Objects in the real world are illuminated by light of different colours and qualities coming from a range of sources and directions, they cast shadows, they can reflect the world around them, they can exhibit different degrees of transparency, they have different surface qualities and we will need to be able to simulate these varied, textured and patterned surfaces. The interaction of all these qualities can give us a rich understanding about models and the scene they inhabit.

It is now possible to create computer generated images of stunning, photographic realism. Looking at such images, however, one rapidly becomes aware that this super-realism is often achieved within a limited domain where clean geometry and pure light prevail; probably with man-made objects in an artificially lit interior. The search is on for ways of dealing with less amenable subjects and, as always, the search can be as much fun as the solution. It is my hope that readers of this book will contribute to that solution. A way of giving 'difficult' subjects a similarly lifelike treatment *will* be found, and it is interesting to speculate as to whether the modelling paradigms available to us now will be adequate for the task, or whether a completely new vision will be required.

A model displayed in wireframe form (top), in quick shaded form (centre) and in smooth shaded form (bottom).

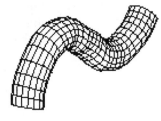

Computer modelling is not just about mimicking the world, however. Indeed it is often our choice not to observe rules which are absolute in real life. For example, in our computer-generated world we can decide whether an object will cast a shadow and we can create scenes where some objects cast shadows and others do not, or where some light sources cause shadows to be cast and others do not. We can decide what will be seen in reflective surfaces and can apply different rendering principles to different parts of the scene.

Rendering is, therefore, about making visible the objects and their given surface attributes under the chosen illumination and is made possible by the application of mathematical rules which determine how light will interact with the scene. A number of rendering algorithms exist, with varying levels of sophistication, and operating at different levels of computational expense.

2.4 THE ROLE OF THE DESIGNER

The medium is properly used when it either extends the range of things the designer can do visually or makes easier, quicker or cheaper an existing part of the design process. Whether the presentation and manipulation of a 3-D logo is poetic or crass depends on the skill of the designer and the sensitivity of whoever commissions it; it is not a property of the medium itself. It is, however, often the case that a medium stimulates ideas and visions to grow in a particular direction. If the designer is constrained by the hardware and software available, with a machine designed for typographical aerobatics and with a 'chrome' rendering option, then the results may be predictable and the existence of those features on his machine will have been partly the result of market forces. The good designer will always be breaking new ground and consequently pushing hardware and software to its limits, but he will rarely be in a position to write software to push beyond the current limits of his application. There is, therefore, at graphics' leading edge, a growing liaison between designers, programmers and computer scientists.

CHAPTER 3

APPLICATIONS

There are unlimited applications for computer modelling and it is
not practical to try to list them all. It is, however, worth isolating a
few disciplines that make use of the medium and then to use them as
examples to consider how their requirements can differ from one
another. At this stage we are looking at the broadest range of uses of
modelling, and in some specialised cases this discussion takes us
beyond off-the-shelf applications currently available on the Mac. It
is, never-the-less, likely that Macintosh hardware and software plays
a major part in the work of all the areas mentioned.

3.1 ARCHITECTURE

Probably the most obvious single use of computer modelling is in
architecture. Towns and buildings are usually straightforward to
model on a computer, and this ability is increasingly utilised by
architects, not only to experiment with different structures but also
to demonstrate their choices to the client before large amounts of
money are spent. Having modelled a proposal within its local
environment, it is then possible to move around the model, viewing
the building from any position, viewing the surroundings from
within the building and assessing the total physical relationship of

the building to its surroundings. The shadows cast by the building, by its neighbours and by trees on site can all be anticipated with far greater ease than previously possible, and on a sophisticated model it might be possible to simulate airflow around and through the new site.

It is equally possible to travel through the building to preview the internal appearance and layout, to try different permutations of lighting, different decors, changes of ceiling height and position of windows, for instance. The same data base from which the model is constructed might be accessed by an expert system to calculate percentage area of windows, heat loss under different conditions and conformity to changing building regulations. Animation offers the possibility of anticipating traffic flow problems by watching them develop on screen, or of seeing the shadow from the new office tower creep round to engulf the nearby housing estate, and it is clear that this will become a major planning tool. An architect designing a child care centre has already been able to 'test out' his design by moving around it 'as a child', in this case exploiting technology (described later) which enabled him actually to move like a child as well as see from a child's viewpoint.

In a simpler case, the remodelling of a foyer or a domestic kitchen can be previewed much more clearly by a client who has no experience of reading plans, than could be traditionally, where those plans were likely to be supplemented only by an artist's impression or single perspective view. A floor plan can be entered into the computer and 'extruded' to make a basic 3-D model in a few moments, after which you can 'move around' anywhere inside or outside that space. This offers the improved efficiency of making and viewing changes in company with the client and together with others in the design team. A reservation about computer modelling is that it has an immediate believability and appearance of finality which a rough sketch avoids. There is also a superficial credibility about a clean computer model which might disguise flaws and design weaknesses from the layman. The rough sketch, however, is somehow pregnant with possibilities which the computer model has tidied out of the way, and it can be most fruitful when the two techniques can coexist.

It may also be desirable to avoid the time and expense of building a traditional model, particularly at the stage of competing for a job, by substituting a computer model. This can be a major economy if the plans are already on a computer since that same data can be used to generate the computer model.

3.2 3-D DESIGN

The 3-D designer may be creating anything from a high speed train to a hairpin, but is increasingly likely to be doing it on a computer. This likelihood has increased since the introduction of much more intuitive modellers, which allow looser, more 'sketchy' ideas to be translated into three-dimensional objects. A problem still exists about matching the flexibility and openness of a thumb-nail sketch on the back of an envelope with a formal 3-D modeller, but the application of artificial intelligence in pen-driven devices such as Apple's 'Newton' could offer a clue to bringing the two together. It might, however, prove to be inadvisable to try and have the computer guessing at the meaning of a scribbled drawing, since it can be the very ambiguity of the sketch that provokes fresh ideas to develop.

As a design matures, it becomes increasingly important that it can be understood unambiguously, and a standard modeller can bestow complete mathematical accuracy on the three-dimensional design. When the process moves from design to manufacture the computer model can be passed on down the line to be used in the design of production tools and can possibly be used for ergonomic or stress testing.

A packaging designer will need to be able to wrap flat images around the product and its container and will probably then need to be able to insert the product either into a simulated environment or into a photograph of one. These requirements bring the need to integrate 2-D and 3-D material in the same environment. Finally, the model might go on to be used in an animated TV advertisement for the product.

A further development might be for the manufacture of the object to be controlled by the same program that created the model. In CAM the computer is connected to the machine (such as a lathe) which produces the component and the data describing the object (which could have come from the CAD half of the same package) determines its operation. A number of production methods exist for getting from the data to an object; the object itself perhaps being a prototype model which will provide fresh information that is in turn used to modify the original design. This is the world of CAD/CAM (Computer Aided Design/Computer Aided Manufacture) and one of the CAD/CAM packages available on the Mac was used by Apple to design the Quadra 800 case and its new ergonomic 'split' keyboard.

3.3 ENGINEERING

The designer of a high speed train will be one specialist working in a team with other specialists such as engineers. In the construction of a bridge or oil refinery, however, the design function may rest with the engineer alone. The engineer might also require a model which gives him access to specialised information, in order to assess component stress for example, and might use techniques such as finite element methods to that end. Although a very specialised field, it is interesting to note, in such a case, how the model can be constructed to provide specific and measurable feedback to its creator.

It is also worth considering to what extent a discipline such as engineering might be (and has been) impacted by computer modelling. In aeronautics, for example, engineers can now study the effects of stresses and strains on the airframe by simulating meteorological extremes, G-forces etc., and subsequently check modifications against the same conditions. This leads to an understanding of the operational limits and to the definition of the aircraft's flight envelope.

RFT (Right First Time) engineering is gaining converts, particularly in industries such as aerospace which have high development costs. Firstly, initial specifications are run through a computer to identify early errors and thus make cost savings. Secondly, design and testing procedures are enacted on screen when possible, in order to minimise the need to make real prototypes and to shorten the time it takes to reach a final product. The latter stage is largely dependent on 3-D computer modelling.

3.4 SIMULATION

An American firm specialises in creating animated computer
simulations for use in lawsuits. It recreates car crashes which have
involved the litigants, incorporating parameters based on those
present in the actual accident in order that the incident can be
studied in court. This is in accord with one definition of simulation:
the reproduction of the conditions of (a situation etc.), as in carrying
out an experiment. It is more problematic as a piece of legal
evidence if an alternative definition of simulate is tried: to make a
pretence of, to feign. A simulation must embody truth about the
situation it seeks to reproduce but at the same time need not pretend
to be that actual situation. Whilst recognising that we are looking at
organisations of pixels denoting two automobiles on a flat screen, we
can derive useful information about what two real vehicles would do
in a given situation, providing the representations have been
programmed to make accurate responses in terms of the masses,
forces and frictions involved in real life. Simulations seek to model
reality with different levels of fidelity. This is modelling 'plus', since
the model has not only spatial dimensions but also attributes that
affect its performance in the temporal dimension, such as mass and
centre of gravity. These features only come to life in an animation.

As well as being able to recreate an incident from the past, it is
practical, and more usual, to want to create a simulation of a
theoretical event. What would happen if one of the cars had been
travelling twice as fast? At what point would a bearing fracture if it
were put under an increasing load? By providing the right forces to
a model which 'knows' how to respond, we can watch the event
unfold before us, then vary the parameters and observe the changes.
This also allows us, in the right circumstances, to build and
animate a scene by describing the physical rules which will apply,
rather than having to control manually every element.

A special case of simulation is the flight simulator. A 'top-of-the-
range' flight simulator will model the experience of flying an aircraft
with such accuracy that flight sickness can be a genuine problem. At
the cost of several millions of pounds, the pilot can sit in the aircraft
of his choice, confronted with an authentic cockpit display, with a
full set of 'working' controls, a realistic view of his chosen airport
visible through the windscreen, appropriate engine noises, and can

'fly' the plane in any chosen conditions, with the correct flight characteristics. Hydraulic rams under his 'cockpit' tilt and rock him just as a real aircraft would do, and the combination of physical and visual stimuli is so convincing that it is necessary to concentrate very hard in order to have any doubt in the reality of the flight experience. In some military simulators, the addition of snug hydraulic suits through which pressure can be increased on the body, and seat belts which can exert sudden tension on the pilot, allow the stresses of acceleration and increased G-forces to be reproduced.

Even the relatively crude visual display of a flight simulator on a home micro is considered, by qualified pilots, to have a useful level of realism, and a Quadra power workstation still more. It is now permissible for trainee pilots to log hours towards their licence on inexpensive software such as 'Flight Simulator' from Microsoft. Flight simulators, of course, are more than just sophisticated fairground rides. They save aircraft, lives and money by allowing for efficient ground training, where landings and takeoffs from obscure airports can be practised repeatedly, responses to in-flight emergencies rehearsed and pilots 'converted' to new types of aircraft. Military pilots can practise bombing runs, in-flight refuelling and landings on aircraft carriers without risk of dangerous and expensive mistakes. These principles can also be applied to other types of vehicle and equipment – locomotive cabs, oil tanker bridges and anti-aircraft guns can all be simulated using similar techniques, and in each case the operator's world is produced by computer modelling.

Our interest is centred on the scene presented in the visual display, and a number of clever shortcuts may be implemented in order to be able to move realistically through a scene in real-time. Dusk and night simulations require less detail to feel realistic, and point light sources alone (which are easier to manipulate than polygons) may provide much of the visual information about an airfield at night. Instead of 'building' a city from polygons it might be possible to 'stick' pictures of the city onto highly simplified shapes. Similarly it is sometimes appropriate to produce authentic looking clouds by 'sticking' cloud pictures onto simple blocks, and shadows will often be acceptable if they are exist as silhouettes on an idealised ground plane, though failing to adapt to contours and obstructions.

3.5 MEDICAL

The ability to extract data from scans taken of patients and construct
from it three-dimensional computer models is proving an important
new diagnostic tool. Previous technology only presented two-
dimensional pictures of internal structures, and it was necessary to
resort to surgery in order to confront organs in three dimensions.
This new method makes it possible to build skulls, vertebra, hearts
and brains in the computer and then to manipulate them on screen.
Volume visualisation (described later) permits a three-dimensional
model of a body to be peeled back in layers to reveal the organ the
doctor requires to see. Any ambiguities about the exact form can be
further removed by animating the part, though it is likely that this
will not (currently) be in real time if using a highly detailed model.

     In all cases of medical imaging (and indeed any specialised area),
it is important to recognise that the computer operator must be
working with someone who knows what is being looked for and
what needs to be seen. Whilst you and I can look at a computer
model of a group of articulating vertebrae and be impressed with the
clarity with which their movements are shown, the animation is
medically useless if it does not reveal what the doctors need to see.
It is the person with medical skills who must decide what is needed
and the job of either the system or the operator to manipulate the
data to provide it. Increasingly friendly and intelligent systems
make it likely that the doctor and the operator will be one and the
same person, but at the current stage of development that is unlikely
to be the case.

     The reconstruction of shattered bones or rebuilding of a
deformed skull involves a three-dimensional jigsaw that can be
rehearsed on the computer model. Also of assistance to plastic
surgeons is the ability to experiment with manipulations at a model
stage, for instance checking on a model that bone removed from the
foot can be used to build a part of a jaw. General operation
simulators are being developed which will permit doctors to practise
surgery in simulated three-dimensional reality. This idea will soon
extend to operations being carried out by doctors hundreds of miles
from the patient and will be a serious part of future space flight
scenarios.

3.6 TV GRAPHICS

Although there is nothing unique about the computer modelling and rendering techniques used in TV graphics to distinguish them from those used in most other areas,they are, however, the most public manifestation of the art. TV graphics have been taken on board so readily by producers and designers wanting their programme introduction or promotion to have more punch than its rivals, that it has almost become the de facto standard. They have also become heavily used by television advertisers, notable for the size of budget they can sometimes make available. As a spin-off, this has unfortunately brought to millions of people, in the privacy of their homes, some of the most vulgar and needlessly expensive images of the century. The best examples of the genre have, however, become minor classics which enlighten and contribute to the discipline of graphic design.

It is hard to generalise about the use of computer modelling on television as its function and form will vary according to the context. Modelling technology has effectively provided an additional step in the evolution of video graphics and there are several areas where it is currently popular. A seminal example from UK television is the Robinson Lambie-Nairn ident for Channel 4 which was created in 1982 and is still running more than ten years later. Station 'idents' (logos, motifs or graphic sequences to identify a station), programme title sequences, information graphics and advertisements all make heavy use of the medium and it is almost universal, at the moment, for news programmes to employ computers in the production of their introductions. News programmes are something of a flagship for the stations and are an important way to establish their house style. The graphics may need to evoke qualities of honesty, seriousness, topicality and grittiness, define the relevant locality, reinforce the station's image and be accompanied by a matching soundtrack. The images used are usually iconic (the globe, the parliament building), the typography prominent, the animation smooth and pacey, and the overall feel often symbolic (reaching out across the airways, flying to the nation's pulse).

Strings of 3-D letter forms can be seen to lend themselves to geometric manipulation in space and are able to retain a high degree of legibility throughout major transformations. Such manipulations are well within the ability of Mac hardware and software and the Macintosh is increasingly finding itself a place in the production environment. It gives way, at the moment, to more specialist machines for a number of tasks, including heavy rendering operations, but is considered to be very cost effective. The video handling capacity of the newer Macs is also attracting great interest from TV production departments.

3.7 SPECIAL EFFECTS

Special effects (FX) can be a special case of TV and film graphics. As the credits roll on many feature length films today, reference will be seen to computer special effects. The ability to generate impossible visions 'realistically' is all in a day's work for the computer and has come to be widely exploited. Until recently the classic examples have been in space films, where computer modelled spacecraft, planets, meteorite showers and the like can be created and choreographed with some ease, often intercut or merged with live or model shot material. Increasingly, however, computer generated effects have become almost standard and films like 'Jurassic Park' rely heavily on them throughout. One advantage of computer generated sets, as opposed to hand-built models, is that they can be destroyed as often as you like and then restored at the touch of a button. This has to be set against the additional time currently taken to construct and render a complex computer model, though improving hardware and techniques will soon give the computer method a clear edge.

It has been estimated at Industrial Light & Magic, a company renowned for special effects production, that only about 2% of their effects currently use computers, and that whilst that percentage will increase,they will not take over entirely from the model makers who have honed their skills over a number of years. One of their stocks-in-trade is dirt and the ageing of models, which often seems alien to computer graphics programmers, and is not always easily implemented when required. It is also difficult, at the moment, for computer models to match the subtlety of lighting that exists on a real set, and the primary requirement of special effects is that they

MUST match the look of the rest of the film. A major advantage of computer graphics and animation, however, is that the 'virtual' camera and lights have zero dimensions. There is nowhere that the computer camera cannot go, no gap is too narrow for its passage and it can pass through walls to order. Similarly, scenes can be illuminated without the physical presence of real lights to contend with, so there are no cables to hide, nothing to keep out of shot, and no problems with heat or power.

In 'The Abyss' a remarkable special effect from Industrial Light & Magic models was a pool of water growing an arm-like tentacle which retained all its clear, reflective and transparent properties while it extended, moved towards actors, transformed its end into a face, and is touched by an actress. Its smooth, gently rippling motion made it totally like water and yet able to do things wholly impossible for water. The brilliant sequence took six people, with the assistance of part timers, six to eight months to produce seventy-five seconds of film (close to one second of animation per person per month). It also took four-and-a-half hours to render each frame, with a number of steps to ensure that fog, shading, reflection, refraction and highlights were all correctly shown. By coincidence, the research team at London's Electric Image was developing a similar effect at the same time, which serves to suggest that the leading edge of the discipline is internationally spread.

Transformations now commonly use digital technology to advantage and are quite common in fantasy films where a frog might metamorphose into a prince, for instance, or into an icecream. Several recent films, such as the 'Terminator' series, raise the technique to new heights, and the process of 'morphing' from one 3-D model to another is not difficult in principle. You will find in Appendix 1 that basic Mac modellers sometimes incorporate the facility, and that other software is cheaply available to morph 2-D images.

3.8 ART

Until recently much computer 'art' has been bad, often because it has not really been art at all but merely the visual product of computer scientists' experiments. There are, however, signs that the medium is improving and the computer is rapidly finding a place as a tool for artists. It has had its teething troubles (in the same way that photography did) but is starting to establish its own unique identity. William Latham has created sculptures on a computer which could not exist in real life, and the obvious way to view an imaginary sculpture is to move round it in a 3-D model. He uses constructional solid geometry and texture mapping (both described later), to create delicate, magical structures sometimes resembling hallucinogenic seashells, his software being custom written with a colleague. These forms are variously presented as photographs, on computer screens or in animations where the viewer is 'flown' through the intricate, coloured tunnels of the sculpture without the inhibitions of gravity or reality. The ability to waive the laws of gravity and to create 'impossible' objects in 'impossible' environments is potentially attractive to the artist, and the new-found availability of the means of such creation suggests fast development in the area.

The mathematical basis for some forms of art (remember 'op art'?) leave it open to obvious development by computer. This readily applies to work in 2-D and 3-D, where there has been a consistent interest for a number of decades, but it can also be extended into the fourth dimension with animation.

3.9 ANIMATION

Although I have mentioned computer animation several times, I have explained that it is not intended to deal with it in this book. (See *'The Art and Science of Computer Animation'* or wait for a proposed book on Mac animation from Intellect). There is, however, a growing use of computer animation, particularly of 3-D animation, and this must necessarily be preceded by building the 3-D models involved. Indeed, such animation can be broken down into three stages - modelling, choreography and rendering, of which two stages are within the remit of this book. Although computers are increasingly used in 2-D (and 2F(1,2)-D) animation, it is with 3-D that their presence is most significant, since it is here that they permit things to be created which could not be done any other way. The uses of 3-D computer animation are many and growing, stretching from Scientific Visualisation through education to entertainment.

One of the great exponents in the field of entertainment is John Lasseter, who is an ex-Disney animator working with a team at Pixar in California, well known for the computer animations 'Luxo Jnr.', 'Red's Dream', 'knicknack', and the Oscar winning 'Tin Toy'. My favourite of these is 'Luxo Jnr.', a miniature masterpiece in which the medium has become completely invisible and we enjoy the animation for itself. The stars are two angle poise (Luxo) lamps, mother and child, who act out a scene (in which the youngster plays with a ball watched by his parent) with a level of characterisation that is close to human. It is a classic example of the technology being handmaiden to the art, though in this case the technology has been developed to a very high level of sensitivity. Telling details include the understated set and palette (computer graphics too often has all the colour knobs set to maximum), the pinpoint accuracy of the few sound effects, and the proportioning of the child lamp. Instead of being a small version of the parent, it is proportioned in the same relationship of human child to adult: small light shade but same size bulb, shorter support rods and springs but with the same diameter . In this film the angle poise lamps lend themselves readily to computer modelling, being made up of geometrical shapes, and it is interesting to compare with the human baby in 'Tin Toy' where it is apparent that computers are far less willing to model a chubby, flexible child than spheres and cubes.

3.10 VIRTUAL REALITY

Virtual Reality (VR) is a much-hyped medium which allows the user to participate in a computer-generated world. This participatory experience can be either immersive or non-immersive. In immersive VR, the user has the apparent experience of being within, and able to move around in, a computer-generated scene; the current enabling technology being a head set with TV screens in front of each eye (allowing the user to look around the scene) and data gloves and suit (allowing interaction with, and feedback from, the scene itself). Non-immersive VR provides a window through which the user can view the scene and the means to change the view of the scene and to interact with it (in practical terms this is likely to mean looking at a VDU display).

Architects are already adding functionality to computer models of proposed buildings by turning them into 'virtual environments' which can then be navigated by issuing 'forward/back/left/right/ up/down' commands, often using the ubiquitous mouse. This allows the architects themselves, as well as their clients, to 'move through' and view any part of the building (on a screen) from any position. In fully immersive VR the user could navigate the building as if it really existed, walking forwards, turning left, looking up, etc.; also being able to touch and move virtual furniture, or even elements of the building itself, perhaps using an interactive glove with feedback.

This could be considered as more of a philosophical than functional step forward from the existing ability to manipulate, and interact with, a model on screen, but there is great potential for the application of VR. For example, as a means of robotic control in hazardous environments, or a means of doctors practising operations without using real patients, or (as has already been suggested) as a means of those doctors performing operations from Earth on astronauts in space!

Whatever the scenario, the computer model needs to be built and rendered, and companies are already specialising in this task. Relatively inexpensive programs now exist for the Mac which enable the creation, and non-immersive navigation, of models. As with most areas of computer animation, there is a trade-off between the complexity of the model and the speed with which it can be redrawn which provides an obvious impediment to smooth movement through a detailed scene. This will rapidly be overcome as subsequent generations of hardware become faster and more powerful, and meanwhile models can be built on a Mac for export to full VR systems running on the fastest hardware.

CHAPTER 4

FUNDAMENTALS

An understanding of the basics of computer graphics theory helps immensely when it comes to using any software package. It is perfectly possible to use a well designed application without knowledge of the theory underlying its operation, but the additional insight given by knowing how and why things happen as they do offers the user greater control. The manual for the application is likely to explain, for example, that certain modelling or rendering options are very time consuming, but knowing why that is so not only gives a greater over-all understanding of the package but makes it easier to plan more efficient ways of using the package. This chapter aims to give a compact introduction to those areas relevant to our subject, and a brief mention of some other areas that we might be drawn into. It assumes that the reader knows little or nothing about the subject and can be by-passed by those who have dealt with the subject before, although it should still offer a basic source of reference. There are many books dealing with computer graphics theory in great depth and I list my own recommendations in the bibliography.

4.1 DISPLAY

It is easy to forget that the monitor screen is only one of a number of different possible output devices (output is dealt with at greater length in the chapter on communicating with the Mac). As such it displays a representation of what is going on inside the computer to the best of its ability but should not be taken as an exact record of what the machine has calculated. It is possible, for instance, that a sphere is stored with complete mathematical accuracy in the memory of the computer but in displaying it on screen the limitations of resolution and palette size give us only an approximation of that perfect sphere. That might prove satisfactory in use but the increments available to us when navigating the screen are determined by the size of the pixels and these are unlikely to allow accurate alignment of parts of a model, for example. In this case, numerical entry from the keyboard might be used to achieve the necessary accuracy, which the screen would then display as best it could. (The word *pixel* comes from shortening *picture element* and labels the basic dot-like unit from which a screen display is made. Typically, each square inch of screen might comprise 72 rows each of 72 pixels).

Enlargement of a letterform detail clearly showing the pixel structure

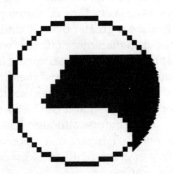

4.2 COORDINATES

In order to move about the screen, and for us and the computer to keep track of where we are (probably indicated by where the cursor is), a coordinate system is used. In the same way that a map reference locates a point as being at the intersection of imaginary lines drawn from one side and from the bottom (or top) of the map, so the pixel column and row numbers address specific screen locations. The horizontal axis is the 'X' axis and the vertical axis is the 'Y' axis. On a display with 624 horizontal lines each of 832 pixels, and with the origin (the point defined by 'X=0,Y=0') sited at the bottom left of the screen, then the pixel addressed by the reference 'X=416,Y=312' would be one of the four pixels surrounding the point dead centre of the screen. These are the screen coordinates.

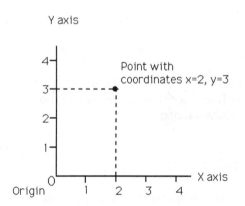

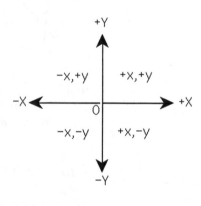

It is clearly necessary to distinguish between a position on the screen and the position of the model within its own world. If we zoom in on our view of the model then the screen co-ordinates referencing a point on the model (unless that point happens to coincide with the centre of the screen) will change, whilst the model itself will not have moved within its own world. A second set of co-ordinates, therefore, describes the position of the model within its own world, and the computer converts those coordinates to screen co-ordinates when displaying the model. As the model is three- dimensional, an extra axis, the 'Z' axis, is needed to indicate depth. The model's

Left: 2-D Cartesian coordinate system. Right: Positive and negative coordinate locations surrounding the origin.

world may be either infinite or limited along each axis. Since this world extends in all directions from its centre (where X=Y=Z=0), then each axis has a positive and a negative direction. For various reasons, the labelling of the axes has differed between different disciplines but for our purposes the only inconsistency we might

Right and left handed coordinate systems, showing the shift of the positive Z axis.

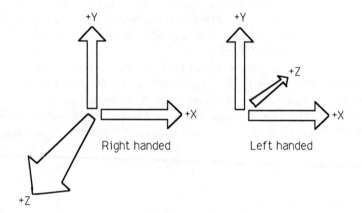

find is in the Z axis which is sometimes positive 'going away' from the viewer (known as left-handed) and occasionally positive 'coming towards' the viewer (known as right-handed).

4.2.1 RELATIVE AND ABSOLUTE

When modelling we are likely only to be presented with world co-ordinates, although the application might use other coordinate systems internally for its own purposes. These world coordinates are often presented as an XYZ readout in the margin of the current window (which updates as positional changes are made), and the co-ordinates of objects can often be accessed and modified through a specific object information box and often through a standard Apple information request using [Control + I]. It can be convenient to establish a rough position by manoeuvring on the screen and then using numeric input from the keyboard for precise positioning.

Positions and movements can be described as either relative or absolute. An absolute position is a specific location in the object's world as described by the world coordinates. A relative position does not refer directly to the world coordinates but is located in terms of distance along X, Y and Z (or a combination of distance and angles) from a known point in object space. This is useful if we wish to move an object a known distance from its current position without wanting to specify the world co-ordinates of the new location.

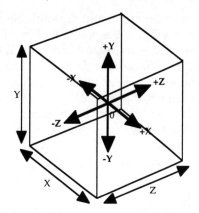

3-D Cartesian coordinate system

4.2.2 CARTESIAN COORDINATES

The 16th century philosopher and mathematician René Descartes gave his name to the Cartesian coordinate system which is the one described so far. This system locates a point by measuring along the X and Y axes in 2-D, and the X, Y and Z axes in 3-D from a given point of origin.

4.2.3 POLAR/SPHERICAL COORDINATES

An alternative to the Cartesian system is the polar coordinate system with which, in two dimensions, a position is located by its distance

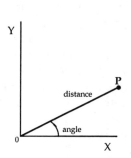
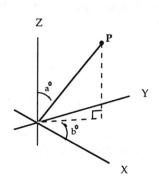

Left: 2-D polar coordinates
Right: 3-D spherical coordinates

from the origin and the angle between the X+ axis and a line from the origin to the point. In three dimensions two angles plus distance from the origin are required, and the method is known as the spherical coordinate system. This can be an intuitive way of moving about a space as it often matches better the way we think about changes of position. It is, for instance, a much more likely way to describe the flight of an aircraft to a location, but has not proved as clear a way of describing the location itself within currently screen-bound
applications.

4.2.4 HOMOGENEOUS CO-ORDINATES

Although not important to us as software users, homogeneous coordinates are mentioned here for the sake of completeness. They simplify the mathematics used to manipulate coordinates by the program, and require a three-dimensional point to be represented by a four number vector. If you look at any such calculations it can be confusing to see a point referenced by one number more than the expected three dimensions (e.g. the point x,y,z is represented by [x y z 1] to allow matrix multiplication).

4.3 RASTER

The image is formed on a normal display screen by a raster, which is a set of horizontal raster lines scanned along each successive row of pixels. A raster image is one which describes its subject in terms of the pixel intensities across its surface. It is, therefore, necessarily two dimensional and whilst it can (like a photograph) illustrate the view of an object from a single viewpoint, it does not 'know' about the object as a three-dimensional entity. A scene or object can be saved from a modeller as a PICT file, for instance, and can be subsequently loaded into a paint program where the bit mapped image (as it is called) can be manipulated. It can probably also be reloaded into a modelling program but only as a flat image to be used as a background, perhaps, or to wrap around an object for surface detail.

It cannot be reloaded into a modelling program and manipulated again as an object since it is only a picture of the object. This rapidly becomes obvious through use but it is not uncommon to find a student new to modelling having abandoned a model in the belief that any file saved will contain all the model's information.

4.4 VECTOR

If the information about an object (or a shape) is stored in terms of the spatial relationships between its vertices then it is in vector form. A file with this information is needed for an object to be recreated in its own three-dimensional space. If a two-dimensional shape, such as a type font, exists in vector form, then the lines describing its outline are objects as oppose merely to being marks in a raster image. The precision with which a vector model can be displayed is dependent on the resolution of the current display device (e.g. a monitor screen or printer) regardless of the precision at which it is stored, which could be absolute. The accuracy with which it is stored determines the accuracy with which it can be mathematically manipulated by the program however.

4.5 SPLINES

It is not easy to draw by hand a smooth line passing through set points but aids have evolved in other disciplines which can help. The 'French curve' is a template of curve profiles which draughtsmen utilise, and from shipbuilding comes a more complete solution. In order to draw the smooth curves of sections through ships' hulls, thin, flexible strips of wood or metal (called 'splines') were held down at key points by weights (called 'ducks'), and their natural, internal tension led them to take up a smooth curve through the weighted points. Mathematical equivalents of the shipbuilders' spline have been developed to provide us with a ready method of establishing a smooth path defined by a few controlling points. This is in contrast to a circle generated by a mathematical equation, for instance, whose smoothness depends on the number of points

A spline curve is modified by moving a single control point 'P'.

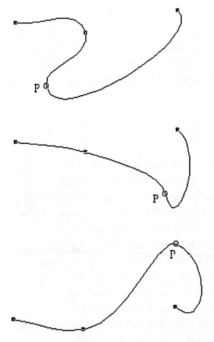

which have been used in its generation and display.

A curve can, therefore, be approximated by a raster display or by a continuous sequence of vector lines but can only be accurately described mathematically. Bezier, working for Renault, developed one of the most commonly-known formulations in order to be able to describe the curved panels of car bodies. The Bezier curve is one of a number of different splines which are defined by an equation using control points to establish varying degrees of curvature along a line. Moving a control point changes the curvature, but the nature of the change varies according to the formulation used. Sometimes the change is local to the point moved, in other cases the whole of the curve is affected. It should be noted in passing, that most types of spline curve do not normally pass through their control points. Current modelling packages are tending to use NURBS (non-uniform rational b-splines) which are the most flexible for many purposes. A surface can be created from a net of splines, the Bezier patch being an example in which adjacent patches with the correct continuity combine to create a complete surface.

Splines are extremely valuable now that modelling has developed beyond simple geometric shapes and tries to deal with contoured surfaces. They enable the creation of three dimensional objects and surfaces whose contours can be smoothly and easily changed by the movement of control points. Most modelling packages now support splines, though with different degrees of sophistication. The use of splines to define fonts allows many packages to create or import two-dimensional type for subsequent conversion to three-dimensional letter forms.

4.6 MODELLING

There are a number of ways of creating and describing 3-D objects such that their data can be stored and manipulated. Some methods log the history of the object's creation, some store a mathematical description and some list the position and connection of the object's vertices. Some deal with solid objects and some deal only with the surface facets of the object. Some descriptions accurately record the object but 'freeze' it so that the possibility of future manipulations becomes limited. All these methods have their own rationale and relevance, and most appear in current Mac modelling packages, but their structure is often hidden from the user.

4.6.1 METHODS

Any object, even a simple cube, can be created within modelling packages in several ways. The significance of the method used might affect how that object can be treated or how it can be used in the process of creating further objects. For example, the data created in making a cylinder with the B-rep 'spin' method will be for a faceted object whilst a cylinder in a CSG system will be understood as infinitely smooth. Since data types can be converted internally by the program, it is not necessarily obvious which method is being used. Fundamentally different principles for making objects are not, however, normally available within individual packages so it can sometimes be important to select the right modelling type for your particular requirement. This is not too difficult as products are often advertised as being for different markets, such as architecture or design visualisation, and for many unspecialised tasks any method can be adapted to serve.

4.6.1.1 B-REP

The most common method is to represent the boundary of the object, known informally as the 'B-rep' method. With B-rep the surface of an object is polygonised and the description stored as a list of

Typical range of primitives

vertices (the corners of the surface polygons), a list of lines joining the vertices (i.e. the edges of the polygons) and a list of faces identifying the individual polygons. For the purpose of rendering the object, these polygons are usually triangulated (meaning divided into triangles) since triangles are necessarily planar and so unambiguous surfaces. Triangulation is not necessary to the description of the object. However an object is produced, it can be given a B-rep description although this might prove to sacrifice accuracy.

4.6.1.2 PRIMITIVES

Modelling packages usually have available a small library of simple, generic three-dimensional models called primitives. These can be represented internally as individual entities (rather than as polygonal descriptions) which use little memory. Typically these will be a cube, sphere, cylinder, cone, torus, wedge, plane and perhaps others, the ability for the user to add more sometimes being available. These primitives can be scaled and modified within the application, often both interactively (such as with a mouse) and by numerical input, so that a sphere can become an egg and a cube can become a customised parcel.

These primitives provide building blocks for more complex objects, a simple camera being made, for example, from a cylinder abutting a cube

4.6.1.3 SWEPT FORMS

There is some inconsistency about the use of the term 'swept form', or more correctly 'swept surface model'. It has started to be used to describe a freeform subset of the general class of swept surfaces, but will here be used to refer to the whole class. The class can be summarised as being created as the result of a two-dimensional (XY) section being 'swept' through the third (Z) dimension.

4.6.1.3.1 SPUN

A two-dimensional template, either a closed or open shape, can be
rotated about an axis (conventionally around the Y axis) to create a
B-rep form. The traditional example is the creation of a bottle and

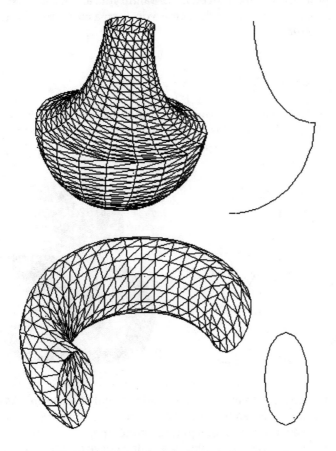

*Spun forms and their
templates
Top: With axis of
rotation meeting the
template
Bottom: With template
distanced from axis of
rotation*

wineglass, or, if a circular template is located outside the centre of
rotation a form like a doughnut is made. In these examples the arc
through which the template must be rotated to make a complete
form is 360 degrees, but most modellers allow for partial rotation in
order to create a form such as a melon slice. In the event of less than

full rotation, it is necessary to decide whether the sections at either end of the sweep are to be solid surfaces ('capped') or whether the form is to be open ended ('uncapped'). This modelling method is called spinning or lathing.

It is often possible to rotate the template about a changing point. If the point of rotation moved in a straight line along the Y axis, whilst rotation was about the same axis, then a corkscrew form would result.

4.6.1.3.2 EXTRUDED

If a template is swept in a direction orthogonal to the plane in which it lies, the resultant form is described as extruded. As an example, a square section could be extruded to make a cube, or a type font

Template and form
extruded from it

could be extruded to make a three dimensional letter form. As with spinning, the ends can be capped or open, so an uncapped cube could be seen as a length of square section pipe. If the line of extrusion is not straight (typically a spline curve option is an alternative) and/or if the template is also revolved, then complex twisting forms can result. The template may be held orthogonal to the path (like a pipe going around a bend) or else translated along the path (maintaining the same orientation).

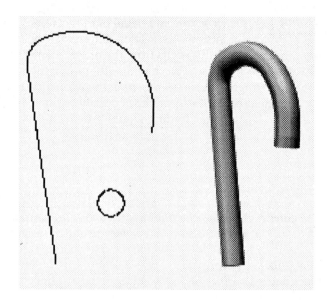

4.6.1.3.3 FREEFORM

Freeform is another word that finds itself variously applied to different aspects of modelling processes. Sometimes it is used to refer to the quality of a surface or form which is asymmetrical about all axes and sometimes to describe a surface or form which has a loose, sinuous quality as if drawn freehand (as opposed to being constructed with an obvious geometry). In some packages a specific freeform tool is available, and this normally enables the construction of an object by defining separate templates orthogonal to each of the three axes.

4.6.1.4 LOFTED

In the lofting process, consecutive cross sections through an object are joined by triangulation, a standard technique for creating an optimal surface of triangular patches between the edges of the sections. The cross-sections could be thought of as being like the geographical contour lines that define a hill, and the triangular patches as being the sides of the hill itself, the smoothness of the surface depending on the closeness and detail of the sections. The alignment of matching points on each section determines the model's coherence and usually results from the order in which the points are created, though in sections having different numbers of points the modeller might not connect them in the way intended by the operator. For this reason it is sometimes possible to specify which points are to be aligned. Lofting would provide a good way of constructing a ship's hull from its sectional members.

4.6.1.5 SKIN

The ability to construct the 'skeleton' of a form and then wrap a surface skin around it to create an object is very useful. The skin function available in some modellers appears to be merely lofting, but in more sophisticated form a skin uses a scaffolding of defined points at the intended surface of the object to create a splined surface.

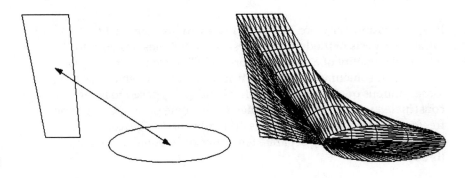

Two templates used to create simple skinned form

4.6.1.6 CSG

A modelling method popular in CAD systems is that of constructive solid geometry (CSG). In this approach an object is represented as a combination of simple primitives such as cube, sphere and cylinder. These basic solids are used as building blocks for more complex objects by means of a system which uses mathematical descriptions of the spatial relationships the primitives have to one another. Boolean set operations of union (+), intersection (-) and difference (&) describe the logical operations of adding two objects, subtracting one from another, or defining the overlap between two objects. The primitives can be scaled and it is also possible to define primitives by the use of 'half-spaces', which are infinite surfaces dividing three dimensional space into solid or void to define objects (any point exists in either the solid, the void or on the division and several half spaces can combine to define the space enclosing an object).

CSG is very economical in the information it stores, as the primitives are stored as mathematical forms rather than by listing all the vertices, etc. For example, it might require the storage of 45,000 co-ordinates alone to describe a moderately smooth B-rep sphere (in addition to all the necessary edge and face information) whilst a perfect sphere can be defined mathematically by four numbers – the three co-ordinates of the centre plus the radius. Complex objects are stored in a tree-like data structure that records the primitives used and the sequence of operations carried out on them.

Real world accuracy is one advantage of the system. This can be seen if a comparison is made between the CSG and B-rep methods for building a model having two rotating drums in contact with one another, such as might be required by an engineer. Because the CSG method uses mathematical descriptions of the primitives, the drums will have a constant diameter; however the B-rep method creates a polygonised approximation of a curve which means that the drums will always be faceted (however small the polygons used). This means that if the B-rep drums were brought together they would either have edges or facets in contact and would not be able to revolve freely. The comparison is somewhat confused by the fact that although a system is using CSG it will probably convert its models to B-rep in order to display

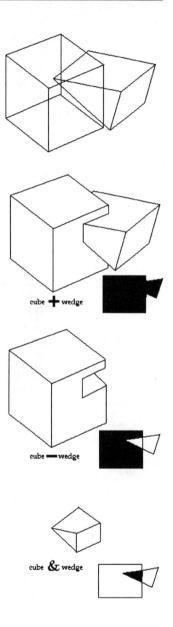

cube ✛ wedge

cube ━ wedge

cube **&** wedge

Boolean set operations

them on screen for ease of rendering. (We will see later that it is possible to use raytracing to render directly from the mathematics that constitutes the CSG objects, but that this particular method is too time consuming to be used for any but the final display).

4.6.1.7 VOXELS

A simple method which is of increasing interest, though used only in specialised modellers (such as for medical use) at the moment, is that of volume modelling. It is included here for the sake of completeness but is not used in any non-scientific Mac software that I know of. Correctly known as spatial occupancy enumeration, this

2 forms made from voxels

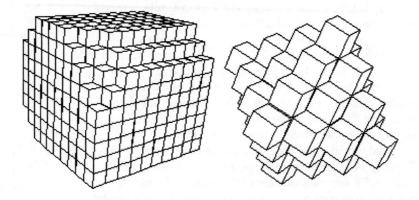

method divides three-dimensional space into cubic units called voxels, of whatever size is suitable, and the object is described by recording the units it occupies. A voxel is sometimes described as a three-dimensional version of a pixel (although the former is really a unit of object space and the latter a unit of screen space). Because, although blindingly simple, the method currently requires extensive data storage in order to describe an object at a useful resolution, various storage and search techniques have to be used with it. Volume models are very easily rendered, and the ability to 'peel' the models back in layers can be most useful.

4.6.1.8 FRACTALS

Fractals are becoming used in modellers to simulate structures like landscape where credible detail can be achieved by fragmenting a surface or object in a pseudo-random manner without recourse to a large data bank. The subject is too large to discuss here, but its use in high-end machines to generate clouds, mountains, rust and such like is sure to percolate through to our Mac software.

The development of 2-D fractal (left) and 3-D fractal (right)

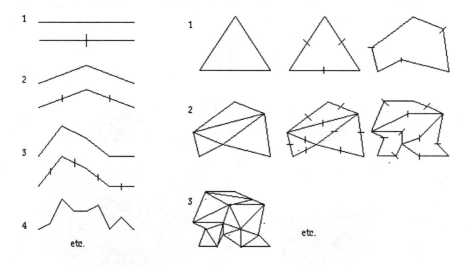

4.6.1.9 PARTICLES

Particle systems are not used in Mac software yet but are, again, mentioned here for the sake of completeness. They are a particular favourite of mine (I have a long term ambition to produce a Mac application for handling them), and consist of a large number of particles, typically between ten thousand and a million. Each particle represents a single point in three-dimensional space, and as a group they can simulate 'fuzzy' phenomena such as clouds, flames, grass or a waterfall. The particles are very easy to define, create, colour and move and they have proved very useful in scientific simulations for showing gas and water flow.

'Typhoon' particle system where each particle is represented by a line showing its recent path

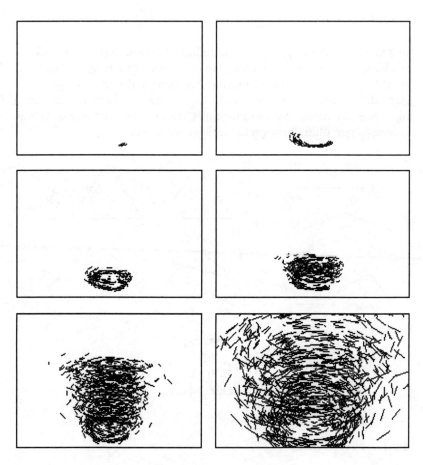

4.6.1.10 GRAMMAR-BASED

Once more outside the scope of existing Mac software, grammar-based systems use inbuilt rules to generate objects and have notably been used to simulate plant growth. The method is listed here as it presents a contrasting paradigm to the more conventional modellers, but though the structure of an object evolves differently using this method, it must still be made manifest through use of a previously-described method.

4.6.2 JOINTS

Not all the models we might want to build are made exclusively of separate, unrelated objects. Often objects have several connected parts, either physically jointed (like a door in a door frame) or in a fixed but distanced relationship (like a planet and its moons). Modellers normally allow these relationships to be established, firstly by creating links between objects (using a parent/child metaphor) and then by defining limitations to the freedom of movement of the links. It is thus possible to define a forearm as being the 'child' of an upper arm and the upper arm as the 'child' of the torso (which is its 'parent') in order to create an arm which has joints at elbow and shoulder. The two joints can have their movement limited around the X, Y and Z axes by set amounts to create a hinged elbow and a ball-jointed shoulder. When the parent object is moved its 'children' stay connected, but in any positional relationship permitted by the joint constraints.

4.6.3 FLEXIBILITY

But what if the object we wish to create is a jelly (jello). We can build a model of the jelly in any position it might take but the internal flexibility of the form is only evident over time and so this is more of a problem to an animator. There are ways of defining variable distances between vertices (which can be connected by mathematical 'springs') but these are not available in current Mac modellers. It is, however, possible to duplicate some symptoms of flexibility through the judicious use of scaling and editing functions in successive views of an object.

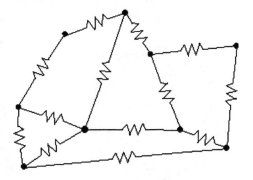

Springs and dampers making the skeleton of a flexible object.

4.6.4 DEFORMATION

In high-end modellers there is now often found a facility for transforming the shape of objects, not yet available on the Mac but likely to appear at some point in the future, called freeform deformation (FFD). Instead of attempting directly to transform what might be a very complex object, the transformation is applied to a cage of control points which imprison the object, thus enabling correct relationships within the object to be maintained. It is as if the object were set in a block of flexible resin which could then be bent and modified, the captive object accepting the same transformations as the block.

4.6.5 EDITING FORMS

Basic modelling methods typically create even or symmetrical forms, which can be combined to create more complex models. This is often an inadequate or inconvenient means of creating the desired contours, and the ability to manipulate the object or its surface more intimately is highly desirable. Low level editing at the level of individual facets, lines and vertices is desirable and starting to become available. It enables the operator to create an approximation of the required object using traditional methods and then to reposition, rescale, remove or supplement existing details on the model. This manipulation can entail dragging a single vertex to a new location, moving a group of vertices, adding vertices (and

A spherical object edited by dragging a vertex (top left), a facet (centre right) and a line (bottom left)

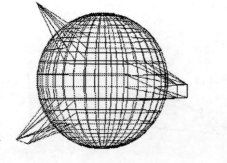

44

correctly connecting them to the rest of the object) or carrying out similar operations on lines, facets or defined sections. Editing should also permit cutting planes to slice objects into pieces, holes to be bored through objects (though this might be carried out in the model construction phase) and vertices or defined parts to be removed. Adding and subtracting features, as opposed to just reorganising them, carries with it the more difficult problem of retaining the desired coherence of the object, since if a vertex is removed the existence of lines and facets that rely on it must be dealt with by either the operator or the system.

4.7 VIEWING MODELS

Having created a numerical description of the desired model it is necessary to display it on the monitor screen. Since we probably have a mental picture of the object, it might not be immediately obvious that we need to decide on a form in which to display it. In fact the process of creating the object is normally an interactive one in which a screen image is used and so the decision will probably be made before creation starts, but we need to be aware that there are many forms the image can take and that choice usually involves a compromise between time and legibility.

4.7.1 LEGIBILITY

The range of ways in which an object can be presented is quite consistent between packages. The criteria for selecting a viewing method vary at different stages of the modelling process, but the relatively long time taken by some methods is often a factor. In the building stage it is often necessary to have effectively instantaneous feedback on the screen for every change of position or scale of an object made. If, as will often happen, a mouse is being used to drag one object towards another, the operator relies on the screen updating in real time in order that the objects' relative positions can be continually assessed. During this operation a 'bounding box' is often automatically created. This is a heavily abbreviated representation of the model by a box corresponding to its maximum dimensions. Owing to its simplicity, its movement on screen can be in real time.

Later in the process the position of objects may be finalised but the effect of lighting on them may need to be seen and this requires a different process, the longer time taken being acceptable.

4.7.2 WIREFRAME

The simplest representation, and quickest to display, is a wireframe model in which all of the edges are shown as lines. This can be confusing to view, however, as we are able to see the back as well as the front of the object and this lends itself to the manifestation of optical illusions. Because it was the earliest form of representation of an object on a computer screen it is still sometimes called for when a scene is required to have a 'computer generated' feel to it.

Some improvement can be achieved by using intensity modulation to strengthen close lines and make distant lines fainter, but unless it is transparent, the front surfaces of a real object obscure the back surfaces, an important factor in our visual understanding of the object. (In fact, even a transparent object usually has the back surfaces modified in some way by being viewed through the front ones, either changed by a shift in colour or tone or by refraction). A wireframe view can only be constructed, of course, from a model which has been built from vertices, such as in the B-rep system, or else can be converted to such a system at this stage.

4.7.3 HIDDEN LINE

An improvement on a wireframe model is a hidden line version in which the front surfaces obscure those behind, resulting in a marked decline in ambiguity. This ability to create a more realistic view is so important that many algorithms have been created to do the job. The manner in which they work depends on the way in which the model data is held and on the level of accuracy required. There is usually a trade-off between sophistication and speed, as a general purpose algorithm (which might not be able to deal with

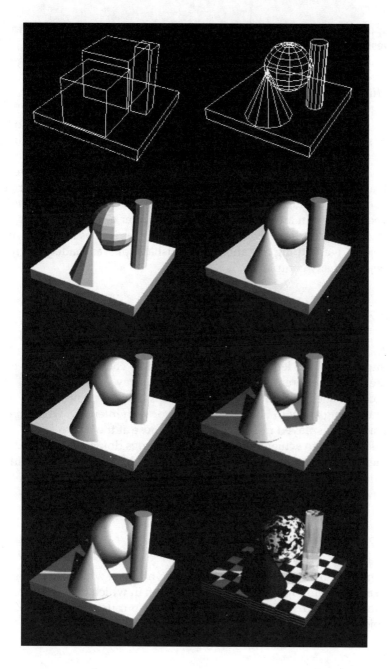

A model displayed using (from top left to bottom right): bounding boxes, wireframe, Lambert shading, Gouraud shading, Phong shading, raytracing, raytracing with optimum smoothness, surface textures.

special cases) is likely to be much faster than one which is built to test for, and resolve, all conflicts it might meet. Applications sometimes provide a quick method for draft work, at which stage errors might be more acceptable than time delays, and a more efficient method for final work when the extra time taken is an acceptable overhead.

The simplest way of using hidden line removal to improve on a wireframe model is by back-face culling in which surfaces pointing away from the viewer are removed. The direction in which a face is pointing is established by checking the angle between the viewer's line of sight and the 'surface normal', a perpendicular to the surface in question, using vector mathematics (both surface normals and vectors have many applications in computer graphics). The back-face cull is a rather crude method, however, as it does not deal with objects overlapping one another and usually proves inadequate for objects of any complexity.

4.7.4 DEPTH CUEING

As was mentioned when describing wireframe models, an improvement in legibility can be achieved by coding areas close to the viewer differently from those furthest away. This can be accomplished with either colour, perhaps having red near parts graduating away to blue distant parts, or with intensity, where near parts are displayed more brightly than those at the back. The calculations to achieve these ends slow things down and are not, therefore, normally used during model building but can be useful at a final stage, particularly if a wireframe view is required. It is not, however, a feature often found in modelling packages.

4.7.5 SOLID

A more realistic impression of an object, and one which is far less likely to be ambiguous, is a representation in which the facets are shown as solid. This matches more closely our understanding of objects in the real world. It is in the nature of a solid model that hidden surfaces are obscured and a number of methods are used to achieve this effect.

Commonly used is the 'z-buffer' method in which the spatial depth of each surface is checked at each pixel location, and the closest surface (i.e. the one with the smallest Z value) is displayed. Another is the 'painter's algorithm' which displays the furthest surface and then works forward through space 'overpainting' with closer surfaces (although the distance of a surface can be ambiguous if it is not parallel to the viewing plane). It is inherent to some rendering methods, such as 'ray tracing', to solve the hidden surface problem.

4.7.5.1 CODED AND LIGHTED

Although the obvious way to show an object as solid might be to treat it as if its surfaces are illuminated by a light source within its own world, it is equally possible to shade facets systematically. If all facets facing in a given direction are coded in the same way, either with the same tone, pattern or colour, then a logical model is produced which has much of the visibility of a lighted model. Such a system might be employed to single out all surfaces of an architectural facing North, for example.

4.7.6 PERSPECTIVE

We see the real world in perspective and the ability to give our model a perspective projection strongly enhances its ability to be understood clearly. Most modellers have the ability to change the degree of perspective by altering the angle of view and distance from the model, usually using a camera metaphor. (It is worth noting the error of the commonly-held belief that changing the focal length of a camera lens changes the perspective of a view. It is the change of distance from the subject which the change of lens permits, that effects the perspective.) The perspective observed through a wide-angle lens when close to an object is dramatic, and that seen with a telephoto lens at a greater distance is much less pronounced.

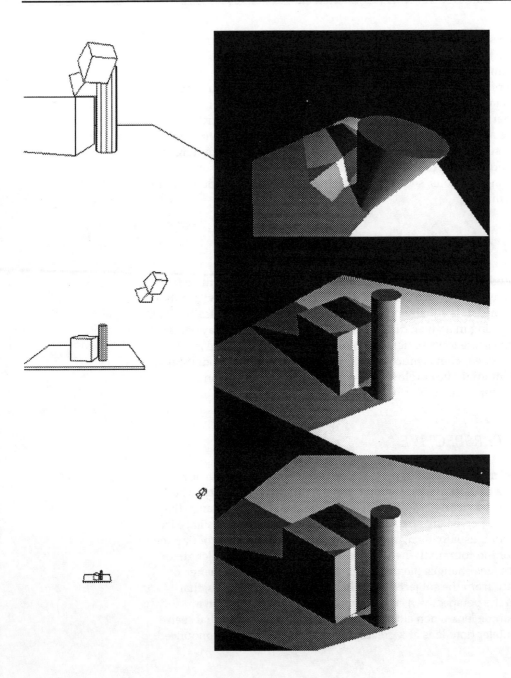

There are occasions when traditional (single viewpoint) perspective can be a problem to us, however. When trying to set one object so that it is just resting on another, perspective can confuse the issue and modellers should allow you to select an axonometric projection in which perspective is eliminated and the task is made simple.

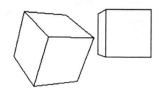

4.8 RENDERING

Chapter 2 looked at the nature of rendering and the way in which it could simulate, with ever increasing realism, the conditions of the real world. It should be noted that packages often devise their own terminology to describe lighting and rendering methods but they can usually be recognised as similar to those types and methods listed here. Whilst modellers now have rendering features built in, the most comprehensive facilities may be found in a separate renderer to which models can be exported. It might also be the case that the modelling features you prefer are not in the package that has the rendering facilities you want, and if you can afford the luxury of more than one package you might transfer models between applications.

Above: Perspective projection (top) compared with axonometric projection (bottom).

Previous page: Changing camera view focal lengths to simulate wide-angle (top), normal (centre) and telephoto (bottom)

4.8.1 LIGHT SOURCES

There are several lighting types, available in even the simplest applications. A spotlight is a light source in which the beam spreads out from a specific point like a torch. The beam may be restricted in its arc (as if by a shade of some sort), the angle of the light beam being alterable in a special panel. It can also be subject to the 'inverse square law' in which the light intensity decreases in proportion to its distance from the source and this fading can usually also be set in the lighting panel.

A point light simulates a source such as a light bulb which radiates light in all directions, and a variation which simulates the sun is sometimes available (i.e. the rays are given direction but are treated as parallel and of consistent strength).

A third light type is 'ambient', which is calculated to illuminate all surfaces with consistent strength and without direction and is often found useful in relieving the totally shadowed areas created by directional light sources in simpler lighting models.

4.8.2 *LIGHTING MODELS*

As you might expect, or else will soon find from painful experience, the lighting models available range from fast, crude renderings that are almost immediate, to slower, more subtle methods that can take hours, or even days, to complete. There is a constant trade off between subtlety, smoothness, resolution and speed. For this reason modellers usually let you work rapidly with a basic render but give you the ability to apply the top quality render to a selected part of the scene as a check before committing to a time-consuming full scene render. It is thus possible to confirm details such as the extent of shadows or the degree of reflection, and to make necessary adjustments, at an early stage. The speed at which renderers work is tied to the hardware configuration in use, but updates to modelling software often improve on the efficiency of algorithms used. This is particularly useful as it is acknowledged as a weak spot of modelling on current Macs.

4.8.2.1 *LAMBERT*

The simplest shading model is Lambert shading, which uses the cosine of the angle between the ray of light hitting the surface and the surface normal, to establish what the intensity of the surface should be (hence its alternative name of 'cosine shading'). As the light source comes to be closer to a perpendicular from the surface, so the angle decreases and the surface becomes lighter. When the light is at right angles to the surface the angle is zero and the light intensity is at maximum. Despite its simplicity, it adds enormously to our perceptual understanding of the object and, since it can be applied extremely quickly, is usually included as the basic shading method in applications. It does, however, produce flat shaded polygons which emphasise the artificiality of the model, and lacks any gradation across planes. Sometimes labelled as 'fast shading'.

4.8.2.2 GOURAUD

Henri Gouraud gave his name to an improved shading model published in 1971. It averages the light intensities at the edge of each polygon and then interpolates along each scan line across the plane lying between these averages to give a smooth, eggshell-like gradation. An extension of his model also allows the individual facets to become hidden by interpolating across facet edges. Sometimes labelled 'smooth shading'.

4.8.2.3 PHONG

Two years later in 1973,a paper by Bui Tuong Phong introduced a method which added specular highlights to smooth shading. Phong shading calculates the intensity at each point along a scan line from its approximated normal. (The approximation is arrived at by interpolating from the normals at the edges on that scan line, which are in turn interpolated from the normals at the points bounding that edge.) Surfaces with different levels of shininess can be simulated by employing a gloss parameter to determine the size of the highlight area. This 'specular' highlight depends on viewpoint, unlike a diffused surface which is independent of the eye position. Sometimes labelled as highlighted shading.

An odd effect of both Gouraud and Phong methods is that an object, such as a polygonised sphere, can be beautifully smooth across its surface, but will still have an horizon made up of the straight polygon edges. This requires additional treatment which is unlikely to be available in a basic modeller, although the smoothness can be improved by increasing the number of facets in the model. It is also necessary to make sure that objects which are meant to look polygonal do not unintentionally have their edges smoothed over.

4.8.2.4 BLINN

Some modellers incorporate a shading model named after computer graphics guru James Blinn, which improves on the Phong model by approximating specific materials by the addition of some extra calculations (derived from real materials) and applications usually have a library of surface types, such as silver and brass, available. The characteristics of the library surfaces can normally be altered, with different degrees of subtlety, and new surfaces created.

4.8.2.5 RAY TRACING

A more recent method called ray tracing employs a different technique to great (and now popular) effect. The principle is simple: tracing a ray back from the viewing position through each pixel to the first surface it meets. The ray is then reflected from this surface into the scene, reflecting off subsequent surfaces until it reaches a light source or leaves the scene. The pixel is then set according to the intensity and colour of the light remaining after the contribution of intervening surfaces. A lot of computation is required, increasing with resolution, and a limit must be set to the number of times a ray can be allowed to reflect before a final result is accepted. The more reflections each ray is allowed, the more accurate the result. The method produces arresting images and automatically deals with shadows with refraction and with transparency but is currently too slow to be practical in many situations unless fast hardware is available. It is good at dealing with specular light but poor with diffuse light.

4.8.2.6 RADIOSITY

Even slower, though good at dealing with diffuse light, is the radiosity interchange method which developed with the field of architectural design in mind. It works from the assumption that the light energy striking a surface must equal the energy reflected, transmitted and absorbed. The first requirement is that the whole scene be divided up into surface patches (which may prove to be the way it has already been modelled) and each patch effectively treated as a secondary light source. Extensive calculations consider the effects of every one of those patches on every other and would be almost impossible to compute if it were not the case that most of the patch pairs will prove to have a nil relationship.

This method produces very credible subtlety within shadows and penumbra, and has the advantage that the computations are independent of viewer position. This is very convenient for an animation through the scene since the calculations need only be done once (provided that nothing within the scene changes during the sequence). Whilst convenient for animating movement through a fixed scene, it would be impossibly painstaking for moving anything within the scene, since all the calculations would have to be repeated for each frame.

4.8.2.7 PHOTO REALISTIC

Sometimes a renderer will have an 'ultimate' quality setting which gives the highest levels of refraction, smoothness, etc. intended for images destined for publication. The same qualities might be attainable by fine tuning other rendering models, but the default for this setting produces what the manufacturers consider the best image that their renderer can provide. The results can be spectacularly good but very time consuming to produce.

4.8.2.8 SPECIALISED

New lighting models are being developed all the time to deal with some of the subtle and complex lighting situations that can arise in real life. By way of example, we can look briefly at two that have been presented recently. Mark Watt (at Digital Pictures, London) has used a variation of backward ray tracing (where the ray starts at the light source rather than at the eye) to render specular to diffuse phenomena such as the interaction of light with water. His method incorporates information about caustics, which deals with reflection and refraction by curved surfaces. With this technique he has produced some elegant and convincing animations of the delicate patterns that dance around on underwater surfaces. It is fascinating to see how evocative they are of other qualities we are all familiar with in swimming pools, recalling the memory of actually being in the water.

Nakamae looks at rendering road surfaces under various weather conditions, which has particular relevance to the development of driving simulators. His team at Hiroshima University has presented animations of road surfaces drying out, in which muddy puddles evaporate (requiring analysis of the minute undulations of the asphalt), but more exciting are those of cars driving at night. In order to simulate the effects of on-coming headlights he had to allow for diffraction due to the pupil of the human eye and even that due to eyelashes. The results are uncannily effective and the most significant clue to the computer origination of the sequence lies not in the rendering but in the eerie smoothness of the car's motion.

Specialised lighting models such as these are not available in existing software, but research such as this will find its way through to packages of the future.

4.8.3 SHADOWS

It is useful to have shadows dealt with automatically as happens with ray tracing. It is equally possible, however, to calculate shadows separately and a number of algorithms have been developed to do this. An architect might want to know how shadows are going to be cast by the sun without wanting all the other visual information that ray tracing would give him. It might also be useful to calculate the position of all shadows in a model (rather than those seen from one viewpoint) so that the view could be moved around a model without the shadows having to be recalculated for each position. Such shadowing is not likely to be found in general purpose modellers, but features such as the ability to create penumbra (soft-edged shadows) is sometimes included.

4.8.4 SURFACE CHARACTERISTICS

Since most users will not want all models to be rendered in a
smooth, featureless monochrome, there are a number of methods
available in most modellers to apply surface treatments to objects.
These are usually selectable from a library included in the package
which can be added to or edited at will. Colour, pattern, texture and
images can be laid onto the surfaces of objects which can also be
tuned for reflectivity, refraction, transparency and other qualities.

4.8.4.1 PROCEDURAL AND NON-PROCEDURAL

One useful distinction that can be made between different types of
surfaces is whether the texture is defined by a mathematical
function, which contains simple 'rules' by which any amount of the
texture can be generated as needed, or whether the area of texture is
stored complete. In the first case (procedural) there is very little to
be stored by the application and the texture can be created
indefinitely, optional random elements giving variety if required. In
the second case (non-procedural) the whole texture map has to be
stored in every detail. A chequerboard pattern can be generated
procedurally, marbling can also be generated procedurally with a
random element introduced, but a picture of a bunch of flowers has
to be created elsewhere and stored.

4.8.4.2 TEXTURE MAPPING

Texture mapping is the process of transferring textural information
from two-dimensional 'texture space' (where it is stored or
generated) to three-dimensional 'object space' where it is applied to
the required surface. The mathematics to do this vary in complexity
depending on the recipient surface. Transferring a flat picture to the
flat surface is relatively simple, wrapping it around a primitive with
a simple geometry is somewhat more complicated, and applying it to
a complex 'hand-made' object is potentially very difficult and time-
consuming. Packages vary in their ability to deal with the more

complex situations. Maps can be applied to surfaces in several ways, the method used being determined by the object's geometry and the effect required. For example, the map can be applied orthogonally (like wallpaper) or as if projected from a slide projector (when it is directional). It can also be 'shrink wrapped' around an object or wrapped as if with a rubber sheet.

4.8.4.2.1 DIRT

Most real world surfaces are not the unblemished paragons of perfection that the computer would like us to believe. In order to add another level of realism some renderers provide the ability to apply dirt to models. Rust can be generated with fractals, for example, and it is even possible to define the parts of the model most likely to be affected by rust and the degree to which each part will sustain the effect. It is only fair to say that this can produce very clean-looking dirt but its appearance is largely under the control of the operator.

4.8.4.3 SOLID TEXTURE

Instead of wrapping the surface of an object with texture, it is possible for the texture to run right through it. If an object is supposed to be made of wood, the solid texture method has the advantage that if the object is cut or opened up, coherent wood grain will be shown at the new surfaces. This method, which is associated in particular with CSG modelling, involves mapping from a three-dimensional texture space to the object space, which is a simple process. Such textures would normally be procedural.

4.8.4.4 BUMP MAPPING

Bump mapping (or perturbation mapping) creates three-dimensional texture by perturbing the surface normals using a mathematical function or a bump map. This means that the

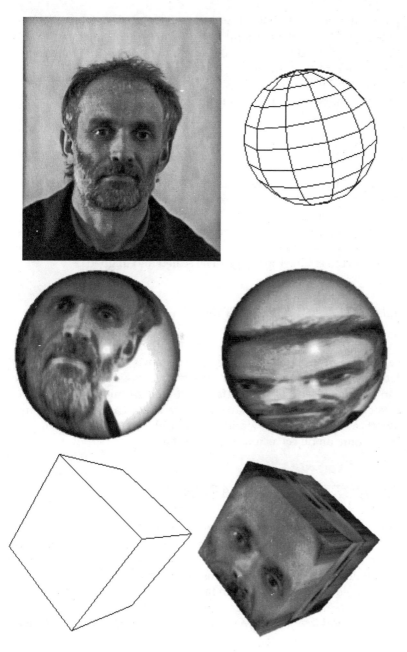

An image and the effect of different methods of wrapping it around a sphere and a cube.

information about the direction each facet on the model is facing (which is used by the renderer to set the lighting intensity on that facet) is disturbed to fool the renderer into thinking that the facets point in a range of directions. This simulates a bumpy surface (orange peel is the standard example) and can be tuned to change the roughness, scale and uniformity of the texture.

4.8.4.5 IMAGE MAPPING

If you are a packaging designer, you will not be satisfied with creating a product with a uniform surface but will need to apply graphics to the box and a label to the product. This graphic image will be created outside of the modeller, in a paint program perhaps, imported and then applied by image mapping. Some control should be offered to enable the image to be scaled and aligned.

4.8.4.6 REFLECTION MAPPING

In order that a surface can be seen to be reflective, there must be something present to be reflected (for instance, an object will not look properly metallic unless it reflects its surroundings). A surface can obviously reflect other surfaces in the scene but it is often useful to set up an environment map (an image which can be reflected in objects as if it were their world: typically clouds) or to wrap an image onto an object as if it were the reflection.

4.9 CURRENT RESEARCH

A lot of work is being done on new rendering algorithms, often in an attempt to match lighting situations found in particular environments in the real world. Although these algorithms may be designed for use within limited disciplines, and thus are not general enough to be of direct interest to us, the research finds itself taken up elsewhere and will lead to more sophisticated renderers, first on specialised high-end machines and later on the Macintosh. The additional subtlety of new algorithms usually brings high computational overheads, which require a powerful machine to be able to handle in a reasonable time. Papers detailing the latest work are to be found in the proceedings of the annual SIGGRAPH conference.

4.10 ARTEFACTS

A number of errors commonly arise in the production of computer-generated images (CGI), usually as a result of the fact that computers, and their display devices, work in discrete steps whilst the world we operate in is smoothly continuous. This results in our often having to match specific points in time and space to the nearest available points in computer time and space, with a small margin of error proving unavoidable. It might, for instance, be that the point in the model's world that we wish to display equates to an ideal screen location which is not exactly centred on a pixel. The best we can then do is to set the point at the nearest pixel, introducing a slight error. This type of error is described by a branch of mathematics known as 'sampling theory' and is particularly evident in CGI as spatial aliasing. A straight line drawn on screen horizontally or vertically will appear perfectly straight since it will run along one row or column of pixels. A line drawn at 45 degrees will run diagonally through pixel locations lying in a straight line; but consider a line lying at an angle close to, but not at, those described. The requirement to match the desired line to the nearest pixel locations results in an uneven, stepped effect. As jagged edges ('the jaggies') can be quite destructive of the illusion we wish to create, much effort goes into removing them, or, more accurately, disguising them.

Anti-aliasing is a technique (which might be considered counter-intuitive) for disguising these effects by softening the edges of the line. Instead of representing the line with pixels entirely of the required intensity, the intensity of each pixel crossed by the line is set at a level between that of the line and that of the background, in proportion to the percentage of the pixel covered by the line. Where the line coincides with a pixel exactly it takes the line intensity; where the line crosses the boundary between two pixels they are both set at an intensity half-way between the line intensity and the background

Anti-aliasing applied to the lower half of a letterform.

intensity. Anti-aliasing is difficult to achieve with a small palette but has become a standard option in most rendering software. Other methods of dealing with the problem are the 'dither matrix', which changes the intensity of a pixel on each scan sequence, and 'pixel phasing', where the screen location of individual pixels can be shifted fractionally by automatic adjustment of the electron beam; but these solutions are less likely to be encountered.

'Temporal aliasing' is a manifestation of the same problem in time rather than space and is relevant to animation. An example can be found in Westerns when the wheels of the stagecoach appear to be turning in the wrong direction.

'Mach banding' is a phenomenon, particularly associated with Lambert shading, in which a surface that should be smoothly shaded appears to have dark streaks on it. This anomaly is a product of our edge detection abilities and is most easily improved upon by decreasing the size of the polygons in use.

'Illegal colours' can be a problem at a production level, since it is possible to generate colours on screen which cannot be accurately recorded onto video tape or broadcast. A wave form device monitor, which is like an oscilloscope, can be used to spot the offending colours.

'Precision errors' are inherent to digital computers. The computer can only allocate a limited amount of memory to each number it uses, and if this space is insufficient to store the complete number it becomes truncated. The imprecisions thus created can accumulate to create noticeable errors, but is unlikely to present a problem for us in well-written software. It is interesting to notice, however, that in one application I have used, if 10 inches are converted to millimetres and then straight back to inches again, the result is not exactly 10 inches. (In another context, these rounding errors have been blamed, in the past, for false nuclear alerts!)

4.11 ANIMATION

Although animation is not our main interest in this book, I make brief mention of it here since a number of modellers include an animation facility and this might well be the final target of any model-building exercise.

There are a large and growing number of disciplines in which animation is becoming a commonplace tool. As model builders we can use movement through and past our scene to add information which a static view will not give. In real life it is often the case that an object is ambiguous until either it moves or you move relative to it, and by animating either the viewing point or the object a clearer understanding of the model can be gained. In areas such as architecture, the ability to move around inside of a computer model of a proposed building is increasingly sought and the feedback from such an exercise can lead to modifications of the original design.

An animation is a sequence of separate images, called frames, which are presented in sufficiently quick succession to give the appearance of movement. Rather than set every individual frame (25 to 30 per second are used for a smooth animation) the operator will normally set important frames (known as 'keyframes') and leave it to the computer to calculate the frames in between these. A continuing problem with computer animation is that it looks like computer animation. Movements often have a queasy, mathematical smoothness which is unworldly. This is good for showing spacecraft, and perhaps acceptable for flying logos (since they are not of the real world), but is often poor for simulating things from real life.

'Keyframe' and 'timeline' are the two main methods for controlling animation in current Mac systems.

4.11.1 KEYFRAME

A keyframe is a frame from a sequence at which point a significant event, such as a change of direction, takes place. In a keyframe system everything in the scene is set in its correct position at each keyframe and the system is told how many frames to generate between keyframes. The keyframes can be returned to and edited. In the simplest case of an object moving in a straight line between two points, the keyframes would be the start and finish frames. If the object was to move to this new position and then revolve ninety degrees about its centre, the three keyframes would be the opening frame, the frame in which the traverse stopped and the end frame showing the object after it had finished its rotation. A high degree of subtlety can be used when defining the movement between keyframes, often using splines for smooth sweeping movement and 'cushioning' for measured acceleration and deceleration.

4.11.2 TIMELINE

An alternative control method is to define the position of each object (which can include the camera or lights) at any given moment in the sequence. In this case each object in the scene is represented on the sequence control panel against a horizontal line divided into time increments. The position (or other attributes) of each object at any moment in the scene can be set on its timeline and is clearly seen relative to any other object. It is easy with this method to make adjustments to individual elements in a scene without affecting others and to make changes to the relative time taken by elements to enact changes. This system is sometimes extended to include timelines for a soundtrack.

Timeline animation window from Infini-D.

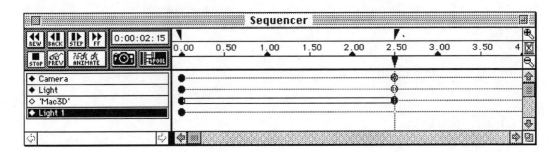

4.11.3 SCRIPTED

The keyframe and timeline systems described allow the objects in a scene to be positioned on screen using the usual controls that we are familiar with from modelling. An alternative is to write a script for the required movement, which is less intuitive but sometimes clearer. If the appearance of the scene is our overriding interest then we need to see it on the screen, but if the concept of the changes is more important, then a script might be simpler. I believe that the best animation systems provide control at both levels, but the facility is not often available within modellers. This is not unreasonable, however, as it is asking a lot of a package to be a fully featured modeller, renderer and animator.

4.11.4 KINEMATIC

Kinematics is the study of movement without regard to cause. At the time of writing all Macintosh animation systems are kinematic, which means that it is up to the animator to deal with the degree and consequences of all movements within the scene. The acceleration of a falling ball, the amount it squashes when it hits the ground and the height to which it bounces must all be defined using the experience and intuition of the animator.

4.11.5 DYNAMIC

Dynamics is the branch of mechanics which deals with the way masses move under the influence of forces and torques. In a dynamic animation the system 'knows' about the mass of the ball, about the force with which it is started in motion, about gravity and about the ball's flexibility so it is able to calculate the entire bounce sequence from the start conditions that it is given. Such a system can recognise collisions and can cause objects to make the correct response to them (which might be impossible in a complex kinematically-driven scene).

Dynamic systems are the object of much current research (and are fascinating to use) but the calculations involved can take a very long time and they are not the most appropriate in all situations. If the ball has to bounce across the screen in a commercial, arriving at a prescribed spot and taking exactly three seconds to do so, it can require a lot of fine tuning of the forces in the scene to achieve the desired end. Systems which combine elements of kinematic and dynamic control are available but neither they, nor full dynamic systems, are yet available to us on the Mac.

4.11.6 METAMORPHOSIS

Text morph example

As well as being able to change the position, colour and surface qualities of an object over time, its shape can also be modified. The change from one form to another is a metamorphosis which can be easily achieved. If the initial object is established at some point in the sequence and then altered for an appearance later in the sequence, the system can often incrementally create changing objects at stages between the two extremes. It is necessary in the systems we will see for the object to retain continuity during the metamorphosis since the system will be tracking the changes in position of the vertices, which rules out editing that removes parts of the object (or metamorphosing between completely separate objects). An inventive operator will, however, usually find a way to achieve the required effect, and producing animation is often about cheating.

It should be noted that the 'morphing' which is currently fashionable in TV advertisements and such like is achieved in two dimensions not three, by interpolating between still and moving images of the objects, not between the objects themselves. Software has just been released for the Mac which does this.

CHAPTER 5

THE MAC FOR MODELLING & RENDERING

This chapter introduces the basic components of a computer system with particular thought for its use in the context of modelling and rendering. Where appropriate it refers specifically to the Macintosh. Since the inexperienced user is catered for, it is anticipated that some readers will choose to pass the chapter by.

5.1 THE OPERATING SYSTEM

As a user you are protected by the operating system from the need to deal directly with the electronics in your computer. A part of the operating system on the Macintosh is built into a microchip but this works in conjunction with a set of software elements which sit in the System file and determine how you can interact with the machine. Since this is software it can easily be replaced by improved versions at regular intervals, the user merely needing to swap the old system file for the new one obtained from your dealer. System 7 is the latest version (at the time of writing) with significant changes, minor changes being indicated by numerical suffixes (i.e. 7.1, 7.2.1).

The operating system on the Mac uses the 'Finder' program to create a GUI (Graphical User Interface) that allows you to talk to the machine easily. This offers a 'desktop' on your screen when the machine is switched on, using windows, icons and menus that can be accessed by a pointer controlled, usually by a mouse and being known as a WIMP environment. Many details of the interface (such as desktop colour) and of your interaction with it (such as mouse sensitivity) can be set using Control Panels in the System folder.

The Mac's GUI is one of its great strengths and probably the single feature with which it is most associated. Although the original research was done elsewhere, Apple was a great innovator in this area, bringing a new ease to the way in which computers can be used. This friendliness won many admirers, and a GUI is now the most common interface for personal computers, largely replacing the command-line interfaces which preceded it. There are situations where the old interface is more useful, and (in some machines) more efficient, but the convenience and accessibility of the Mac's interface is legendary.

5.2 MAC HARDWARE

'Hardware' describes the physical components of a computer system; the machinery itself (as opposed to 'software' which instructs the hardware what to do). The whirring box on, or under, your desk, the monitor, the keyboard and the mouse are the basic hardware components. The range of Macintosh computers offers a range of configurations and it is relatively easy to achieve the usual compromise between cost and functionality. A strength of the Mac system is the ease with which hardware elements can be integrated and upgraded, avoiding the traps and pitfalls which have caused problems for the unwary in the PC market (where specialist knowledge can be needed to set up equipment effectively).

5.2.1 CPU

The CPU is the heart of the computer, where the instructions specified by the program are carried out and where the operation of all other elements of the computing process is coordinated. It is built as a tiny integrated circuit (IC), often referred to as a chip, and has shrunk so much in the last 30 years that a computer as powerful as the Quadra sitting beneath my desk would then have filled a room. There are several families of chips which are commonly used, and each has particular features which cause manufacturers to build machines around it. The Motorola 68000 chip is a 16 bit chip which has provided the basis for several graphics-orientated computers including the Apple Macintosh. ('Bit', incidentally, is short for 'BInary digiT' and is the smallest unit of storage in the computer.) As the chip has developed its added capabilities are indicated by a higher reference number, so that the Motorola 68020 is a full 32-bit device, the 68030 adds technical enhancements (like advanced memory management) and the 68040 develops further still (incorporating a high degree of parallelism).

Macintosh have developed their range of machines using each new Motorola 680x0 chip so far, but are about to introduce a new generation of machines based on RISC technology (Reduced Instruction Set Computers). A RISC chip is optimised to run the bare minimum number of instructions very fast, concentrating on those used most often; infrequently-used instructions are constructed from combinations of the few present. Computers often find themselves referred to by their chip number as it gives a general indication of their performance. It is interesting to note that the 68000 chip incorporates 68,000 transistors (guess where it got its name from) but the 68040 builds in a massive 1.2 million transistors. VLSI technology (Very Large Scale Integration) permits the fabrication of this number of transistors on a single chip.

The speed at which operations are carried out by the CPU is determined by the 'clock rate', measured in megahertz (MHz), a megahertz representing one million cycles per second (the 68000 chip typically being run at about 8 MHz). The faster the clock rate the faster information is processed, but since different machines do a different amount of work in one cycle, it is not sufficient merely to compare clock rates. Bench marks are used to compare the speed of different machines, and time each machine as it completes the same tasks, but whilst these tests are accurate they are not necessarily helpful. It might be that the tasks accomplished in the bench test are not relevant to the application in mind, that the machine is optimised to produce good bench test results, or even that the machine is too clever for the tests. The speed of operation is now often described in 'mips' (millions of instructions per second) and 'mega-flops' (millions of floating point operations per second), with alternative prefixes 'giga-' (one billion) and 'tera-' (one trillion) increasingly being used to whet the appetite. The Mac literature is refreshingly free of macho mips ratings, and for graphics applications it is often more useful to know how many polygon fills it can achieve in a second or how many vectors it can draw in a second, a calculation directly related to the end product and which takes into account any special graphics hardware aboard.

The basic chip is often supplemented by others which do specialised jobs and take part of the workload from the CPU. The most common is the maths co-processor, which relieves the CPU of much of the burden of mathematical calculation, and is often now standard or available as an optional extra. As modellers we might be particularly interested in graphics co-processors which take over graphics chores. These supplementary chips are optimised to undertake their limited functions more efficiently than any general purpose chip and allow the whole process to be markedly speeded up.

It is, unfortunately, necessary to acknowledge that modelling and rendering require the computer to do a lot of calculations and therefore are best performed on a powerful machine. High quality rendering, in particular, is too time-consuming to be considered in a production environment on the smaller machines, and indeed the software will often require a co-processor. The simpler modellers will run on any machine, however, and the area can be thoroughly explored without resort to the most expensive hardware; you just need to accept that things proceed more slowly.

5.2.2 MEMORY

Computer memory is where data is stored, either permanently or while calculations are carried out with it. Its size is usually described in kilobytes and megabytes ('K' and 'Mb'), which stand respectively for thousands and millions of bytes (though strictly the value of a kilobyte is 210 or 1,024 bytes and a megabyte is 220 or 1,084,576 bytes). Sometimes memory capacity is described in words rather than bytes, a word being a unit of memory storage which can vary from machine to machine. A typical word on a personal computer is 8 bits.

Most memory is random access memory (RAM) in which memory locations can be written to and read from without having to work through a sequence of storage locations, and its contents are normally volatile (disappearing when the machine is switched off). Read only memory (ROM) is non-volatile, can only be read from (as a protection from being overwritten), and is therefore typically used to hold information such as the operating system.

Only five or six years ago a typical home computer might have had 64K of RAM, but now 4Mb is a common minimum and 20Mb a good starting point for professional applications. The cost of producing RAM has fluctuated markedly and has had an obvious knock-on effect on the price of machines. Top end Macs, particularly in environments using graphics, might choose to start with 64MB installed; 256Mb being the maximum RAM capable of being fitted in a current Mac. Modelling and rendering programs can require at least 4Mb of RAM as a working minimum and work far more comfortably with four times that amount. RAM chips can, however, be easily purchased and installed as your requirements grow.

32-bit addressing under System 7 allows 'virtual' memory to be created, in which case some secondary storage can be treated as if it is (slow) RAM. Space on the hard-drive can be allocated in the 'Memory' Control Panel to be used as virtual memory, which can be useful for opening additional programs or for handling large documents. It is more effective when using several small programs simultaneously than when using one large program. RAM can also be allocated to function as a disc cache, which can speed programs up. It does this by holding commonly-used information in fast memory and thus avoiding the need to access it from slow secondary storage.

32-bit addressing allows for faster data transfer in Macs which can support it, but only with software that is '32-bit clean'. In order to be compatible with older, incompatible software this feature must be switched off in the 'Memory' Control Panel.

5.2.3 STORAGE

Since the information in the computer's memory will be lost when you switch it off (or it crashes!), it is necessary to store it in a more permanent form. You MUST, repeat MUST, acquire the habit of saving current files at regular intervals lest an error (or a power failure) wipes out hours, days or weeks of work. As well as saving to your hard disc you must also back up your important files to a secondary storage device in case you should have a problem with your hard disc. You will accumulate much information (text files, picture files, model files, etc.) that needs to be stored for future reference, and the file you lose is always the vital one. The backup storage can be to a removable medium or to a 'mirrored' hard drive, in which case all data is simultaneously stored on your main and mirror drive.

Secondary storage is most commonly provided by disc drives which hold information on magnetic 'floppy' discs loaded into the drive, recently having increased to a typical 1.44 megabyte of storage capacity on a 3.5 inch disc. The term 'floppy', incidentally, is a hangover from the previous generation of discs which were physically flexible. Discs allow random access, which means that data can be taken from anywhere on the disc without having to run through all the preceding material. Hard drives use permanently mounted discs with very fast access times (typically holding 40 to 250 megabytes but available up to several gigo-bytes) and can be mounted inside the main computer box or bought separately and plugged in externally.

Removable hard drives, in which a fat cassette slots into the drive mechanism, provide a convenient means of storing data in 44Mb or 88Mb units, and these are heavily used for passing files to computer bureaux. Those using the 'Syquest' mechanism are the most popular, but the 'Bernoulli' version is often considered to be more reliable, though more expensive. Large removable drives of up to 2G (gigabytes) are now available. Tape provides an alternative magnetic storage medium, but being a linear access method, is too slow for use in an application (imagine having to go through a dictionary from page one every time you want to find a word!) and is mainly used for relatively cheap back-up and archiving. DAT drives use this technology.

Laser technology has dramatically increased memory storage capacity and is just starting to become commonly available for computers, having already established itself in CD players for HiFi systems. Standard rewritable optical drives hold 128Mb on a removable 3.5 inch disc and double capacity drives are being introduced, whilst larger optical drives hold 650Mb. 'Juke boxes' of discs provide even greater capacity. These discs provide more stable archive storage than magnetic material, are competitively priced and will probably become the most common removable media on the next generation of computers. The magneto-optical (MO) 'floptical' has just been introduced to read both standard floppies and 21M discs. Data is stored magnetically but optical techniques are used to increase density and permanence. CD ROMs are increasingly used as a read-only medium for disseminating up to 600Mb of data and CD ROM drives are likely to become standard in future computers. The medium is particularly suited for applications using video/ animation data which require a large amount of storage with fairly quick access times. It is now being used for holding applications accompanied by many examples and demonstrations and also for holding font libraries. Machines allowing CD ROMs to be written are dropping in price and will soon become widely accessible.

Fast solid state secondary storage is also becoming used and its progressive availability is likely to be inversely proportional to the price of the material. Since the CPU can handle information faster than it can take it from secondary storage, slow access times can cause processing bottlenecks which becomes a very real concern, for instance in animation.

The main factors governing the choice of secondary storage are: your typical file size and the number of files to be stored; the speed with which you need to be able to access the data; and the security of the data; also the cost of the medium and, in the case of removable media, the cost of the mechanism itself. Prices are currently dropping for all secondary storage devices, and in many cases, dropping fast. A small 40Mb hard drive is now a tenth of the price it was several years ago. A rough comparison of storage cost in £ per Mb as at the end of 1993 follows, based on the lowest generally available price (excluding VAT). In the case of removable storage the medium and mechanism are costed separately. Devices with the fastest access times and extra features will normally cost extra.

Type	Capacity	Mechanism cost (£)	Medium cost (£)	Medium cost (£-Mb)
Floppy	1.4Mb		0.8	0.6
Hard drive	40Mb		100	2.5
	85Mb		129	1.52
	240Mb		250	1.04
	1Gb		780	0.78
	2Gb		1370	0.68
Tape	160Mb	600	16	0.01
DAT	2Gb	1200	20	0.01
Syquest	44Mb	230	44	1.0
	88Mb	320	65	0.74
CD	600Mb	275	read only	
Floptical	21Mb	330	16	0.76
Optical	128Mb	750	33	0.25
	650Mb	1690	89	0.14

5.2.4 I/O

As mere mortals we cannot commune directly with the computer and need means of getting information in and out. The Mac is provided with a good range of ports (manifested as sockets) for the attachment of input and output devices. These devices are described in the chapter on communicating with the Mac and include hardware such as the keyboard for input and the printer for output. Different machines in the Macintosh range offer different ranges of ports but many are common to all machines.

The Apple Desktop Bus (ADB) connects devices such as the mouse, keyboard, graphics tablet (and sometimes 'dongles' - hardware security devices sometimes found on modelling packages) to the Mac.

The SCSI port (pronounced 'scuzzy') connects external devices such as scanners and external drives and allows a number of devices to be 'daisy-chained' (meaning connected one to another in a chain). SCSI plugs/sockets are 25 or 50 pin, and the first and last devices in a SCSI chain need to be 'terminated', the first terminator often being built in and the last having a plug-in terminator. (I've never been aware of any problems with an unterminated SCSI chain but, apparently, I've just been lucky.)

The serial ports connects to printers, modems and to a net work.

The video port connects to a monitor.

The power ports accept power from the supply and provide power for devices such as the monitor.

The sound ports connect to microphone and speakers, etc.

The external disc drive port connects to an external disc drive.

5.2.5 NETWORKING

Networking is too specialised a subject to be dealt with in this book but the basic principle is straightforward and very useful. A number of Macintosh computers can be connected to one another using their built-in networking capability, allowing them to communicate with one another and with other devices on the network. This means that files can be transferred between machines, machines can share printers and other input and output devices, and common files can be held on a file server and accessed by all machines on the network.

Of particular interest to us as modellers, often wanting maximum processing power, is the ability of one machine to call on all the computing power on the network in the service of its own calculations. In an office with twenty networked Macintoshes, this means that a single machine could be left running through the night with the power of all twenty machines at its disposal. Software is increasingly 'network aware', meaning that the software is designed to make use of this facility and can divide up the workload among available machines for optimum processing speed. Network rendering is becoming a common, and welcome, feature in modelling packages, often being made available through supplementary software.

Machines being used by the controlling computer can still be used for other jobs as their CPUs will only be engaged by the controller if they are idle. During word processing, for example, the CPU is heavily under-used and is therefore largely available for use by others on the network. Another side of network awareness is that software will now often check to see if illegal versions of itself are being run on the network and will refuse to function if that is the case.

5.3 EXPANSION

Many machines in the Macintosh range have 'slots' available inside the main casing ('Processor-direct' slots and 'NuBus' slots) to take expansion cards. These cards are printed circuit boards for video and graphics applications, networking and communications, additional processing power, and other purposes. It is well worth trying to anticipate future expansion requirements when buying your Mac and ensuring that you have a machine with enough slots to allow it to grow with you. If you want to squeeze maximum speed from your machine, work with video and use a large colour monitor, you will need enough slots available for all the extra boards you are going to need.

5.3.1 ACCELERATORS

I work on a Quadra 950, and after experience of 'lesser' Macs, was delighted with its speed of operation. Briefly. It is a well-known law of computing that the machine you need is the one that is just a little more powerful than the one you use, and this law is never clearer than when working with graphics, especially rendering. Since a high resolution, full colour, ray traced scene can still take hours to render, this impatience is, perhaps, understandable. However rapidly algorithms and hardware are improved, they are likely to lag behind demand, and only interactive, photo realistic, real-time image production is likely to satisfy.

In pursuit of these ends, a number of manufacturers make cards that speed up aspects of your machine's operation. At their most complex they can seem like computers in their own right (and can cost as much), whilst there are more modest improvements to be obtained at lesser prices. These cards are often sold on the basis that they will make your machine run faster than a model higher up the product range, and it is always worth checking that the cost of doing this is not greater than trading in and buying the machine whose speed it will emulate.

General purpose accelerators are available with various specifications, and in some cases (as with the well known 'Radius Rockets' and 'YARC' boards) can be added either singly or in groups. When grouped, dedicated software can then arrange for each card to be treated as an independent computer, allowing tasks to be distributed among all the cards.

More specialised cards aim to improve the machine's performance in one specific area, such as speeding up the operation of 'Adobe Photoshop' (a widely used photo design and production tool). Some modellers/renderers can be supplied with their own boards and in the case of 'Shade', for example, multiple boards can be added for very fast processing. Increasingly, modellers and renderers are designed to make use of accelerator boards, if installed. The financial cost can easily be worthwhile in a production environment where time is money but is often outside the range of the casual user.

5.3.2 EMULATORS

It can be desirable to make your Mac pretend it is another machine, most obviously a PC, perhaps in order to be able to run software specific to that machine. Whilst the Mac currently has far more modelling/rendering software available for it than the PC, a company might have a mixture of machine types or specific requirements that require a PC solution. There are also industry standard packages that are not yet available on the Mac. Software emulators can be slow and hardware emulators can cost more than the machine you are emulating, but the ability to have both Mac and PC windows open on your desktop at the same time can be useful.

An interesting emulation from our point of view is that of 'MacIvory', which adds a Symbolics 'Ivory' processor to a suitable Mac (such as a Quadra) and produces a platform which will run the powerful Symbolics modelling/rendering/animation software.

Since it runs under the Finder, you can switch between it and Mac applications running on the same machine. Whilst not cheap, it gives you the chance to run state-of-the-art software found in many leading production houses, and Mac Ivory effectively offers high-end technology at budget prices.

5.4 CONTROL HARDWARE

If the process you are working on involves machines other than the computer, it can be convenient to have the computer control them. It can even become essential that the computer controls them. When producing images to be laid down on video tape, it is often necessary for the computer to spend minutes (or hours) generating each frame (video runs at 25 frames per second in the UK and at 30 frames per second in the USA). An animation controller, which can be a NuBus board like the DQ-ANIMAQ, will control a suitable, professional standard VTR (video tape recorder) so that it advances a single frame and receives each image as it is generated. It can also control a VTR which is inputting single frames to the computer, possibly in order to post-process or composite images. Animation controllers can also be external devices or software.

5.5 FILES

When you save your work, entering a name in the file-save dialogue box, the data is stored in a particular structure or 'file format' under that name. The structure used will be determined by the application, which may offer you a choice of formats. Sometimes these formats have been developed for the particular application alone and sometimes they are generic, in which case they will be encountered in many other applications. Generic formats obviously allow you to open files within different applications and thus take advantage of their different features, but specific formats are sometimes created to allow the storage of special information relating to just one application. For instance, a modelling file might include the state of the background, lighting and animation script that relates to its own application rather than just numerical details of the model which could be universally understood. For that reason, if a generic format is used for the sake of portability, it can be sensible also to store files in the native format so that all the information is retained for future use.

Some file formats originated with early applications in the field and have been adopted by later programmers; others provide updates to previous file formats. We might distinguish between the requirements of files containing words, model data and 2-D images, although all are stored physically in the same way. Many applications have their own proprietary file type, some having proved sufficiently useful to be supported by other applications. The following are some of the most common 2-D and 3-D file types relevant to our discipline.

Adobe Illustrator: An object-orientated 2-D file accepted by many modelling programs for import (as a template, for example).

Aldus Freehand: An object-orientated 2-D file accepted by many modelling programs for import (as a template, for example).

ASCII: Stores text (but not its formatting) using the almost universal ASCII codes.

DXF: Developed by AutoCAD for storing 2-D and 3-D CAD files. It has become an industry standard, but because current modellers have features that DXF was not designed to handle, the manual for an application will explain the manner in which its models will be stored in the DXF file. Whilst the universality of this format enables models to be exported to many applications, it can mean that some features available in its host environment (such as interactive NURBS) will be lost in the translation.

EPS/EPSF: Encapsulated PostScript is mainly for storing 2-D object-orientated images but can store bit mapped graphics as well. Resolution independent.

GIF: Graphic Interchange Format, designed for transmitting compressed images.

Photoshop: Picture file created by Adobe Photoshop . Includes Alpha channel information.

PICS: For storing animations made of PICT and PICT2 images.

PICT: Can store object-orientated and bit-mapped images of up to eight colours. It is Apple's standard image format. PICT2 is an update of the PICT format which can store 32-bit colour but is still usually referred to as PICT. A useful format because it is supported by almost every Mac application.

QuickTime: Animation format using the QuickTime system extension for System 7. Several compression algorithms are supported and its open architecture allows more to be added in software or hardware. Other platforms have also adopted QuickTime; which will make file exchange easy.

RGB: Raw Red/Green/Blue data file.

RIB: Pixar's format for storing rendering and modelling files. Used by RenderMan and widely supported on a number of platforms.

SCITEX: CMYK file for high-end image processing.

Swivel 3D: Stores 3-D model files with articulation information. Created for Swivel 3D but now widely supported by modelling applications.

TGA: TrueVision Targa file (2-D). Widely used in the PC world.

TIFF: Tagged Image Format, the standard for scanned images. It can take advantage of LZW compression but compressed files cannot always be recognised by the receiving program. Since the TIFF file is also standard on PCs, file transfer is straightforward.

It is important, when considering new software, to ensure that it can import and export the file types that it will need in order to work with your other applications (and with outside applications if necessary). File conversion utilities (like deBabeliser) can bridge some gaps.

5.6 COMPRESSION

It is possible to maximise the use of storage space by compressing information when it is stored and then decompressing it when it is retrieved. For graphics applications, one commonly used compaction technique is 'run-length' encoding. Rather than separately store the actual intensity of every pixel, run-length encoding stores the intensity of a pixel and the number of following pixels with that same intensity. Imagine a single pixel being ON at the centre of a 640 x 400 pixel display. Instead of individually recording the state of all 256,000 pixels, it would be sufficient to record that the first 127,999 pixels were OFF, the next one was ON and the remaining 128,000 were OFF. The efficiency of the technique is greatest in images with blocks of similarly set pixels and would become inefficient in the rare case that no pixel was the same intensity as its neighbour. It is, therefore, more efficient in dealing with computer-generated images (where the pixels in a solid block of colour are consistent) than in dealing with video images (where visual 'noise' limits the likelihood of adjacent pixels being the same). A number of other methods for compression are available and some applications can select from a library of different techniques after assessing which is most efficient for each given image. The encoding and decoding can sometimes be achieved in real time using either software or dedicated hardware methods.

Animation, and the increasing use of video, highlight the problem. If you consider the amount of storage required to store one second of high-resolution, 24-bit colour animation, it is clear that efficient compression algorithms are essential if we are to be able to develop the medium. Even at 640x480 pixels, one second of 24-bit, 30 fps video requires 30 MB of memory, and one minute needs 1.8 gigabytes. Assuming the storage is available, there remains the problem of getting that much data to the screen fast enough for real-time display. A common method of compacting animation is to store the first frame in its entirety and, thereafter, to store only the changes between subsequent frames. This is extremely efficient when few pixels have changed between frames, which may often be the case in computer-generated sequences. It is likely to be far less efficient in handling sequences from a video source, since random changes are likely to occur to pixels throughout a sequence, even in areas of apparently unchanging colour.

Compression algorithms are described as 'lossy' or 'lossless' according to whether they achieve their compression at the cost of sacrificing any information. It is often acceptable to lose some information in order to achieve greater compression and this proves to be one of several areas of compromise in visual computing. Applications increasingly offer a compression option (such as LZ compression for TIFF files) at the time of saving a file but beware of using a compression type which the receiving application cannot understand. Take care also if you have QuickTime in your System folder, because JPEG compression will be offered by 'aware' applications, but the same application will not be able to decompress the file on another Mac without QuickTime installed. Compression will increasingly be built into hardware and new chip sets due shortly support JPEG, MPEG and H261 standards (described next).

As well as using compression within your own system, it can be vital when communicating data to other systems on a network or down a phone line. POTS (Plain Old Telephone System) has been considered to lack the bandwidth needed to handle the demands of intensive transmission (such as good quality video) and alternatives (such as ISDN) are often needed. A new compression system is now promised which will send 320x240 pixel colour images at 15 fps over POTS.

5.6.1 JPEG

The Joint Photographic Experts Group (JPEG) algorithm for still images can compress an image by 25 to 1 with minimal loss of quality, but can take 15 minutes to compress a 25MB image in software (on a 25-MHz 68030 machine). Built into hardware, however, specialised compression processors have the performance to sustain video rates. The algorithms must, of course, be able to decompress as efficiently as they compress and the JPEG algorithm is an example of a symmetrical algorithm which uses the same number of operations for both processes and hence the same time. It is becoming increasingly available as a hardware add-on, and much higher compression rates are possible if some loss of information (often imperceptible) is acceptable.

5.6.2 MPEG

The Motion Picture Experts Group (MPEG) algorithm for motion picture images has been slower to arrive than JPEG but is now being seen in add-on boards. Because of its delay in arrival, a 'moving' JPEG has evolved in the meantime. In order to take video in to the computer in real time, to store it in an acceptably limited amount of space, and to export it in real time, a lot of efficient compression is required. Interestingly, and perhaps surprisingly, whilst MPEG is designed for use in areas such as video it is not suitable for non-linear digital editing, which is at the heart of the promised desktop video revolution. This is because the temporal compression compresses moving image data by storing only the difference between one frame and its preceding frame, instead of storing all of each frame. The information from the previous frame is therefore required in order to construct the current frame, and this can only be achieved through linear, rather than random, access..

5.6.3 H.261

H.261 (also known as Px64) is a specification for a method of sending compressed video over digital phone lines and local area networks, particularly addressing the needs of video conferencing. It is likely to become significant since it has been adopted by a number of major companies such as AT&T, Motorola and British Telecom.

5.6.4 IFS

Iterated Function Systems are used to derive a simple set of fractal rules from complex data, such as a picture, and thus allow potentially extreme data compression. They have the advantage over other compression systems of being resolution independent. Whilst the principles have been talked about for several years and research papers published, applications are only just starting to appear in the high street and their impact has yet to be assessed.

5.7 CUSTOMISATION

Any off-the-shelf computer can make some attempt at modelling and rendering, subject to suitable software being available. We have, however, established that our discipline has special requirements, and it is worth summarising the ways in which we might optimise a machine for our particular task.

It rapidly becomes tedious to have a long delay before a model is

redrawn after you have moved or amended it and then to see that
delay increasing as the model becomes more complex. If the model
is in a shaded mode the delay is longer and watching an image being
ray traced can be like watching your life tick away. It is therefore
desirable to have a fast machine, ideally with a bank of accelerators
added.

24-bit colour is great for photographic rendering, but unnecessary
for wireframe engineering drawing. A large monitor does, however,
make life a lot easier, and I find my 16-inch Apple monitor a very
satisfactory compromise. In order to run it in full colour you need to
add extra video RAM or buy a suitable video card, depending on the
machine that is running it. If I was working on large, complex
models I would want a 21-inch+monitor.

You can't have too much RAM installed but for anything at all
serious you'll need 10Mb. 20Mb is a comfortable starting point and I
haven't yet needed more, but I have not been involved in
heavyweight colour graphics where 64Mb would be useful. This is
not to say that 5Mb plus virtual memory is not practical for our area,
it is just less convenient and not enough to get commercially serious.
Bear in mind that much current modelling software recommends a
minimum of 6Mb and that future packages are likely to want more.

I can't imagine starting without a hard drive, the question is only:
'how big ?' Despite reading that 'size isn't everything', you will find
that 60Mb gets full very fast and 600Mb would be nice. I manage
with 250Mb but off-load files to an optical disc as they build up, and
I'm not building models commercially. Large hard drives do not
encourage economical housekeeping but are very convenient.
Ideally I would have two, large, mirrored hard drives so that all data
was automatically backed up and it would take a catastrophic
accident to lose it all. I would also employ someone to back up every
day to a secondary medium, since I'm no better at doing it than
anyone else. A number of applications provide the option for
automatic backup, and DAT drives provide relatively cheap storage
for gigabytes of data. I'm delighted with my 128Mb optical for
archiving but still store the discs beside the computer instead of in
another room (or town!) as I should, for optimum security.

I use a mouse for drawn input but strongly recommend a
graphics tablet. A tablet is always top of my shopping list but
somehow everything else gets bought first. The degree to which you

need a tablet will be determined by the sort of work you are doing (and also by the background you bring to the work) but the mouse is ergonomically very bad for freehand drawing. Start with a mouse and then discover through doing it how much use you make of it, how much you use numerical input from the keyboard, and how much use you could make of a puck to input data.

You will need to get information out of the computer, but only you can decide whether that needs to be printed, plotted, photographed, filmed or video taped. Be warned that a video set-up can easily cost more than the computer equipment, though this is easier to bear if it is shared by a number of operators.

Although I'd like to claim you can model and render to professional standards on the cheapest, simplest Macintosh, I'm afraid it's just not true. You can get a flavour of the discipline, get to understand its principles and do worthwhile things on simple hardware, but you will need more power to produce the images shown on the covers of the manuals.

5.8 EXPENSE

The cost of achieving a modelling solution can be measured in both time and money, time itself having a price tag in any commercial situation. Direct cost comparisons between platforms are only possible when looking at identical functionality since, for example, the built-in networking ability of the Mac will offer no cost saving if the machine is not to be networked. Similarly, the extra cost of a Mac video over one for a PC is irrelevant if video is not to be handled. It is fair to say, however, that Mac hardware prices have (currently) dropped to a point where they are no longer a problem when making comparisons with PCs and that software prices too are roughly comparable across the two platforms. Reports comparing the cost of Macs with PCs have indicated that installation, maintenance and training are all easier on Macs, and that this leads to them being cheaper over a three-year period.

5.8.1 TIME

If you are quietly investigating modelling as a spare-time interest, and are happy to leave your machine running over the weekend to generate a single high resolution, full-colour image, then the minimum hardware capable of doing the job is adequate for your needs. Indeed, there is an added preciousness about a picture that has been nursed along over several days which is missing from one created in minutes. It also allows time for you to think about what you are doing. This might seem too obvious to be worth mentioning, but when technology speeds up production it also cuts back on the gestation period which is part of the creative process. The result can almost precede any clear intention.

In a production environment, however, time is money, and fast equipment means (potentially) more jobs can be undertaken. Clients are likely to want a quick turn around, with their expectations being partly fed by the technology itself. Acquiring a number of machines and networking them together is often part of the solution, especially in a business of any size, and I am constantly aware of the power I am missing out on by having a single machine isolated on its own at home.

It is also important to have software which will do the job required efficiently and also to be thoroughly familiar with it. One benefit of Mac software has always been the operational similarity between different applications. Apple sets tight guidelines for the creation of software and interfaces for its Macs, and since most manufacturers conform closely to these guides, new software is easy to 'get into', and hence has a quicker learning curve. Although much of the fun of modelling is in solving new problems, it is much quicker when the problem is a familiar one and the solution has been rehearsed.

5.8.2 MONEY

Many computer users spend their lives dreaming of the great things they would do if only they had a bigger machine. It is, however, very satisfying to achieve the maximum from a limited machine and this can often lead to greater ingenuity and invention. Also, with the Macintosh range of machines, one can be quite confident that projects will be able to be carried forward onto more powerful machines if the opportunity arises or that connection to a network will give access to extra power. As a home user the best advice is probably to decide on the software that you need to run and then to find the machine that will run it 20% faster than the speed you genuinely require. This will give a little room for leeway but not stretch finances further than necessary. If you are confident that you are going to need to develop your equipment in the future, then you must also ensure that your chosen machine has enough expansion slots (although both Apple and third-party suppliers regularly bring out conversion kits which might help you). Finally, you can expect to be able to sell or trade-in your machine in order to make another purchase, though you must not delude yourself about the speed at which computer hardware devalues. Too many people wait on the sidelines of computing, waiting for the definitive machine to arrive; whatever you buy will be superseded but that does not make it out of date if it still does the job you want of it.

If you use a computer professionally, then there are good reasons for spending more money on your system. Hardware is usually going to cost less in the long term than your labour or that of your staff, and there are often incentives to be close to the leading edge of technology. It is well worth talking to your accountant about leasing, since this not only spreads the cost and can have tax advantages, but can give you a high level of flexibility in upgrading equipment when you need to do so. In education leasing is increasingly considered now as a means of establishing an immediate hardware base, rather than having to build it up over a period of years (and thus losing out on the use that could have been made of it in the early years). If you are using your Mac as part of your business, it also pays to consider a maintenance contract. Since Mac equipment seems to be generally reliable, it is difficult to bring yourself to spend that extra five percent at the outset, but you have to assess the cost to your business of being without equipment for the period of any repair.

I know of a number of businessmen who have been talked into spending far more money than they need to on their computer systems. They have ended up with very nice systems but specified

far beyond their real requirements. I do my word processing on a
Quadra 950 because that is my machine, but if I only did word
processing I would trade it in straight away for the cheapest
Powerbook – I would be wasting its power. Unless you have
unlimited funds available, there is always a compromise to be made
between the ideal system and the one you can afford.

5.9 ERGONOMICS

At the same time as considering hardware, it is worth thinking about
how and where it is going to be physically used. In the broadest
sense, the working environment must be psychologically sound as
well as ergonomically effective. It is not within the power of the
system's designer to determine whether the operator works in
monastic silence or with Wagner playing at full volume, nor
whether the lighting is from soft uplighters or glaring spotlights,
but these factors form part of the total user interface. It is also the
case that scientific disciplines are likely to be carried out in a very
different environment from that of the creative world and that the
personnel will have very different backgrounds. Someone with a
scientific background, who has probably become familiar with
computers and programming as a general purpose tool, is likely to
be more comfortable inputting numbers through a keyboard than a
graphic designer with, perhaps, no background in mathematics. The
designer, on the other hand, will feel immediately comfortable
holding a stylus that may be alien to the scientist, yet they may both
need to use the same computer system.

When a process such as drawing a freehand circle, with which we
are all familiar using pencil and paper, is being undertaken on the
machine, it is easiest to use a tool that simulates the process with
which we are familiar. In that instance using a stylus is manually
identical to using a pencil (but with the initially disconcerting
difference that you don't see the result of your drawing on the pad,
but on the screen in front of you). A fresh coordination needs to be
acquired between hand and eye. A mouse also requires the hand to
be moved in a circle, but, being gripped differently, excludes the
subtle finger control we would normally expect to exercise. Cursor

keys present a further level of removal from the real-world experience and sitting down to write a program to draw the required circle is probably as far as you can get from using a pencil.

It is not, therefore, possible to describe an ideal environment, as it depends on who is doing what with the system. Certain features can be recommended, however, not just to make the job comfortable, but thence to get the most out of the user. The following should be set according to recognised ergonomic standards:

1. The height of the desk and chair: these must be set relative to the operator when resting the balls of the feet on the ground, and not arbitrarily. The chair should allow the seat to tilt forward.

2. The position of the keyboard, pad, mouse, etc., relative to the operator. RSI (Repetitive Stress Injury) is the subject of medical discussion and keyboards are claimed to be a major problem. Long periods drawing with a mouse can also be a problem (as I have discovered).

3. The size, distance and angle of the monitor.

4. The radiation level of the monitor (new monitors conform to high standards, old ones can often be converted).

5. The monitor's resolution and refresh rate (72 dpi is a standard resolution, but higher is good for fine work; higher refresh rates mean less flicker).

6. The ambient and local light level and type (low light levels allow the monitor brightness to be turned down, thus relieving eye strain, but might conflict with other office needs). Strip lighting can flicker, especially when nearing the end of its life, and seems to be a particular problem when combined with monitor flicker.

7. The continuous time spent at a monitor: various recommendations exist and include the advice to get up and move around during breaks.

8. The combined noise of collected computer and peripheral fans should be recognised.

There are now specific EEC standards which must be met and stricter standards upheld elsewhere, notably in Sweden.

CHAPTER 6

COMMUNICATING WITH THE MAC

It becomes so obvious to tap at a computer keyboard, wiggle a mouse and watch the results of these actions on the computer screen that it is easy to take for granted that this is the way one 'talks' to a computer. It is, however, worth considering the broader view – that these are merely examples of the input and output of data. However sophisticated the data may seem to us, perhaps a photographically realistic three-dimensional scene, the computer can only distinguish between 0 and 1. It is the job of the input and output devices to work with the computer and create an interface that makes our communication with the machine as friendly and efficient as possible.

6.1 INPUT DEVICES

An input device is a piece of hardware which allows us to put data into the system. This input may be coded (such as a typed instruction) or positional (such as perhaps traced off a map). As modellers we might often find ourselves concerned with inputting data both in drawn and numerical form. My first experience of computers (many years ago) was of hours spent punching cards in a noisy, communal punch room, followed by the presentation of several boxes of cards to the computer operators through a mysterious hatch in the wall and a day or two waiting for a print-out to be returned. If one hole was punched in the wrong place on one card then the program didn't run. Not the environment for which most designers would choose to abandon their drawing boards and putty rubbers.

6.1.1 KEYBOARD

The ubiquitous keyboard is so familiar that it is easy to forget how it works. It usually conforms to the same layout of letters, figures and symbols as the typewriter (with some regional variations amongst the non-alpha-numeric characters). The qwerty keyboard (named after its first five keys) is the standard; ergonomically superior key layouts have been designed but retraining presents too great a problem for them to be implemented in most cases. Keyboards are also available which improve on the standard rectangular format and help to avoid the stress injuries which can arise from constant use. It is possible, with a non-manual keyboard, for alternative key functions to be held in software and switched between. Your keyboard Control Panel, for instance, will enable you to choose between a UK and a US keyboard, if both layouts are installed.

Several keyboards are available for the Mac, some with an additional numeric keypad to speed up numerical input, four cursor keys which move the screen cursor left, right, up and down; and 'function' keys which can be configured by the user (or the current application) to do prescribed jobs. Depression of a key, either on its own or in conjunction with another (e.g. SHIFT, CONTROL, ALTERNATE, COMMAND) generates a unique electronic digital code which is interpreted by the computer's CPU. The code is normally the international standard ASCII (pronounced 'askey').

If a key is held down too long it will send its message more than onceeeeeeee (this is because the keyboard is checked by the CPU about 50 times a second to see if any key has been pressed). Whilst the system may not respond to the repetition of messages from some keys, it is likely to do so with all the alpha-numeric keys, which can give rise to errors. Once a key has been recognised as having been pressed, the significance of the code is considered according to an established priority, so that QUIT or BREAK, for example, may be given priority over everything else that is going on. An interrupt which is given priority over everything else is called an 'NMI' (non-maskable interrupt). The key 'repeat rate' and 'delay until repeat' can be set in a Control Panel.

6.1.2 MOUSE (+ variations)

The mouse is another ubiquitous device that fits in the palm of the hand and is rolled over a smooth surface. In a mouse with a mechanical mechanism (the most common type), a ball in the base of the mouse is rotated by the movement across a surface and these rotations are translated into data which moves a screen cursor on a corresponding path. The less common optical mouse establishes its position by detecting reflections from a beam shone downwards by a light-emitting diode, and a reflective surface is therefore required. Mechanical mice collect dirt that interferes with their efficiency and should be periodically cleaned; they work best on a clean mouse mat.

Move the mouse to the right and the screen cursor moves a proportional distance to the right, move it forward (assuming a horizontal surface) and the cursor moves up the screen (assuming a vertical screen). The screen cursor, incidentally, is often not the same as the keyboard cursor and may change its form according to the function it is currently fulfilling. The speed of tracking of a mouse, and its double-clicking speed, can be customised in a Control Panel to suit the operator. The Mac mouse normally has one button at the finger tip end which can be used to 'click', 'double click' and 'drag', these operations having fairly predictable consequences in Mac software. The mouse connects to the ADB chain (usually at the keyboard) by a flexible lead which makes it easy to set for right or left-handed operators. Cordless mice are now available, which are less restricting, more expensive and ambidextrous. In general the mouse can be regarded as a cheap, simple and relatively low resolution device. It is important to remember that the coordinates returned by the mouse are relative to the position on the last occasion that the ball was turned. If the mouse is taken off the surface its absolute position is lost.

The 'tracker ball' is similar to an inverted mouse and is operated by turning the ball with the fingertips. It moves a screen cursor in the same way as a mouse but is, perhaps, less immediately intuitive to use. One of its advantages, however, is that it remains stationary and for this reason has become incorporated into some laptop computers, like the Macintosh Powerbooks. As the size of the ball is increased, so subtle movements become easier whilst big movements require the ball to be spun more. A giant tracker ball has been suggested as a control device for handicapped users who have difficulty making fine movements.

6.1.3 2-D GRAPHIC TABLET

Graphics tablets have a pad, normally between A4 and A0 size, on which the position of a hand-held sighting device called a 'puck', or a pen-like 'stylus', can be detected with great accuracy. They can also be used with digitising tables of much greater size for higher levels of precision. The puck has a small window showing cross hairs, which are to be aligned with the current data point, and buttons to determine the use that is to be made of that data. Either the pad or the puck transmits continuous signals which the other receives, and can be electromagnetic, electrostatic, ultrasonic or infrared. The signals translate into X,Y positions with an accuracy of up to 0.001 of an inch and the pads are widely used as a means of transferring data from a drawing on paper to the computer. Before starting work the digitiser must be orientated to the sheet of paper, so that verticals remain vertical and the origin is correctly located.

If the puck is replaced by a stylus then the same principles allow freehand drawing, such as might be useful in a paint program. Whilst the puck is often used to input data without reference to a display monitor, the stylus operator normally uses the monitor for positional feedback. The use of the stylus is associated more with continuous movement and the puck with the input of discrete points. Some styluses are pressure sensitive, which is a great advantage in trying to match the subtlety of normal hand media, but this facility is dependent on the software's ability to support it. Both puck and stylus are normally connected to the pad with a flexible lead, though cordless versions are now available with the disadvantage that they are easier to mislay.

The digitising pad can often be configured by the user, allowing the relationship between its drawing area and the screen area it maps to be flexible. Some applications cover part of the pad with menu overlays relating to program functions, and when the stylus or puck is used to select from this menu it is said to be used as a 'pick'. The same applies to the use of pick or stylus to move the screen cursor in order to select from any screen menu displayed. The stylus, in particular, is often used to select data from the current screen image for further treatment, for example in a paint program to select one colour from the screen image for use elsewhere.

6.1.4 3-D DIGITISER

The systems described so far have been used for inputting 2-D information, and this may, of course, provide the basis for building a 3-D model. It is, however, possible to input 3-D information directly, though the equipment for doing so is not yet widely found. The position of a stylus tip, moving in 3-D space, can be tracked using acoustic, mechanical, optical or electromagnetic means. An object can thus be traced over with the stylus, but care must be taken to select logically suitable points on its surface for digitising. A new device for the input of three-dimensional information into a computer is a sonic digitiser using four microphone sensors to calculate distance from a stylus tip emitting an ultrasonic signal at a rate of up to sixty times per second. Commonly, the object would have a mesh grid drawn over its surface and the intersection points would be those digitised. The process is, as yet, time consuming and painstaking. Laser scanning provides an alternative method, but all current systems have problems with objects containing inaccessible areas.

6.1.5 TOUCH SCREEN

There are occasions when it is desirable to have the most direct possible relationship between alternatives open to the operator and the means of attaining those alternatives. Such a high level of interactivity is appropriate, for instance, if the public has access to an unattended machine, which they are to be encouraged to use intuitively to get information. A touch screen allows the user to press the screen and get the same response as a mouse-click would normally give; buttons simulated on screen can therefore be 'pressed', and items 'dragged' (if so programmed) with a fingertip. There are a number of different technologies that can be used to build touch screens and the choice is likely to be based on cost, sensitivity, robustness and available size. Monitors can be supplied with touch screens built in or they can be added subsequently.

Whilst there is no frequent case when this is of specific use to modellers, it is increasingly the case that computer models may subsequently be made accessible to the public through such interactive media.

6.1.6 SCANNER

We are likely to need to import complete images intact from a range of sources as well as to create them by hand (for example to use as image maps). Flat art work can be imported using a 'scanner', in which the material is placed face down on a glass plate and scanned using similar technology to a photocopier, producing a file in a common format. Until recently, colour scanners were very expensive but the price has dropped considerably and a 24-bit colour scanner able to work at 600dpi (dots per inch) can be bought very reasonably. Ultra-high resolution scanners are likely to be found only in bureaux, but desktop machines are coming out with 1200dpi, although it is worth remembering that scans at that resolution create very big files. The desktop machine's usual image size is about A4, and small hand scanners are available which cover a width of about four inches, whilst being dragged manually down the image. Problems in using them can arise if the copy is slightly misaligned or, in the case of the hand scanner, the dragging is not even, but the latest software improvements have largely overcome these faults. When text is imported, the use of OCR (see below) software can produce a portable ASCII file (allowing, for example, a newspaper page to be scanned in and converted to a standard ASCII file which could then be reset using a typographic package). Recently, machines have appeared on the market which make use of the shared technology of colour scanners, printers and photocopiers to do all three jobs (currently at 400dpi) with consequent cost saving.

6.1.7 NEW INPUT DEVICES

Three forms of input which are in their infancy are 'OCR' (optical character recognition), in which an intelligent system reads printed (or sometimes even hand-written) text; direct speech, in which a system understands human speech (in a currently limited vocabulary); and the 'DataGlove', which translates movements of the operator's hand (encased in the DataGlove) into comparable movements in the three-dimensional space of a robotic hand which might exist or merely be a computer model. The DataGlove is one tool of 'virtual reality' in which the operator is able to enter into a three- dimensional computer-generated space. (The potential and implications of virtual reality are so great that it will be dealt with later in the book.) A directional hand tool (a palm-held ball shape, tapering to a pointer, with input buttons) is one of the devices which has been developed to allow someone in a virtual environment to 'fly' through the virtual space that surrounds him.

6.1.8 VIDEO

It is common to import material from a video source, which might be either direct through a video camera, or using pre-recorded material through a VCR (video tape recorder). The suitability of this as an image input medium depends on the use to which the image is to be put, since broadcast video resolution can be fine for producing material for TV viewing but not necessarily for reproduction as a print. The quality of the image is determined by its spatial resolution (768x576 for broadcast TV in the UK) and by its colour depth (i.e. 24-bit represents 'full' colour). A specialist video card is needed to enable the computer to interface with a video input but these are now starting to be built into new machines, especially those intended for multimedia work. A top quality card can cost as much as a top of the range Mac.

Live action can also be grabbed-in, the main problem being the massive file sizes taken by large screen, full colour video at 25 frames per second in the UK using the PAL system (or 30 fps with the NTSC system in the USA and some other countries). These problems are now being alleviated by hardware compression boards capable of taking in live video and storing it at 7Mb per minute with 160:1 compression. Apart from top professional equipment, video boards are rarely designed to be of broadcast quality but this technology is now becoming available at accessible prices. Apple is now building video-handling capability into a number of models at very little extra cost in order to encourage its wider use, and the market's interest in multimedia is hastening this development.

6.1.8.1 STILL CAMERA

Increasingly available are still cameras designed to capture static images on a digital medium, using either discs or RAM, at a potentially high resolution. If the material shot is exclusively destined for use in the computer then this is a fast, reusable medium, though still relatively expensive since it is in its infancy. There is much talk about digital photography superceding traditional paper-and-silver methods, and it seems certain to do so in a number of areas. Being able to grab images of the real world directly into the computer, manipulate them digitally and integrate them seamlessly with other media, suggests a very productive environment.

6.1.8.2 LIVE CAMERA

A vertically mounted video camera is usually to be found in the corner of computer graphics studios standing ready to import flat art work, usually being a professional 'three-chip' camera. It has the advantage over a scanner that it can also be used for three-dimensional subjects and it is easier to view the image on screen while it is being manipulated, but is not necessarily of a suitably high resolution. A domestic camcorder can equally well be used, though at a slightly inferior quality. For preliminary visualisation work, and often for work destined for domestic video, the simplest equipment is adequate and easy to use. A camera can also be used for grabbing-in live action if a suitable video board is installed.

6.1.8.3 VTR

Pre-recorded material can be input from a video tape deck; either a separate unit or one integral to a camcorder. The same issues of quality apply. If it is required to input video frame by frame, perhaps so that each frame can be treated in a paint system, then professional equipment and a video controller are needed. These are likely to be far more expensive than your Macintosh, though demand is pushing prices down fast.

6.2 OUTPUT DEVICES

Being able to input data only allows for a monologue and in order to communicate with the machine it must be able to 'talk back'. It does this via a possible range of output devices. A printer or plotter can provide 'hard copy' on paper, film and video cameras can record still or moving images, or real time feedback can be given by the monitor screen. Output can also be of data to a storage device but devices such as disc drives have been dealt with in the previous chapter.

6.2.1 VDU

The basic VDU (visual display unit) is normally a standard computer monitor (although a video card might also display its output on a video monitor or television). Its screen is such an integral part of the way we work with computers that it is often forgotten that it is an output device and not a window on the computer's mind. It provides a quick and understandable, but not always accurate, view of the state of progress within an application. A normal monitor cannot, for instance, show a straight diagonal line without the 'staircasing' effect of a pixel screen, and an image of photographic quality can only be shown at the much lower resolution of the screen itself.

A number of properties of a monitor are worth considering, particularly size, resolution and colour. The resolution is usually expressed in dpi which indicates how many pixels there are to an inch; the more there are, the smaller they obviously are, and the clearer the picture definition. Typically a Mac screen will have 72 dpi, which is described as high resolution, though 80dpi is not uncommon. Note that it is the dpi figure which indicates the screen's resolution and not the pixel count, which is often quoted instead. A 20-inch screen with 1024x768 pixels is the same resolution as a 14-inch screen with 640x480 pixels, and a lower resolution than a 15-inch screen with 640x870 pixels (72 dpi compared with 80 dpi). You will notice that the first two sizes mentioned are of a horizontal format compared with the vertical format of the third monitor. Horizontal is the standard, but for DTP it is convenient for the screen format to match that of the layout. This 15-inch monitor is, therefore, designed with a whole screen, vertical A4 sheet in mind, the 20-inch monitor permits the viewing of a double A4 layout. Screens which rotate from vertical to horizontal give you some advantages of both formats. Portable machines have different screen technologies, and although they are improving fast, cannot match the clarity of conventional screens yet; as I write this, Apple has just announced its first colour laptop, with 256 colours.

A large monitor can make working life much more comfortable, but the size actually needed is best defined first in terms of the job to be done and then translated into inches; bear in mind that monitors are generally described by the diagonal measurement of the tube, which will be greater than the available viewing area. If your work involves a lot of fine detail then the highest resolution helps, though the zoom factor in all applications can be used as an aid. (The viewing distance of the monitor is also a factor.) The equipment you buy will usually be chosen by compromising several factors. The other major factor with monitors is colour.

The most basic screen will display only black and white and simulates greys with graded black and white patterns. A greyscale screen can generate a range of greys but no colours. An 8-bit screen can produce 256 colours and a 24-bit screen generates more than 16 million colours (although you won't have enough pixels to use them all at once). For close to photographic quality a 24-bit display is needed, but the results at 12-bits (4096 colours) are quite good and can be very good if the palette is judiciously chosen. The difference in palette size is most easily seen in areas of gentle gradation, where small palettes give rise to banding. It can be a waste of time and space to generate images with larger palettes than can be displayed on the monitor for which it is eventually destined (is it worth ray tracing at 24-bits for your monitor if the image will end up in an 8-bit application?). For precise colour work it is possible to accurately calibrate the colour seen on the monitor to the colour produced by another output device, such as a printer.

Unfortunately you cannot just plug any monitor into any computer and start work, the machine must be capable of driving the display. There are limits to the size/bit-level of monitor that any Mac can drive with its basic capacity and it may be necessary to add video RAM or a separate video card in order to drive the monitor of your choice. A phenomenon that can seem strange at first is to see two monitors being driven by one computer, so that the cursor passes from one screen to the other during horizontal movements. This is facilitated by the Mac operating system, and set in a Control Panel, and can be useful, for example, to display a number of application menus and control windows on one screen whilst having the main image window on a second screen, avoiding a single cluttered screen.

Video work requires further consideration, and if you anticipate that this will be a requirement, it is as well to check out your proposed purchases thoroughly. A computer monitor is non-interlaced, which means that every line on the screen is scanned at each pass, whereas a TV screen is interlaced, meaning that only alternate lines are scanned on each pass. The most noticeable results are that our computer monitor is comfortable on the eyes, having no perceptible

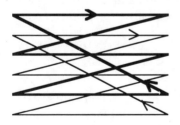 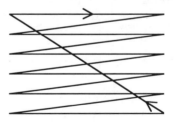

Raster scans
Left: interlaced
Right: Non-interlaced

flicker, and that a TV image will not display thin horizontal lines without dramatic flicker. This requires consideration when producing images for video, as static, single pixel horizontals must be avoided. For example, a Mac window looks terrible on a TV because the window 'frame' is made up of single pixel lines which flicker badly, although the contents of the window might look fine. Anti-flicker filters are fitted to some video boards to alleviate this problem and are a great improvement for general use, but the resultant signal is no longer strictly of broadcast standard. A multisynch monitor is often required since it can adjust to different refresh rates, and it is worth noting that for video work, a resolution of 576x768 pixels matches a TV screen. A computer can also generate colours outside of the range that a TV can handle and rich saturated colours are usually to be avoided. It is possible to run images through a PAL filter (as in the UK) or NTSC filter (as in the USA) which will strip out 'illegal' colours, but since TVs are often poorly tuned, it can prove safer to err on the side of conservatism rather than risk glowing reds. The net result of these differences is that images generated only for the computer often look terrible when transferred to video.

Since you are likely to spend a lot of time working at your VDU it is an important purchase, but the technology is so improved that there are many fine monitors available. I'm delighted with my 16-inch Apple monitor and was surprised to find that it did not receive great reviews in comparative tests, but this indicates that there is a high subjective element in screen choice; it pays to have seen and used your screen before purchase. Other considerations in making your life comfortable are: a high refresh rate to minimise flicker (75Hz is common and satisfactory), anti-glare coating (particularly in a bright environment), low radiation levels (modern monitors conform to stricter guidelines), and a tilt and swivel base (almost standard and ergonomically essential).

6.2.2 PRINTER

An obvious output device is the printer, of which there are several types. The cheapest and most popular is the 'dot matrix' printer, which strikes the paper through an inked ribbon with a number of fine pins. The pins are carried in a moving head and the image is made up of a number of small dots, the resolution of which is determined by the number of pins in the head and the subtlety of the software driving it. A basic printer has nine pins, twenty-four pin machines are now common and higher pin numbers have recently become available. Many dot matrix printers can be equipped with colour ribbons (comprising bands of magenta, cyan, yellow and black) through which the pins selectively strike, but the results are not very convincing and are liable to be inconsistent as the ribbon fades. The dropping price of other technologies is causing the dot matrix printer to be superseded especially for non-text applications but it provides a cheap means of getting rough print out.

Laser printers employ electrophotographic technology (first developed in photocopiers). They are more expensive but produce very good quality results in black and white, until recently with a typical resolution of 300 dots per inch (dpi) but increasingly with 600dpi as standard. They are also available with higher resolutions and with colour - at a price. The human eye can distinguish separate dots up to about 1000 dpi. Ink jet machines (which shoot precise jets of coloured ink onto the paper) and bubble jet machines (which burst bubbles of ink onto the paper surface) are reasonably priced, quiet, and give clean colour, whilst thermal transfer printers (which use special paper) are effective but relatively expensive. It will always be the case (with foreseeable technology) that screen colour will fail to match printed output accurately, owing to the different ways in which the images are formed, but calibration brings them closer.

The means of creating colours on the screen is fundamentally different from that used to create printed colour. Screens optically mix from the three 'additive' primaries of Red, Green and Blue (RGB) to make all colours; the three primaries combining to produce white. In the 'subtractive' system the three primaries of Cyan, Magenta and Yellow (CMY) are overlaid to make any colour; the three primaries combining (theoretically) to produce black. In practice the print process requires the addition of black (K) pigment and the system is referred to as CMYK colour. Since the RGB screen image will often be representing a CMYK printed image, accurate matching of the two systems is vital, though not always easily achieved. Improvements to System7 address this issue, but since the colour gamut of the two systems is different, a perfect match is not always possible. Pantone have produced a set of matches between printing colours and screen colours, which is helpful in areas such as DTP, but a precise match requires particular combinations of screen and video card under controlled conditions.

6.2.3 PLOTTER

Plotters produce hardcopy by drawing on paper with pens which can move along the X axis and be raised from, or lowered to, the surface of the paper. Either the pens can also move along the Y axis or the paper can be moved along that axis past the pens. 'Flatbed' plotters hold the paper flat in either horizontal or vertical plane and can vary from A4 size to ten feet long. 'Drum' plotters take less floor space than horizontal flatbed plotters to produce large plots on cut or continuous roll, paper, by wrapping the paper over a drum roller, or by moving it from one roller to another. The plotter usually has between four and ten pens, selected under software control. Since the pen can produce only lines and dots, and must combine these styles to produce shading, it is best suited to linear or diagrammatic images only. The software that drives the plotter cannot convert raster images to plotable form. The best plotters are very high resolution devices, widely used in industry.

6.2.4 VTR

Video tape is the most commonly used medium for recording moving images today. A large number of formats are already available and more are developing, with great increases in quality. Whilst it is still generally true that the larger the tape width the greater the potential quality, improvements in tape technology mean that excellent results are now practical on narrower tapes which are associated with smaller (often cheaper) machines, though not necessarily to broadcast standard. Traditionally, tape has been used for analogue recording, but increasingly digital technology is invading the market place and can be expected to grow in influence over the next few years. Digital storage allows images to be subject to manipulation without loss of quality and is in the form needed to be handled by computers. At the time of writing we are less than twelve months away from TV quality digital storage at reasonable prices. There are many video formats which reflect the range of qualities, sizes and prices of systems available for use from home to professional broadcast standard. A significant distinction is between

those that store the red, green and blue signals separately
(component) and those that merge them together (composite). The
highest standard professional formats are component but broadcast
transmissions are currently composite.

Assuming that video is being used to record moving images, the
ability of the computer to generate them (or store them and then
replay them) in real-time is crucial. Although mentioned already, it
is worth noting that when the computer cannot always calculate and
display subsequent images at 25 (or 30) fps, and if that is the case
then the frames must be 'dropped' individually to the VTR. This
capability requires a professional machine and also an animation
controller, which can be either in software or hardware. Both are
likely to be expensive.

6.2.5 STILL CAMERA

Setting up a still camera and photographing from the monitor screen
is a cheap and simple way of saving images. The camera must be set
up on a tripod, daylight balanced film used, a shutter speed slower
than the screen refresh rate used, and ambient light must be
prevented from falling on the screen and causing reflections
(usually by improvising a hood to enclose screen and camera). It is
also desirable to run tests to find the ideal exposure and best screen
contrast to set, the maximum contrast available on the screen being
outside the range of film to record accurately (colour prints
having a lower contrast ratio than transparencies). The maximum
resolution will be that of the screen, however, and the scan lines
may be more obvious in the photograph than on the screen itself.
There is also likely to be some distortion of the image owing to the
curvature of the screen.

In order to guarantee the highest possible quality images, special
film recorders have been developed. These contain a very high
resolution black and white monitor with a flat screen and three
coloured filters, to which the camera must be accurately aligned.
The three colour planes in the frame buffer are separately displayed
through the appropriate filter and recorded onto the same piece of
film. The resultant resolution is far greater than on a colour

monitor since the black and white screen is not restricted by the shadow mask required by the former. Bureaux are available to produce slides at a resolution of 4000 to 8000 lines.

6.2.6 FILM CAMERA

The same principles apply to recording sequential images on cine film, with the added problem that the camera must be capable of reliable single framing, preferably under the control of the computer. It is not practical to film moving images of any quality from screen in real time because synchronisation problems between the shutter and the scanning are added to those described for still images. Recording directly from screen with a video camera normally produces poor images, although some professional cameras allow the shutter to be adjusted to the screen refresh rate for optimum synchronisation.

6.3 THE SCREEN INTERFACE

The role played by the screen interface has been touched on when describing the operating system and the specific problems of a modelling environment, first mentioned in the opening chapter. Its importance cannot be understated, and in the chapter dealing with specific applications I will often refer to the way in which the programs allows you to interact with them. The ease with which you are able move around and between the different features of the application and to set properties such as position, colour and surface, contributes to your enthusiasm for the job at hand and to your level of productivity. One particularly interesting problem in a modeller is the need to navigate 3-D space (and 4-D space, if you include the temporal dimension of an animation) by reference to a 2-D screen.

The need to position objects in space by rotating them around X-,Y- and Z-axes has found different solutions. Sometimes the three axes are controlled similarly but separately, perhaps by knobs or by mouse after the appropriate axis icon is selected; but more often rotation about the axis orthogonal to the screen plane (i.e. the Z-axis) has a different control. Rotations around the X- and Y-axes are typically controlled by virtual sliders aligned along the X- and Y-axes, or by horizontal and vertical movements of the mouse (because horizontal movements to left and right can be seen as analogous to turning a freely held object around the Y-axis and vertical movements around the X- axis). It is less easy to find a method of mimicking rotation around the Z-axis which is consistent with those of X and Y, and a less intuitive use of the same devices is often implemented. Research on the problem has produced a number of inventive solutions which represent the movements in terms of circles or spheres and different manufacturers have their own preferences. The movement of the object might be made in real time, in which case control of positioning can be interactive and it is likely that numerical positioning will be available for greater accuracy. The axes around which the object rotates by default are normally the world axes, which are unlikely to coincide with any of the object's axes (except when the object is in its canonical position or has been shifted without rotation). The pressure sensitive ball device, that has already been mentioned, represents one mechanical solution to the problem.

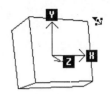

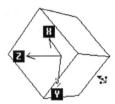

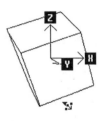

None of these methods matches our own use of binocular vision to interpret spatial position. Our brain uses the difference in information received from our two eyes to understand depth and even slight head movements can be enough to clarify spatial ambiguities. Stereoscopic viewing is available for use in conjunction with computers but tends to be used for viewing the final result rather than for interactive creation and manipulation. The method used involves replacing the single screen image viewed by both eyes, with separate images for each eye. Spectacles can hold separate mini-screens in front of each eye or can be used to filter separate information for each eye from a single screen by the familiar red/green lenses or by polarising lenses at right angles to one another. Alternatively, the screen information intended for each eye can be presented in turn whilst the lens covering the opposite eye is blacked out electronically, the synchronisation being controlled by the computer presenting the images. If the information for both eyes is shown on a single screen, then the display can be confusing for a viewer without the appropriate spectacles.

In MacTopaz labelled axes of rotation are shown. The object is rotated by clicking on the appropriate axis and dragging to position.

Virtual reality tools will allow you to enter into the same space as your objects and manipulate them from there, though this may not always prove preferable to viewing the scene from the outside. One should distinguish here between 'immersive' VR in which the operator enters into the computer created space, and 'non-immersive' VR where the operator observes the space through the window of the screen, but can manipulate objects within it. It is open to discussion whether the latter is a sufficiently new paradigm to be called VR.

Another spatial problem arises in setting the position and direction of light sources in the scene and there have been a number of very different methods employed by various applications. If the light source is not directional then only the position of the light itself has to be established, and methods vary from placement in top/ side/front windows to dragging a patch which represents the light around the surface of a sphere which stands for the boundary of the object's world. It is also possible to position the light, not by setting its position in space, but by demonstrating its effect on a symbolic object in the scene, as seen from the current viewpoint. A directional light has to be similarly positioned in space but also has to have the direction of its beam established, and probably the angle of the beam as well. This is quite effectively done in some applications by siting the light in the 3-D environment and dragging out a line representing the beam direction vector from the light to another point in 3-space. If the beam angle is variable then lines can be used to represent the edges of the beam instead of the beam's central direction, which has the advantage of increasing the accuracy with which a beam can be positioned.

CHAPTER 7

DESIGN METHODOLOGY

Since a computer model never actually builds itself, it is desirable to consider the methodology – the orderly arrangement of ideas – that needs to be brought to the modelling process at all stages.

7.1 PLANNING

There are usually at least half a dozen different ways of creating a model within any one modeller.   Even a b-rep cube, for example, can be created by extruding a square template, by lathing a four-sided object from a half-a-square template, by skinning, by lofting or by selection from a library of primitives, to name just a few obvious methods. The most appropriate method to use in building an object will depend mainly on the facilities offered by your modeller, on the relative efficiency of the available methods and on the use that is to be made of the object.

If it is intended to 'walk-through' the finished model it will probably be advantageous to create it in its simplest practical form (i.e. with walls having no thickness and doors having no moulding) so that it can be redrawn fast enough to achieve a sense of movement through the space. If the final model is to be rendered as a high resolution colour slide, then detail might be more important than file size and a long rendering time acceptable. If the model is to be exported to another package then it is necessary to check that it will lose no important properties in the process of saving to the chosen file type. If a number of separate elements go to make up an object they might be 'locked' together, but will the individual elements be able to be 'unlocked' if a change is later required?

All these possibilities, and many more, are obvious when pointed out, but can easily be overlooked if the project is not planned. Whilst there is probably no 'wrong' method of working, there are certainly methods which are more productive and less prone to unwelcome surprises than others. It is necessary, therefore, at the outset of the project to have at least an idea of what you aim to do, and, ideally, to have a clear plan of what you are going to do. Experience will contribute much to any decision about working method, particularly when there is a high level of similarity in models that you build and you will establish a routine. Half the fun of modelling, however, is in working out the best method of building a new and unfamiliar object, and, on completion, in realising a better method for 'next time'.

It is also possible that an open-ended and experimental approach will yield fresh discoveries but in real terms a balance is needed between such an approach and that of mindless repetition of a known formula.

7.1.1 'WORLD' MAP

I find it helpful to have a quick sketch alongside me which shows a cube representing the modeller's universe (or relevant part of it if it is infinite) marked with the axes and their rulers. The sketch could, of course, be drawn on the computer and viewed in a separate window, but I seem to be happier with paper. On this I roughly position the object(s), light(s) and camera(s) and with this guide alongside me I rarely get lost in the 3-D space. This might sound like an absurd confession, but in the modellers that I end up using most often it is still easy to get disorientated when moving the camera around and to lose a clear sense of the relationship of the objects to the light sources, for example. The orientation can be regained and/ or the relative positions reviewed, within the modeller, but not always conveniently. Some modellers are much better about preserving a sense of position than mine, but other relationships can be misinterpreted and I wouldn't throw away your notepad yet.

7.2 MATCHING METHOD TO TOOLS

It is necessary to recognise what your modeller is good at doing, what it is not so good at doing and what it just can't do. You can probably build something very similar to the model you want with any modeller but working to its strengths saves time and heartache. Whilst spinning and extruding are common to most packages, there is a limit to the objects that these processes alone will create, and it is no use being impressed by sample models of wine glasses and office desks if you are going to want to create frogs and curtains.

Manufacturers usually give an indication of the sort of customer at whom their product is aimed, though they are likely to suggest as broad a range as possible. It is usually clear, however, if a product is intended for architects, engineers, visualisers or for less dedicated use. This book should provide some assistance, magazine reviews are helpful (and copies can often be obtained from the product's distributor) and colleagues opinions can be sought. Take care that colleagues do not have a limited and/or dated view of the current field since there can be little incentive to watch the market place changing once a purchase has been made (though many Mac users are sufficiently enthusiastic about their work to keep up to date). I have also often noticed a reluctance to acknowledge that a product on which a lot of money has been spent is no longer (or perhaps never was) the best on the market. The most helpful magazine reviews might well be those in trade magazines rather than in the Mac press, since their reviews are made in the context of a specific discipline range.

Once you have a modeller, and after you've run through the tutorials that come with it, you need to explore a little to find its limits. Some of the facilities you might look for are:
- the ability to create complex curved surfaces (probably with splines)
- the ability to create non-symmetrical objects

- the ability to join objects
- the ability to cut objects
- the ability to enact Boolean operations on objects
- the presence of low-level editing tools

If these facilities are not present as such, you can start thinking of ways to skirt around their absence, probably with varying degrees of success. For instance, if you can't do a Boolean 'addition' operation, can you 'glue' or 'group' or 'link' the relevant objects, and if so, does this alternative give you sufficient functionality? If you can't obviously create asymmetrical objects, can you rethink your object in terms of a collection of symmetrical parts? If you get stuck for a solution then perhaps you have become locked into one way of thinking and need to try and see the problem again simply – as if with the eyes of a child (or move to sections 7.5 and 7.6).

7.3 THE NAMING OF PARTS

Your model may be made up of a hundred separate parts. You might have several versions of your model stored on the hard drive. When you create another part and are prompted to give it a name, resist the urge to call it 'x1', 'thingy' or 'new bit' because, descriptive as the names seem at the time, their meaning will be forgotten by tomorrow, if not sooner. 'Upper leg – left' is more meaningful than 'ulL'. Give everything a name which would identify it to a stranger, or else have a clear and consistent coding system for part names (e.g. W=window, 3=third floor, N=north facing, etc. according to your needs). The extra time taken in typing in a clear descriptive name is saved many times over when it comes to locating something in the future and the Mac allows file names of a useful length (up to 31 characters), unlike some other machines I can think of. Using the date as a suffix can be helpful in distinguishing between versions, although the System keeps track of the file's date anyway.

If you need to load two different versions of an object in at the same time, beware that the application might perceive a clash of names if both versions have the parts or objects similarly named. Whilst this can be solved by renaming, it can be tedious to find the only way to proceed is to be presented with every name in sequence and asked for an alternative.

Applications, especially drawing packages, often support 'layers', which can be thought of as transparent overlays to which different parts of a drawing or model can be allocated. These can provide a good way of separating different elements from one another. For example, the floor plans and pipe runs for a building can be held in separate layers and viewed (or operated on) either individually or overlaid on top of one another.

7.4 SALVATION

Everyone knows that you must save your work at regular intervals, that you must make a back-up copy on to a separate medium, and that you must keep a second copy of important files at a different location from the primary copy. Everyone also has his/her own story about losing an hour's or day's or week's or lifetime's work because the cat stood on the delete key or workmen cut through the power cable. I have become good at saving regularly to the hard disc, but always wait longer than I should before making copies on to another medium (despite now having an optical drive to make things far easier). When you lose your work, however (and you will), you have only yourself to blame.

If you can afford it, a great first line of defence is a pair of mirrored hard drives (described in section 5.7), where all data is simultaneously stored on two separate hard drives. There is also plenty of cheap software which will automatically save files at pre-set intervals (I use a simple public domain program), and such software will often perform backups to predefined storage devices. (Take care with software that does a regular 'Save' without presenting a dialogue box because if you have loaded an existing file to use as the basis for a new one the first save operation will overwrite the old file and you therefore need to 'Save As' a new file name before starting to modify the file). Establishing a habit of saving every 15 minutes and backing up at the end of every work session is a good start. In a communal environment your work can be destroyed in so many different and exciting ways that saving it regularly becomes vital and paranoia on the matter is to be encouraged. A code of practice should be given to anyone joining the community – and enforced.

It is also necessary to consider the lifetime of data held on different media and under different conditions. Data doesn't stay intact forever on most common media and even ensuring a ten-year life span requires thought. Magnetic storage on tape or floppy is not only vulnerable to obvious magnetic influences like the big magnet in your monitor or magnetic fields in your graphics pad (depending on the technology it uses) or to heat sources like the radiator beside your desk; data simply vanishes over time as the molecules rearrange themselves. Optical storage has a longer life span but for critical archiving it might be necessary to get expert advice on storage variables such as temperature and humidity.

7.5 LATERAL THINKING

After a basic introduction to modelling I ask students how they would model a square, moulded picture frame with mitred corners. Quite correctly they create a 2-D template representing a cross-section through the moulding, extrude a length of moulding, clone it to create four lengths, rotate the lengths in units of 90 degrees, and align the lengths. Some students use a Boolean operation to mitre the first length before cloning; some forget the mitring until after cloning; some ignore mitring entirely. They have created a frame the way they would if they were in the woodwork shop and the result is as required.

But how about creating the 2-D template (off centre) and then spinning it with the spin sides set to '4'? You arrive at the same thing with a lot less effort, but having used a process which does not mirror the real world frame-making method. After the superiority of this second method is acknowledged I ask how the students would change the frame from square to rectangular. A scaling operation along the appropriate axis is proposed but when we try it we find that whilst the frame is now rectangular, the moulding at the ends orthogonal to the direction of 'stretch' has itself become stretched (and is now fatter than the other pieces of moulding). Several alternatives then arise to solve this problem, but the exercise has been sufficient to show that thinking around the problem can pay off and that there are both advantages and disadvantages in making computers mimic real-world methods.

Consider also a simple cylindrical block. A cylinder can most obviously be an extruded circle, but what differences would the cylinder have if it were the result of a spun rectangle? The faceting of the end caps would be visible in wireframe view and might be more amenable to editing, but would this be an advantage or not? Since the program would need (internally) to triangulate the end caps whether these were visible or not, would the file sizes be any different?

7.6 CHEATING

The shadows of the moving aircraft cast on the ground in flight simulators add a great deal to the realism of the scene, but look closely at the shadow and you will probably see that it doesn't follow the contours of the ground it pretends to be cast upon and might completely ignore the hangar it should be wrapped around. I have been told a number of times in computer animation houses that cheating is the name of the game – creating something as simply, quickly (and cheaply) as possible to fool viewers into thinking they have seen what you want them to have seen. Unless you have moral objections, and believe that the viewer is being cheated by shortcuts to achieve a believable result, then it is a good idea to join in and save yourself some work.

The philosophy of the movie world is not, however, appropriate to the engineer, who will usually need to construct accurately all elements of his model in such a way that they can be built in real life. He might, however, be able to 'economise' on the rendering without compromising the model's integrity. Consider the maxim that 'Efficiency is intelligent laziness'.

CHAPTER 8

MACTYPICAL

No two modellers have exactly the same features or the same interface. They all have their strengths and their weaknesses, their advantages and their disadvantages. As a potential purchaser you will probably look for a package combining all the best features you have seen from every modeller but will necessarily settle for something less. You will find, however, that after a few months of working seriously with your chosen modeller you will know it well enough to be able to make it do most of what you want, having discovered ways of getting around apparent limitations of the package. You will also discover that upgrades add features previously available on other packages that you thought you had missed out on. Improvements in file standardisation make it practical to move models between modellers in order to benefit from different features, although there are some limitations to this ability and you incur the expense of buying two (or more!) modellers. If you are buying more than one package it is likely that your purchases will specialise in either modelling, rendering or animation and that you will treat them as a suite of programs.

Appendix 1 looks individually at many of the modellers, renderers and modeller-renderers available for the Mac today. It also briefly comments on animation facilities in these programs and at dedicated animation software, since you might well want to use that facility, but this is dealt with in depth in a second book. This chapter describes an imaginary modeller, referred to as MacTypical, which combines a range of modelling and rendering features culled from those available on the market and which can then be used as a yardstick for describing the real software. It is a little more generous in its features than any single real modeller but should still provide a useful comparitor.

MacTypical comes on three discs, has a 250-page, spiral bound manual and is accompanied by a separate tutorial manual with its own examples disc. All is contained in a shelvable box the size of a fat book, sleeved in a jacket with glossy photographs showing the wonderful images it can create and listing its stunning features. The jacket does not tell you how many man-hours were spent making and rendering the models in the pictures.

The program is in compressed form on the discs and is easily installed in 15 minutes. The main application takes up 2.5 Mb of disc space and together with its files and samples this rises to 7 Mb. Four Mb of RAM are required to run the program and 8 Mb are recommended; having 20 Mb or more will prove an advantage. The latest version of MacTypical runs under System 7, is 32-bit clean and is compatible with the 040 CPU. It does not use a 'dongle' (a small hardware 'key' that must be present for the program to run) but discourages illegal copying by requiring the user to enter name and company, etc. when the application is first installed.

8.1 MACTYPICAL INTERFACE

On first running the application, the default screen is divided into four windows labelled as showing the Top View, Front View, Right View and Camera; to the left is a vertical column of 22 icons in pairs and at the top of the screen is a familiar Mac menu bar. It proves possible to customise the screen display by adding, removing, resizing and redesignating windows to suit your own preferences, so that you might choose to have a large Camera window, small Top View and Left View windows. The icon bar can be repositioned and additional 'floating' windows can be selected from the menu bar to display information about the position, orientation and dimensions of objects (in numerical form), and about surface qualities of objects.

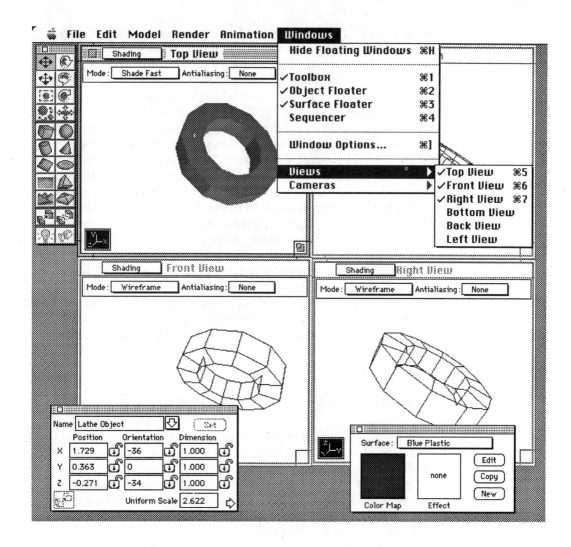

These windows not only describe the properties of objects you create but offer you one method of modifying them. The colours used for background and wireframe object display can be changed and other details customised for future use.

Infini-D interface showing many features of MacTypical

The icon strip accesses the toolbox, the icons being 'clicked' on to select a range of tools for creating, scaling, moving and linking

119

objects and for adding lights and cameras. Specifically, creation icons either select primitives, an environment for creating spun objects, an environment for creating extruded objects, or environments for creating asymmetrical objects. Movement icons allow the rotation of objects around a selected axis, or movement of an object in a specified plane. Link icons allow for the connection (and disconnection) of objects to (and from) one another in defined relationships. Many of these icons can be selected in conjunction with a key-press (Shift, Command, Option or Control) in order to constrain the selected operation. For example, the use of the Shift key with a movement tool limits the selected object to movement along one axis only, as opposed to free movement in one plane if the key is not pressed. Lighting icons add extra lights, and camera icons add extra cameras, all of which can be positioned nywhere in the scene and pointed in any direction, using the movement tools.

System 7's 'Balloon Help' is used, so assistance is available by moving the cursor to the queried item. The menu item 'Preference' allows the application to be customised somewhat; for instance it can be decided whether certain warning boxes will be shown, whether the cursor will automatically 'click' to a grid and what colour the default background will be.

8.2 MACTYPICAL OBJECT CREATION

The primitives available directly are the cube, cone, sphere, wedge, plane and torus. Having selected the appropriate icon, a click with the cursor in any View window creates an example of that primitive at that point. A double click on the icon brings up an object information box which allows the object's properties to be ascribed before it is created; this box will also be presented if an object in the scene is selected and the standard Mac information box request (Control + I) is made.

The extrude icon takes us to a separate screen; in one half of the screen a two-dimensional template can be drawn, and in the other half a three-dimensional view of the object created by extruding that template immediately appears. A strip of icons at the side of the template windows allows the selection of tools for drawing the template with either straight lines, freehand lines, splines, open polygons, closed polygons, rectangles or ellipses. The template can be edited and templates can be imported from other suitable applications. (MacTypical uses System 7 to permit 'subscription' to other applications, so that the template could be created in a draughting package and future attempts to edit the template would call up that package.) The default extrusion path is straight but it can be set to a user defined spline. The template can be held orthogonal to the extrusion path or else translated along the path (maintaining the same orientation).

The spin icon takes us to the environment for creating spun objects, which is largely similar to the extrude environment. Here a template is drawn in one window and a three-dimensional object is created in the second window by rotating the template around an axis. The default axis is vertical and straight but can be altered and the degree of rotation can be changed from the default 360 degrees. The environment for building freeform objects has four windows with views similar to those on the main screen and with tools similar to those in the spin and extrude environments. The modeller constructs objects from the three templates in the Top, Front and Side windows and allows for great flexibility of model building. Another environment for building non-symmetrical objects creates skins around a number of templates positioned in three-dimensional space. This is like building a ship's hull around a row of ribs.

Three-dimensional text can be created by calling on the text tool icon (which requires TrueType fonts to be installed). This presents a dialogue box in which the text can be typed and the font and style chosen. On exiting this box, the text is extruded into an object in your scene. The text can then either be treated as a single object or can be separated into individual letter objects.

The objects created by all these methods appear in the scene that is being built up and they can be dragged and rotated to the required positions. To do this the appropriate movement icon is selected, the object is selected in the correct view window, and the cursor is moved with the mouse button held down. It can be specified whether the object will be shown moving in full detail as the cursor moves or whether a bounding box will substitute for the object in order to ensure that the object moves (effectively) in real time. The bounding box is the default display and is usually only to be replaced by the detailed object when very accurate alignment of parts is to be made by eye. When this is needed, the view in the chosen window can be switched from perspective (which is the default) to orthographic (a non-perspective representation), in which mode exact relative positions are made clearer. Many alignments can be achieved numerically by using the object information window, in which the XYZ coordinates of the aligning objects can be set to match one another. Another alignment aid permits a point on one object to be selected and aligned with a point or plane on another object; after this the first object can be rotated about the point and/or slid along the plane to its final position.

In MacTypical, objects can be joined to one another by defining several selected objects as a group (which can then be given a separate name), by 'gluing' them together irreversibly or by 'linking' them. If a roof is to be fused permanently to the walls of a house, then grouping or gluing will cement their relationship; if a lid is to be fixed to a cabinet then a joint which permits the lid to hinge open and closed might be needed. The link tool enables objects to be connected flexibly, the amount of permitted movement being definable (numerically) around, and along, each axis. A chain of connected objects can thus be set up with hierarchical links, the first object selected being known as the 'child' and the object to which it is connected being called the 'parent'; the next object connected becomes the 'parent' to the rest (though in this example it could be thought of as the grandparent). Scaling of a parent automatically scales the children (and grandchildren) as well.

MacTypical doesn't yet combine Boolean joins with these others (though it's next version might include this feature) and it is necessary either to collaborate with a solid modeller or to improvise.

A valuable feature, which MacTypical has only just acquired, is that of vertex-level editing. This permits objects which have been created using all the above methods to be refined at a low level. Points, lines or faces can be selected individually or in groups and moved or deleted. Deletion requires some thought, as the application will have to make sense of the remaining object information and might not do so as you had intended. Additional points, lines and faces can also be added but it requires a clear understanding of the existing object for this to be achieved without error.

As one would expect, objects can be copied and deleted at any time (backspace key providing a shortcut for deleting the selected object). If copied, the duplicate can be defined as having either a wholly independent existence or as being a clone which will adopt any changes subsequently made to the original object. The clone function can be useful if you need to work with multiple identical elements whilst retaining the ability to modify those elements. Cut, Paste and Copy functions work in the same way as in other Mac applications – saving to, and restoring from, the clipboard.

Every object is created with a centre point, about which it rotates. This centre of rotation can be repositioned anywhere inside or outside of the object. It permits the hinge of the cabinet lid to be set at the correct position and rotation of a knee to be at the point where the lower and upper legs meet. The world also has a centrepoint (where $X=Y=Z=0$) and objects can be rotated about either the world's centre or their own centres of rotation. The object's centrepoint is also the point about which scaling operations are conducted and it can be useful to be able to move that centre to the edge of the object. One instance where this would be useful is where the size of an object is to be adjusted after it has been aligned with something else in the scene. If the centre of rotation is at the point of alignment then changes of scale will not affect that alignment; if the centre of rotation is at the object's centre then a reduction in scale will leave the object separated from its contact point, and an increase in scale will leave it overlapping its contact point. In either case a realignment will have to follow.

8.3 MACTYPICAL NAVIGATION

It is possible to move your 'point of view' around in the three-dimensional world of your objects. Each window has a row of icons which enables you to reposition your view either up, down, left, right, into or out of the scene. Clicking on the desired icon moves the viewpoint one increment in the selected direction; the increment size being multiplied or divided by ten if the Option or Control key is held down. Further icons zoom in and out of the scene, zooming having the effect of enlarging the scene (relative to the window) but without moving the actual viewpoint. Moving the viewpoint changes the perspective, zooming does not.

In the three view windows (or however many view windows you have chosen to have) the view remains orthogonal to the defined view axis. This means that however you navigate in the Top View window you will always look down on the scene; you might move to the left or up or closer, but you cannot creep around into a side view for instance. In the Camera window you are viewing the scene as if through a camera which inhabits the object world and has the same freedom of movement as the objects. It is therefore possible to

Navigation tools in Infini-D in camera view window (top) and object view window (bottom). Note the ability in the object view window to switch between perspective and orthographic projection systems.

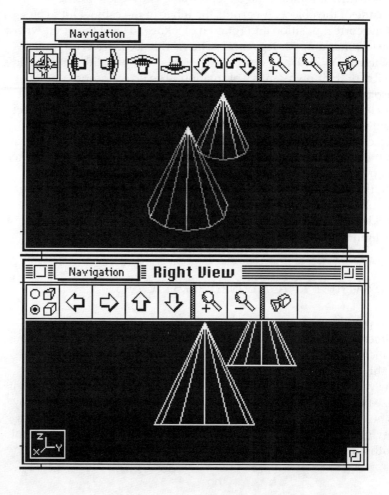

position the camera anywhere in the scene (including inside an object) and to point it in any direction. The angle of view of the camera 'lens' can also be adjusted to give any effect from 'fish-eye' to 'telephoto', and a number of customised camera positions can be set within the same scene. The advantage of setting up several camera positions is to be able subsequently to switch between views with ease. In the Camera window a set of icons, additional to those in the view windows, enables the view to be rotated about the scene.

It is important to distinguish between moving an object and moving the point from which you view that object, as they can produce the same image. The difference will be apparent if the object being moved is not alone in the scene as it will appear in a different relationship to the other objects, and the effects of lighting, reflection and shadows will be seen to change if a shaded view is selected. As most manipulation of objects will be done in wireframe, however, it is easy to get lost in a scene by mixing object and viewpoint movement.

8.4 MACTYPICAL RENDERING

The objects in the scene can be viewed as bounding boxes, wireframe, hidden line or solid. If solid they can use either a fast (Lambert) shading, smooth (Gouraud) shading, best (Phong) shading or ultimate (ray traced) shading model. The selection of rendering method is selected from a pull down menu found in the View and Camera windows, each window being set independently of the others. The criterion for choosing a rendering mode is usually a compromise between wanting a fast screen update and wanting detail in the scene. At the model building stage the speed of wireframe, combined with its ability to let you see through objects, usually makes it the choice, ambiguities being removed by occasional changes to fast shading and perhaps best shading for checks on smoothness. When the models are positioned, solid shading is necessary to check the effects of lighting and the more sophisticated shading models are needed to check surface qualities and shadows (the calculation of shadows can be switched off). Since ray tracing is time consuming, one of the main icons accesses a tool which permits a smaller, selected part of the scene to be ray traced; this makes it practical to check details, such as the interaction between reflective surfaces, without resorting to a full scene render.

The rendering is carried out in a separate window, allowing the main window to be worked on during the rendering process. This rules out one excuse for a tea break but allows the user to be more productive! A software extension also allows the rendering process to be shared by all the machines on a network, which could mean big time savings. An 'alpha channel' is available so that information about transparency and anti-aliasing, for example, can be carried forward in files to other applications which are equipped to use it.

8.5 MACTYPICAL SURFACE EFFECTS

Surface properties can be individually assigned to objects. A floating window allows the selection of surface properties from an existing library of twenty-four (including gold, red plastic, mirrored, wood grain, marble, etc.) and the editing of these properties to create new ones. Factors which can be altered include shininess, metallicity, specular highlights, glow, reflectiveness, transparency, diffuse shading and index of refraction. The maps which set up surfaces like wood grain or tiling can be edited or new ones created and colours can be selected from the whole of the available palette. It is thus possible to create a green, highly reflectant, semi-transparent wood grain surface on an object; a dull, translucent, blue marble with red veining, or dull, glowing brass.

Images can be mapped onto surfaces; possibly being patterns or pictures. This allows a can to have a label wrapped around it, a product to have a brand name on it or a room to be wallpapered.

Complex surfaces can be created by combining several layers of surface information. These can include bump, transparency and reflection maps, as well as more esoteric effects such as provided by highlight and glow maps. The ability to set varying levels of transparency enables features of several different layers to be combined in the final surface, sometimes using the alpha channel of an image. Different mapping methods allow maps to be applied in several ways in response to the shape of the object being mapped.

Consider, for instance, the difference between wrapping a square box in patterned wrapping paper and using a projector to shine the same pattern onto the box. In the first case the pattern would be parallel to the plane of each side; in the second it would distort according to the angle at which the projected beam hit the side. MacTypical offers the options of mapping methods matching planes, cubes, cylinders (with or without capped ends) and spheres as well as a 'wrap around' method. Editing facilities allow for precise orientation, scaling and alignment of maps to objects.

8.6 MACTYPICAL LIGHTING

By default a mid-level ambient light bathes the scene and a single point light is directed at the centre of the universe. These settings can, of course, be changed and any number (subject to memory) of other light sources can be specified. In order to position lights, they can be temporarily seen as objects within the scene and scaled, moved and orientated as any other object. Alternatively, they can be specified numerically. The direction of any light's beam is shown by arrows which can be cross-referenced in the different view windows for accurate alignment. Lights can also be pointed automatically at any specified object.

Each light can be assigned a specific colour, brightness, beam angle and focus, and its natural ability to cast a shadow can be turned off if preferred.

8.7 MACTYPICAL EXTRAS

Other characteristics of the scene can be controlled for specific effect.

Fog can be specified in any colour and density and within prescribed spatial limits (equating to 'visibility').

Environment mapping simulates the reflections calculated during ray tracing but using the faster Phong shading method. An image is imported or created to serve as the environment map or a QuickTime movie can be used to create a dynamic map (such as rippling water).

Depth of field can be simulated (showing restricted focus, as in a photograph).

Other Macs on a network can be called on to share in all the calculations involved in building a scene and can substantially decrease rendering times (according to the number and power of the machines in the network).

Terrains can be constructed using functions such as Noise or Julia sets, the latter producing a fractal surface. These terrains can then be treated as any other object.

The level of anti-aliasing can be defined, the requirement of improved smoothness being set against increased rendering time.

Sparkle can be created by setting 'flares' of brilliant light on objects, simulated by radiating lines, though these are primarily intended for use during animation.

8.8 MACTYPICAL ANIMATION

Although not a specific requirement of modelling, the animation facility included in MacTypical can be very useful and is therefore briefly described. As well as creating an animation for its own sake, an object can often be explained or understood more fully if it is moving or if one's view of it is changing (the human brain is good at interpreting pictures but if they are moving it is brilliant). It is also possible that the object being modelled has moving parts or that modelled objects have a changing relationship, and in either case animation can make this clear. Similarly, it might be useful to be able to change surface properties of an object or its lighting, such as in an architectural model where the change of shadows cast during the day is potentially important.

It is a 'time line' system which lets key moments in an animation

Time line animation score in MacroMind Three-D

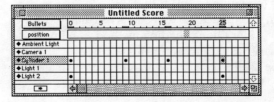

sequence be set at discrete points on a horizontal line calibrated with time increments. Each object in the scene, including cameras and lights, has its own horizontal channel aligned with all the others and most object or scene properties can be changed at any time during a sequence. Changes to different objects can thus be readily synchronised with one another. As the creation of an animation is in progress, its current state can be viewed in any view window in any viewing form or, for maximum speed, with objects displayed merely as bounding boxes.

Changes occurring during the animation can be made abruptly or smoothly, splines being available to 'round' changes and 'easing' being available to create acceleration changes which match most movement in the real world.

Constraints can be imposed to limit the actions of objects, either locking the behaviour of objects to one another or restricting directional or rotational movement.

Changes made to the properties of an object over time (other than positional changes) are often described as morphing, the term being a contraction of 'metamorphosis'. Morphing of surface and form can be achieved by MacTypical's ability to interpolate between two end states over a period of time.

A hardware animation board is supported, allowing animation to be laid to tape one frame at a time as it is created, though this requires both the board and a professional video tape recorder.

Animation features are deliberately kept short here as the whole subject of Mac animation is to be fully dealt with in another book.

8.9 MACTYPICAL FILE SUPPORT

MacTypical can import and export files of several types. It can import bit-mapped images (PICT) for use as maps, object-orientated drawing files (Freehand and Illustrator) for use as templates, and objects stored as DXF, Swivel 3D or MacTypical 3-D files. It can export screen images as PICT or EPS files, objects as DXF or MacTypical 3-D, animations as PICS or QuickTime, and scenes as RIB files for subsequent rendering in MacRenderMan. Another MacTypical file type will save all information about the state of the application at the time of saving, including both the scene and the interface, so that a session can be resumed at any time.

CHAPTER 9

CASE STUDIES

In order to get a feel for the process of modelling on the Macintosh, the production of the images on the cover of this book can be used as a case study. This provides the opportunity of detailing specific modelling sessions using software described in the book, and of looking at the problems and solutions that presented themselves. None of the models are compex but their construction requires the use of the main modelling and rendering functions, and the use of several different modellers gives room for some comparison. I have described the actual route used to create each image including, therefore, comments on alternatives and improvements which revealed themselves. As with all modelling projects, there any many other ways to achieve very similar final effects.

Front cover image from this book

9.1 MAC 3D

The front cover image was modelled and rendered in Infini-D, 'tuned' in Adobe Photoshop, and lettering was added in Aldus PageMaker.

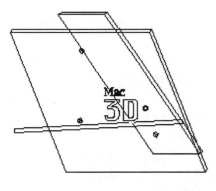

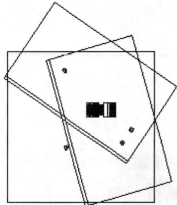

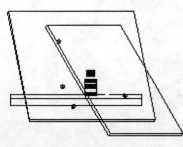

Above: Front, top and right views of scene. Above right: Text extrusion dialogue.

1. The 'Mac 3D' object is very easily created using the 3-D text dialogue box selected from the Model menu. By simply selecting a font from those available on the System, typing in the letters and an extrusion depth, and clicking 'OK', a letterform object appears in each of the four model view windows. The 'Mac' object and '3D' object are created separately in order to allow for different scaling and alignment.

2. The environment is made up of three flat

Text	
Text:	3D
Font:	Schoolbook ▼
	Extrusion Depth: 0.600
	Cancel OK

surfaces created from rescaled cube primitives. The Cube Tool icon is selected and a single click in any window creates a cube (centred on the cursor), a dragging action scaling the object to the desired size. Selecting the Squash & Stretch Tool allows the cube to be reduced in size on one axis alone to produce a fat, square sheet. (A similar object could have been made as quickly by scaling a cube using numerical input in the Object Floater window, or by extruding a square template.) Sheets were preferred to infinite planes since it might have been decided to allow the edges to show.

3. The sheet object is duplicated twice by selecting it with a cursor click, then using the Duplicate command from the Model menu.

4. The three sheet objects are realigned so as to surround the Mac 3D objects, by use of the Rotation and Move Tools. A single sheet object is selected, the appropriate Rotation Tool selected and then the object is dragged around the chosen axis into the chosen orientation. The V-plane Move Tool is then selected (the Rotation Tool automatically deselects but the object remains selected) and the object dragged into place. I choose to use the V-plane tool to move the object vertically and horizontally in one window and to change to a View window at right angles to the first in order to move in a third dimension. I could, alternatively, stay with one window and use the H-plane Move Tool to move the object in and out of the plane of the window.

5. A quick render is undertaken at this point to ensure that no mistake has been made in the interpretation of position of the wireframe objects, as this viewing mode can prove ambiguous. The menu bar set into the top of each window frame is opened to select 'Shading', and 'Fast Shade' selected from the Mode Menu which then appears; the Antialiasing Menu setting is left at 'None'. On releasing the mouse button the rendering starts and this status is indicated by shading changes within the cursor arrow. The rendering takes just over one second on my Quadra. (When a longer period of rendering is passing, a status strip appears at the bottom of the window to show the approximate percentage of rendering time elapsed.) A quick render is tried in each window.

6. Since everything seems to be as expected, the positions of the objects are fine tuned. The final view is also set up in the Camera window by selecting 'Navigation' from the menu set into the window and then using the Movement and Rotation icons which then appear to position the camera. A camera icon gives access to a dialogue box in which the camera focal length is set to 'Normal'.

7. It is intended that the final image should demonstrate a range of properties that can be created through the rendering process but that it should not try to overpower with a catalogue of every technique available. In particular, reflections and shadows will provide part of the design. The objects are therefore attributed properties which should achieve this end, and then lights set.

The following object properties are set within the New Surface box selected from the Render Menu. The final properties are arrived at by trial and error (the main error proving to be gratuitous colour) and summarised as:

Floor surface – grey 'mirror'.

Wall surface 1 – faint marble colour map and no reflection.

Wall surface 2 – flat grey colour map, soft bump mapping, glow and 60% reflection.

Mac object – flat, shiny grey with diffuse shading.

3D object – polished marble with specular highlights.

8. Lights are positioned and attributed properties so as to create the desired effects. It is at this point that my main error arises - too many lights. It is best to use as few lights as possible and to position them correctly but the temptation is always to add more lights until an effect is achieved; as well as being undisciplined, this leads to greatly increased rendering times. In this case, I was happily playing with the lighting controls in Infini-D and arrived at roughly the effect I wanted after setting five lights. Since I did not, at that time, see much need to keep my rendering times down, I settled for what I had got rather than look for a more economical set-up. This would not have been acceptable practice in a commercial environment, and proved to be unwise in my own.

The lights are: two lilac point lights, a dark pink and a light green point light and a white spot light (medium angle); all lights set to cast shadows. This combination arose from an experiment with red, green and blue spots added to the initial white point light. The initial colours proved too strong and too cool, the angles of the spots proved too cutting and, after some juggling with settings, more lilac was sought. Lights are added by selecting the Light icon in the tool bar and clicking in a window, then set by selecting Edit Light from the Model Menu. They are positioned in the same way as any other object, and in the case of spot lights, display a line showing their direction of beam whilst being rotated. The Point At selection on the Model Menu allows a light to be automatically pointed at a chosen object.

9. In order to judge the full effect, including shadows and reflections, ray tracing is required. Ray tracing of selected areas offers a preview of the image and at this stage a tiled environment map was added to give a little variation to some reflections. This is added from within the Environment dialogue box found in the Model Menu.

Environment map box

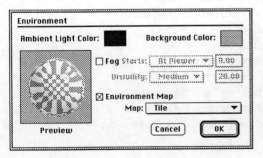

A full rendering is necessary to assess the final effect and with anti-aliasing and 24-bit colour set, the full sized rendering took 24 hours. Whilst many changes could be made based on the results of quicker rendering modes, the full render was repeated more than once for the sake of 'fine tuning'. This render was at a resolution of 75 dpi, which meant that the final version at 150 dpi took about 4 days, producing a TIFF file of 4.13 Mb (just under 1Mb with LZ compression).

10. The final image was manipulated slightly in Photoshop (the contrast of the back reflections was reduced and one colour subdued) and the resolution was increased to 300 dpi by interpolation. Note that this method of increasing the resolution does not produce the same accuracy as rendering at that resolution. Title lettering was also tried out in Photoshop before finally being set in PageMaker.

9.2 BACK COVER – THE SUNGLASSES

The sunglasses were modelled and rendered in MacTopas, and the final image 'tweaked' in Adobe Photoshop.

Back cover image

1. Using the floating Palette window, accessed by the Palette icon in the main Tool Bar, the background is set to white (merely personal preference).

2. The Spline Polygon tool is selected from the main Tool Bar and the outline of one side of the front of the sunglasses drawn. Each mouse click creates a new spline control point and

Top: Template 1
Above: Template 2
Below: First attempt
at lens cutter template.
Bottom: Final Cutter
shown aligned with
lens

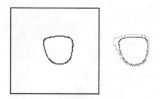

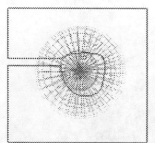

each point is connected to the next by a straight line; once three control points have been established, each subsequent click causes a section of the spline curve itself to be drawn (in colour). The polygon is completed when the first control point is clicked on again. The shape is saved as 'Template 1'.
3. The inside perimeter of the front of the sunglasses is drawn in a similar fashion, and saved as "Template 2'.
4. It is now necessary to turn the shape into an object, so template 1 is selected (by clicking on it with the General arrow curor) and Extrude Object chosen from the Object menu. An edge view of the template is shown and mouse movement then interactively controls a diagram showing the depth (and angle) of extrusion. Once these are as required, a mouse click brings a return to the main work window where the template has now been extruded into an object.
5. Template 2 is now used to drill a hole in the new object and create the rim of the glasses. First the new object is selected. Then Drill is selected from the Object menu ('delete drilling polygon' and 'create internal surface' are selected from the dialogue box which presents itself) and the drilling polygon (Template 2) is selected with the cursor. After a short pause the required object is on screen. A quick render, selected from the main Tool Bar, confirms that the object is as intended.
6. A lens is now needed to fit into the frame, and I suspect that there may be better ways to create one than that used; as usual with a modeller there are always several routes to a solution. This method works, however, and is only criticised for its lack of elegance.
    A slice is to be taken off a sphere in order to produce a circular lens, and the lens then cut to the required shape with the Drill function. The existing Template 2 is, of course, the exact shape needed for a drill, but if used as before would leave a hole cut out of the lens (rather than cut the lens to the shape of the hole). A new template named Cutter is therefore created by using Template 2 to drill a hole in a square shape, effectively producing a negative of Template 2.
    Overlapping a sphere with a square template and then using the Drill function provides a lens 'slice'. The slice is

turned 90 degrees by using the Rotate tool in the Tool bar; selection of the tool causing labelled axis indicators to be superimposed on the object, and rotation being achieved by click-dragging on the appropriate axis of rotation. Cutter is then manoevred over the lens and used as a drill to create the shaped lens. Experiment showed that the application did not 'like' using a drill template with a hole in it and Cutter was ammended to offer a single continuous edge by removing a slice between the outer and inner edges. This created a shaped lens with an unwanted extension which was trimmed back.

7. The lens was aligned with the frame and experiment showed that a cleaner render was achieved by scaling the lens up a little so that it overlapped the inside edge of the frame. This was achieved by stretching the lens in along the X and Y axes using the Stretch tool in the main Tool bar, the percentage of stretch being shown in an information window. The lens and frame are grouped together using the Grouping sub-menu in the Object menu.

8. An arm for the spectacles was made by extruding a spline polygon as before.

9. This was moved into place by using the Rotate tool and by dragging with the General arrow.

10. The second half of the glasses is created using the Mirror function in the Object menu. The first half is selected by dragging a box around it using the General arrow cursor and Mirror selected. An axis, across which the object will be mirrored, is set by click-dragging a vertical line through the bridge of the glasses, and the second half is formed.

11. The arms of the spectacles are positioned by selecting them individually in a top view, rotating with the Rotate tool and dragging them into position. No attempt is made (in this model) to create a realistic hinge.

12. A suitable view is created using the Change Perspective, Zoom, Pan and Revolve options in the Camera menu. These work extremely well. Choosing the Revolve option produces axis labels and works in the same way as object rotation. On selecting one or the other of these

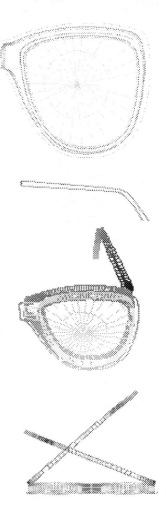

From top:
Frame + lens,
arm template,
arm connected to
frame,complete
spectacles.

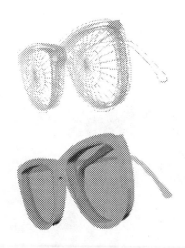

options, a representation of the object made up of bounding rectangles appears. This transforms interactively in response to mouse movement and is 'fixed' with a final click.

13. Surface properties are now attributed to the glasses. These are issued through the Material Palette, accessed by the Palette icon in the main Tool bar. The frames are simply defined as a shiny, opaque pink; the lenses as shiny, 70% transparent brown. Default settings are accepted for the many rendering variables available and options such as fog and flares are left unused. The default lighting is accepted. Phong shading is chosen and a full render executed using the appropriate render button in the main Tool bar.

14. A background image is to be used and this is loaded into a buffer with the Open command from the File menu. Selecting Background in the Material Palette and clicking the Map button produces a list of available images, from which the new one is chosen.

Wireframe and smooth shaded versions of the spectacles

15. A final render using 'high quality' settings produces an image which is saved as a PICT file. This is taken into PhotoShop and tidied up slightly, the main changes being a slight lightening of the images seen through the lenses, and a slight blurring of the background where it is not seen through the lenses.

9.3 BACK COVER – THE BUILDING

The building is one of the sample files that comes with MiniCad+. The only modification made to it was to change the projection from orthoganal to perspective using the Projection selection in the 3-D menu. Limited familiarity with using MiniCad+ suggested that it would be fairer to the package to utilise a file from an experienced user rather than to create one myself. Since the original file showed the 3-D model overlapping a 2-D plan, which I chose to remove, some minor corrections to the image were made in Aldus SuperPaint.

Opposite page: Orthographic projection (top) and perspective projection (bottom) of MiniCad+ building.

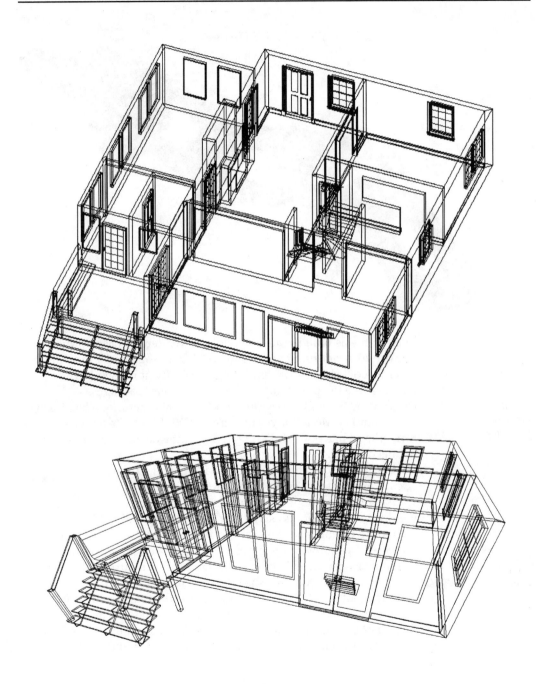

9.4 BACK COVER – THE CHAIN

The final chain

Rectangle (top), fillet size setting (centre) and rectangle with two filleted corners (bottom).

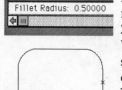

The chain was built in MacroModel and rendered in MacroMind 3D. These two applications are designed to work together, and whilst MacroModel has its own rendering capability, it is useful to demonstrate the possibility of moving between packages. MacroMind 3D will also accept models from other modellers (using its own utility ModelMover to convert DXF files to its own native file format) and has powerful animation facilities which this project does not need to use.

A single link of chain is built in MacroModel by sweeping a circular template along a profile path.

1. Using the Rectangle tool a rectangle is drawn in the workspace window. One corner is established by pressing and holding down the mouse button, and then the required size and shape of rectangle is created by dragging the mouse and then releasing the button. The rectangle is displayed in orange to show that it is currently selected.

2. Using the fillet tool the corners of the rectangle are rounded off. With the tool selected, a default radius for the filleting curve is shown in the tool space at the bottom of the window. In this case the default of 0.25 inches is insufficient and is replaced by typing in 0.5. The cross hair cursor of the tool is clicked on each of the sides

containing the angle to be filleted, and the right-angle is replaced by a smooth curve. This is repeated for each of the four corners.

3. Having created the link profile, the path is made up of eight elements: four curved corners and four straight sides. This can be shown by clicking on any part of the profile with the arrow tool, in which case only that individual part will turn orange to indicate that it is selected. The parts are resolved into a single object by selecting all of them, using the arrow tool to drag a box around them, and then selecting *Join* from the Object menu. (*Select All* could have been chosen from the Edit menu and key combinations can be substituted for both menu commands.)

4. The cross section for the chain link is drawn using the Circle tool. The circle is made by click-dragging from the centre outward.

5. To build a model from the templates the Sweep tool is used. On selecting it and moving the cursor into the workspace window, the instruction bar at the bottom of the screen offers a reminder of the process to follow. First click on the profile to be swept (and it turns orange), then click on the sweep path (it too turns orange), then double-click or press Enter. A shaded 3-D model of a chain link is displayed.

6. A second link is made by selecting the first link and selecting Duplicate from the Edit menu. The new link is displayed with a horizontal offset.

7. The position and orientation of the new link is established using the Rotation tools to rotate about a chosen axis and the Arrow tool to drag to position. There are, in fact, several alternative ways of accomplishing this task and this method was used because it avoided the use of key modifiers which come into their own when a package is more familiar. Using the Rotation tool from the Hand tool group, an axis of rotation is set by clicking at two points along the desired axis, and then the object is dragged around that axis. As orientation was done by eye and did not need to be precise. This worked well as an intuitive method.

8. The two links are then selected and duplicated as a pair, the new pair being aligned as before. The process is repeated until the chain is complete.

9. In order to check that the links are correctly aligned it is necessary to view the chain from other angles, otherwise it might

From top to bottom: Cross-section template and path, link object, duplicated link, realigned duplicate, several links.

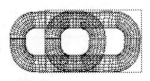

be found that the links were overlapping in places rather than interlocking. If the chain links had been linked heirarchically within MacroModel and their limits of movement defined, one could be sure that their aligment was 'legal', but since they have been aligned by eye, a check is needed.

10. The model is now saved in its native format and taken directly into MacroMind 3D without the need for file conversion. (In order to try the ModelMover a DXF version was also saved and converted to MM3D format, and it was surprising to discover that this conversion took an hour. A record of the conversion, however, showed that the model contained 13150 points, 13072 faces and 26241 edges, which shows how much calculation had to be done by the software. Since the chain is a repetitive form made of simply-defined units, it also provides an interesting reminder of the inefficiency of storage in b-rep form compared with a data type, such as CSG, which stores the model as a mathematic description.)

Chain with one link selected

Top: Bounding box version of chain Bottom: First rendering of chain

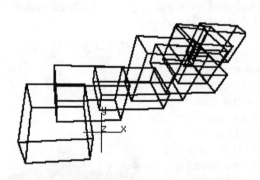

11. Within MacroMind 3D the camera is moved to obtain a suitable view, and to speed up the redrawing each time a new position is tried, the chain links are set to be displayed as bounding boxes. This is done by selecting the camera icon and the appropriate direction-of-movement icon and then click-dragging in a view window.

12. The default lighting is ambient plus one distant light source and a draft render is done to get a feel of how it might look. Three view windows are opened (front, right and top) in order to facilitate moving the lights and they are click-dragged into guestimated position (the camera icon having been replaced by the arrow icon). Each light is selected and Shading Info picked from the Objects menu; the Light Info box then allows setting of light

properties such as type (e.g spot, distant, etc.), intensity, beam angle and colour. The Point At selection from the Object menu allows a light to be easily pointed at a chosen object.

13. Selecting each link individually, the Shading Info item now offers a comprehensive means of setting the surface properties of the object. These are set with each link being assigned a different texture map.

14. Final render of selected areas suggests that everything is as required, a full render is carried out and the image saved.

15. Photoshop is finally used for minor touching up and adjustment of contrast, etc. relative to the other back cover images.

Heavily foreshortened view of chain, with quick shading

CHAPTER 10

THE FUTURE OF MODELLING

The next generation of computer hardware and software is never too hard to predict. It will be faster, smaller and, after it has settled in the market, cheaper relative to its performance ('more bangs per buck'). It will bring no great surprises with it on arrival since it will have been thoroughly hyped before it comes. Its performance will briefly seem incredible, and it will raise the expectations and demands of users, thus preparing the ground for a further generation. In many areas of computing, standards are high enough for most tasks and one has to ask how much a superior technology is really needed. When writing this book, for instance, my Quadra offers little practical improvement over the cheap, home micro I used for my last book; the software alone is worth nearly as much as my previous hardware and software combined and it is noisier, the bigger screen, smoother interface and better keyboard being the most obvious advantages.

When I come to view a model, however, there is no comparison; I repeated a ray tracing of a simple model (at the same resolution and colour depth) which had taken 27 hours on my old machine and it was completed in 72 seconds. This is the result of both improved and optimised hardware and of more efficient algorithms written to exploit the potential of the hardware. Now that I have more than six million colours at my disposal instead of just sixteen, reproduction quality resolution, a high level of anti-aliasing , the ability to scatter light sources about a scene, add fog, image map, environment map, and make everything glossy, reflective, refractive and transparent, I am annoyed to find that my rendering times have gone up again. If anything tests a system's limits, rendering does, and it has become something of an Achilles' heel for the Mac. This is not because the hardware is inferior to anything else (at the price) but because the Mac has established a reputation as a graphics machine and it makes it easy for the user to demand the best. Although the requirement for high quality modelling and rendering is growing fast, and each generation of machines brings big improvements, it will be some time before you can move a light source in a complex scene with immediate, interactive, ray traced feedback. Meanwhile I quick-shade during the day and let the machine ray trace with all the bells and whistles during the night.

It is a less interesting exercise, therefore, to try and predict when things we can already do on our computers will be done better, and more challenging to guess what new feats we will be able to perform. Best of all, is to wonder into what fresh modelling fields we might be taken.

10.1 VIRTUAL REALITY

The obvious uses for this infant technology are remarkable, the less obvious uses staggering, and despite the fact that it only reached the marketplace around 1989, it is expected to revolutionise many disciplines. Surgeons will be able to practise convincing operations on 'virtual' patients, astronauts can already practise space manoeuvres on the ground, anyone can be a 'virtual' racing driver in his own living room, and the animator can define an actor's path through 3-D space with a sweep of his hand. Whilst the ultimate video game scenario is one promise offered, there are many more potential uses for virtual reality, both mundane and outrageous.

Virtual reality (VR) has grown from concepts such as 'artificial reality', a term coined some years back by Myron Krueger, and is currently typified by its enabling encumbrances like the glove, mask and suit. The DataGlove from Jaron Lanier's company VPL is an input device which is worn like a glove and translates hand and finger movements into electric signals. Combined with an absolute position and orientation sensor, the glove translates movements made by the operator's hand into information which can be used to duplicate the movements in the computer's three-dimensional world. It is thus possible to control movement within the computer scene by hand movement, and one obvious development has been to create a computer model of a hand which can mimic the operator's hand. It is then easy to create an object in the computer's imaginary scene and to grasp it with the model hand which inhabits that same scene, under the control of the DataGlove. The glove is also an output device, as tactile-feedback devices can give the operator the same touch clues as he would expect from manipulating a real object. Whilst the glove can be used with a 2-D VDU screen to display what is happening in the scene, this falls short of providing the total control which participation in the 3-D scene would allow. The glove can therefore be used in conjunction with a stereoscopic headset which provides a separate screen for each eye and allows the user to look around the scene as he would in real life, presenting fresh views as it senses the head being moved and utilising all the spatial depth clues that the user would normally expect. This describes a fully 'immersive' VR experience where the user enters into the computer space, but 'non-immersive' VR is more easily provided where the operator watches a single screen to look around and to monitor movements he (or his hand) 'makes' in the scene. A further level of removal has the operator using external devices, such as the standard mouse, to control a proxy that has been modelled within the scene.

The gloves can, as you would expect, be used in pairs and a DataSuit has also been constructed to allow the whole body of the operator to interface with the machine. The most obvious limitation on the feedback from these devices at the moment is the lack of force-feedback. It is possible to feel the surface of an object, but not to feel its weight when 'picked up'. More effective force-feedback devices have been built but not yet in a convenient form to match the relative freedom of the Data Glove/Suit/Headset. Forces and torques can be applied to a hand control but currently only as part of a substantial machine rather than in the compact and mobile form required, though the possibility of using 'memory metals' to push against the skin in the DataGlove has been considered as a response to the force-feedback limitation.

The technology of this new discipline seems to define little more than a fresh interface paradigm, but VR has somehow been presented as a branch of philosophy. However, now that the pioneering enthusiasm has become either more muted or more local, it has become popular to tone down expectations by use of the term 'virtual environment' (which accurately describes the computer-generated space), rather than 'virtual reality' (which seeks to describe the experience of using it). Either way, the 3-D environment built in the computer is a prime example of modelling, and the pressing demands made by VR (even with its current, relatively crude, technology) must impact strongly on the development of modelling and rendering.

The ability to move through a computer scene uses nothing that is new in principle, it merely requires a sequence of views of the scene from different viewpoints. The ability to provide this is a necessary part of any 3-D modeller but in order to give a sense of movement these views need to be presented to the observer at about 25 or 30 views per second (these examples being the standard video animation rates in the UK and USA respectively). If your machine can't render a complex scene in 0.04 seconds then you might need to export your files to one that can.

Whatever the object you are modelling, however, whether it is an office block, a car, a container for washing-up liquid or a teapot, it is likely that you can enhance your (and your client's) understanding of it by experiencing it in three (and four) dimensions. This is one thing that VR offers you. You will also be able to do much more comprehensive pre-production testing in VR than is currently possible, perhaps using yourself as the model for ergonomic analyses: walking through the office, sitting in the car, handling the bottle, pouring from the teapot.

10.2 DYNAMICS

Increasingly it will become possible to give to models properties that go beyond the merely visual. At the moment in a model, the materials comprising a rubber tyre, a steel girder and a silk handkerchief are likely to be differentiated only by their surface appearance. By crediting materials with the attributes that they have in the real world, it is possible to have them reacting to physical forces and interacting with one another and with their environments.

Alan Barr (*Introduction to physically-based modelling*, SIGGRAPH, 1989) defines a physically based model as 'a mathematical representation of an object (or its behaviour) which incorporates forces, torques, energies, and other attributes of Newtonian physics. With this approach, it is possible to simulate realistic behaviour of flexible and rigid objects, and cause objects to do what we wish them to do (without specifying unnecessary details)'. In section 4.11.5 it was explained that, having defined a ball and a surface, we can 'drop' the ball and watch it bounce around until coming to rest. If we also care to drop a properly defined cup onto either a properly defined pillow or onto properly defined concrete, we can witness it either land gently or smash at a level of accuracy prescribed by our definitions. It is immediately apparent that many object are flexible to different degrees, either in whole or part, and that many are articulated (such as a skeleton). When this is mathematically acknowledged in a model, however, snooker balls can interact realistically, articulated figures can trampoline and leaves can gently flutter down in a breeze. Not surprisingly, some things are easier to define than others and many things are too complex for it to be practical to attempt a definition. Nevertheless, in addition to the functionality of such a display, there is always an addictive magic about witnessing even a simple occurrence unfolding under its own (apparent) initiative.

The application of basic physical laws enables the realistic simulation of the motion of bodies and cannot only be applied to separate complex bodies, but can automatically describe the conduct of bodies in collision. It therefore takes little effort to simulate a raindrop falling or a ball being thrown by specifying mass, starting velocity and direction to a system that knows what gravity is, perhaps that there is a cross-wind and how to apply the rules. A little more information is needed to cope with friction and bouncing and more again if the object is articulated, flexible or asymmetrical; but although the number and length of the required mathematical equations grows, the governing rules remain clear. There is a considerable body of literature on the subject and it has been a major conference topic for several years.

10.3 INTELLIGENT MODELS

A term recently imported to computer graphics (from the fields of philosophy and biology) is that of teleological modelling. Derived from the Greek word 'teleos', meaning end or goal, it provides an extension of the current definitions of modelling to include a number of recent developments and provides a model that is goal-orientated. It is a mathematical representation which calculates the object's behaviour from what the object is 'supposed' to do. Alan Barr suggests that it has the potential to extend the scientific foundation of computer graphics and vastly to extend the state-of-the-art for computer graphics modelling. He suggests that teleological methods can create mechanistic mathematical models with predictive capability and produce compact formal descriptions of complex physical states and systems. It seems that teleological modelling does not offer new methods but provides a conceptual framework within which recent (and future) methods governing an object's purpose can be related to existing modelling methods. The teleological model of an object includes time-dependent behavioural goals as part of the object's fundamental representation. This gives us an object that knows how to act (perhaps a doctor's 'model' patient can bleed?).

As well as knowing how to respond physically to the world, and having an understanding of its role in life, it might be useful or an object to be able to exhibit intelligence. It could then recognise imminent collisions and take avoiding action, plan routes and strategies, and respond to rules of behaviour. Artificial intelligence (AI) has been described as the science of making machines (or, in our case, models) do things that would require intelligence if done by humans. It is a new and important science, whose methods need not concern us here but whose influence will be felt in modelling. Already 'expert' or 'knowledge-based' systems can be used within limited domains, such as architecture, to allow models to be interrogated for hidden information; the system's knowledge having been initially collected from human experts.

It is also possible for a system to develop heuristically, i.e. to learn from its own experience. Paraphrasing Norbert Weiner (from his seminal book *Cybernetics*) an object that learns 'is one which is capable of being transformed by its past environment into a different being and is therefore adjustable to its environment within its individual lifetime'. We might build models that develop the initial properties we give them through their own experience and 'children' of these objects could, of course, inherit their more advanced properties. Each generation would build on the understanding of its ancestors.

Systems already exist which exhibit a behavioural response to their world, an elegant example being Craig Reynold's flocking model birds. He describes a flock as being made up of discrete birds yet with an overall motion that seems fluid; it is simple in concept yet is so visually complex; it seems randomly arrayed and yet is magnificently synchronised; and perhaps most puzzling is the strong impression of unintentional, centralised control. In his first models the birds (he calls them 'boids') are simplified to wedges, and by applying a few simple rules a group can 'fly' from a starting point to a given goal, avoiding obstacles en route and displaying all the characteristics of a flock. The wedges were later replaced in an animation by bird-like models which could flap their wings in flight and also display the flocking characteristics.

The behaviour of an object can be described in terms of its response to stimuli within its environment and that response may be qualified by its internal state (if it is credited with one). Several research projects have set up computer models inhabited by 'creatures' that mimic internal states such as hunger and anger and use these states to modify goal-directed behaviour. We can, therefore, think of future models having properties that stretch from red and glossy to angry and confused.

10.4 DIGITAL DOUGH

A pet prediction of mine is the creation of what I have called 'digital dough', which assembles several existing principles to create a new, interactive modelling medium. If a three-dimensional lattice was created to define an object, then the object could be deformed by moving points in that lattice (the 'resolution' of the object being proportional to the closeness of the points). If the points were interconnected with springs then the deformations would transmit through the solid and the consistency of the object could be defined by the tension of the springs. If we now let this object exist in a virtual world accessible through technologies such as the DataGlove, then it can be hand-modelled like clay; a sort of digital dough. By putting on the gloves we can squeeze, stretch and shape the object like a sculptor and, by changing the tension of the springs at any time, can change the object's consistency. This becomes a much more intuitive modelling method than those with a more visible mathematical basis.

If we then take an articulated human figure model and let its parts be made of digital dough, then we have a lay figure which can be hand-modelled to suit any requirements. We can make it short and fat, tall and skinny, with a big head or large feet, can create caricatures or likenesses, and could easily 'tweak' the quantities of dough available in any particular area. Once sculpted to taste, the figure can be animated using all the normal techniques, including dynamics, but the glove technology also offers the option of combining them with interactive positioning. The figure could be moved like a puppet, set in position by hand and/or controlled by a program, and given whatever degree of intelligence we choose. We can define characteristics such as gait pattern with 'conventional' methods or by real-time demonstration using the figures themselves (the figures have become plural, because it is, of course, trivial to clone a crowd). Facial expression can be similarly controlled and artificial intelligence can be attributed as desired. Its proportions could also be entered numerically to ensure the accuracy needed for scientific testing.

It might be useful to house this dynamic, articulated figure as an INIT for use from within any Mac program. It could wait in the desktop, perhaps to be called on as an ergonomic tester of computer models, and as this is the first task for which it is being considered, the ERgonomic figure In our Computer will be called ERIC. The redistribution of a little digital dough could also give us ERICA, and if we don a Data Suit we can join our new creations in their digital world.

10.5 CATALOGUES

Alvey Ray Smith suggested in Byte magazine (Sept. 1990) that 'much modelling will be made redundant by the selection, from electronic catalogues, of ready-made models. The user becomes a "spatial editor" inserting the model(s) into the 3-D scene, sizing and customising to taste'. In a very small way this is already happening with 3-D clip art, but it takes little imagination to see it developing. Builders already design houses by amending plans from house catalogues and 3-D model catalogues could often avoid reinvention of the wheel, though at some threat to originality. In Japan, clients can already have customised kitchen designs created for them as they watch, by designers selecting, modifying and arranging a collection of kitchen components.

Conversely, photo realistic models of items that do not exist can be shown in catalogues, and not produced in reality until ordered. A jeweller already uses one of the packages described in this book to design and sell jewellery before it has been made, with obvious savings in outlay on precious materials, also gaining the ability to tailor items to individual demand.

10.6 AND FINALLY

The magnitudes of forthcoming changes are unpredictable but looking at the pattern of the past forty years suggests an exponential growth curve in computer modelling as in so many other areas. Pocket-sized workstations might not get given away free with petrol but they will become commonplace. This resultant increase in portability will not just add to convenience but will change attitudes to computers; an ever-available, hand-held box losing the preciousness of a desk-bound machine available during office hours.

3-D digitisers will become automatic and commonplace.

Solid modelling will be used more (it is already appearing in computer games). Visualisation, such as medical and financial, will increasingly use solid models to make otherwise obscure data visible.

New modelling methods will evolve to deal with problematic subjects such as freeform, non-geometrical, soft objects (e.g. humans); objects for which there is no straightforward mathematical description.

Increased networking, particularly using telephone and satellite links, will move us towards the long-held vision that all computers could ultimately be linked to produce a single global machine with massive computing power and access to all recorded knowledge.

Modelling at present is exciting but it will become more so in the next few years.

Stay curious, keep an open mind and have 3-D fun.

APPENDIX 1

MODELLING & RELATED SOFTWARE

When I started writing this book I listed software that I would like to describe and identified 34 modelling packages for the Mac, 3 separate rendering packages, 13 animation/post-production packages which might be relevant to modellers, and several programming and control applications. The number has increased whilst I have been writing and the range of Macintosh machines has also increased to include many more with a realistic modelling capacity. Apple itself is also promoting its range far more strongly as modelling/rendering capable and the next generation of machines will further improve on the ability to model and render to the highest standards.

I would have liked to review all of these applications but was soon confirmed in my view that it takes months of regular use to know a package sufficiently thoroughly to describe it fully. Even if the time (and inclination) were available for such a mammoth task, the software pool would always be changing faster than it could be reviewed (more packages being added and existing packages updated and improved) and I didn't want a book that would date so quickly as to be obsolete by the time it came to publication. Compromise was therefore needed, and I chose firstly to limit the number of packages I looked at, and econdly to try to look at the basic principles underlying the operation of different products, with the emphasis on features original to each.

This does not, therefore, try to be a comprehensive review of all Mac modellers but attempts to offer an insight into the different paradigms that have been brought to the computer modelling process by a range of products. I hope also to give some insight along the way, into the requirements of the various modelling disciplines and the way in which these are catered for by the products considered. In discussing the applications I have looked at their modelling and rendering facilities, pointing out unique or unusual features. In order to do each application justice, all the more common features are also listed but without comment. Animation facilities are only mentioned in passing, although in some cases this is their main feature. It is planned to follow this book with one that deals with animation on the Macintosh, at which time these applications will get the attention they deserve.

I have tried to pick a varied range of packages and have found most distributors very helpful, only a couple of my choices being unavailable to review within my time limits, for various reasons. In the course of reviewing all these programs I obviously found favourites that I was immediately comfortable with, and others that felt rather awkward by comparison. I decided that it would be unfair, however, to put too much emphasis on strongly subjective responses, as I come to modelling from my own particular direction, have my own particular uses for the discipline, and have not been able to spend months working exhaustively with each and every application. Also, and most importantly, many of these packages will be updated within the lifetime of this book and criticisms made now might well be answered in future releases. Software prices have been excluded here since they change so fast (one of the applications described having halved its price while the book was being written).

Whilst I hope that this chapter will offer some insight, you should try out your own choice before purchase; and will find that an increasing number of products are available as free (or cheap) demo versions that offer most of the functionality of the full package, and provide an indispensable way of 'testing the water'. There is also a move towards releasing groups of related demo applications, together with sample files and instructions on cheap CDs.

SUMMARY OF APPLICATIONS DESCRIBED

In order to make more accessible the full descriptions of applications that follow, a quick summary precedes them. This makes brief, comparative comments on the likely uses and main features of the various packages.

INFINI-D is an easy to use, general purpose modeller which includes rendering and animation facilities. It displays a good spread of features without becoming complicated and provides a sound introduction to modelling, leaning towards symmetrical rather than freeform objects. It was used to create the front cover of this book and would be an accessible teaching tool. Whilst it is not intended for precision design such as engineering or architecture, it could make a quick and versatile prototyper. A network rendering feature (which is extra) adds great functionality in a multi-Mac environment.

STRATAVISION 3D fits into the same general category as Infini-D but has a slightly more sophisticated feel to it and is lauded for its rendering capabilities. I found manipulation of objects particularly intuitive in this package and like its ability to 'grow' with StrataExtensions. Spline based animation is built in and 'Raydiosity' offers a rendering method even more comprehensive than ray tracing. A wide variety of model types can be comfortably built, though they are not intended to be CAD accurate.

RAY DREAM DESIGNER introduces some innovatory methods for viewing and operating on models, and these naturally take a little getting used to. They seem to lead you towards particular types of object, and it requires familiarity with the package to appreciate its full range. Perhaps because of this I sense more of a 'house style' in the models produced here than in some other modellers. It is, however, well regarded by those who use it regularly. Another general modeller, its ray tracing is amongst the fastest on the Mac and network rendering is available as an extra; it has no animation facility.

SWIVEL 3D PRO is one of the longest established Mac modellers and has a proven track record. It is starting to look a little basic by comparison with the latest breed of modellers but continues to do a reliable job, being particularly known for the jointing facility from

which its name derives. It now integrates closely with
MacRenderMan to provide sophisticated rendering, and has a simple
animation facility. Although lacking 'frills' it contains enough tools
to do many jobs well and is admirably straightforward to use but is
not the probable choice for building highly detailed models.

MACROMODEL is another general purpose tool, but one which
particularly emphasises spline-based modelling both in the creation
of 2-D templates and as sweep paths. It has no animation facility
and limited rendering capability, models being exported to other
packages for these tasks. There are a number of useful features, such
as having several editing levels, though the wide use of keys to
modify tool functions leads to a relatively steep initial learning
curve. The early version of this package has a slightly unusual
balance, since it is strong on flowing, curved objects which can be
difficult to create in many modellers, but seems more complicated in
the creation of basic objects on which other modellers thrive.

ALIAS SKETCH! is another modeller which focuses its attention
on editable, spline-based curves, particularly drawn freehand. It
introduces unusual methods which emphasise freeform shapes and
tend to play down simple, symmetrical forms, although these can
also be produced. Aimed at illustrators, graphic and product
designers, this is not meant for use as a precision CAD product, but
encourages intuitive tuning of form. Rendering is included but not
animation and it has a special feature for compositing objects
realistically onto background images.

MACTOPAS caters particularly for an animation production
environment and its modeller is efficient and unassuming. It feels
very solid and offers a practical range of workable tools without
gimmicks. It does not, for instance, include ray tracing in its
rendering arsenal because the process is too time-consuming for
realistic production use, but concentrates its efforts on extensive
mapping and Phong rendering options which will produce
satisfactory results much faster. Details like soft shadows, flares and
cutting templates all work well, and the animation includes helpful
features such as scripting. Given its intended market, the modeller
does not aim to be CAD accurate but offers the control to create
chosen effects in a straightforward way.

FORM•Z is a general purpose solid and surface modeller with a
high level of functionality. It incorporates minimal rendering and no

animation. Being a solid modeller it adds Boolean functions to surface building methods and this significantly extends the ways in which the user can think about model building. A rich and accessible range of tools is available through a strongly iconic interface, and the breadth of functions requires familiarity to do it full justice. A particularly comprehensive range of editing and modification functions is welcome and details such as terrain modelling enhance its power.

MODELSHOP II is a well-established modeller catering for the architect/designer. It is a fairly unsophisticated package by current standards but benefits from a simplicity of operation which makes it very friendly. Basic shading and animation are included, though models would normally be exported for detailed work. Viewing methods use architectural paradigms with plans, elevations and projections; perspective views are set up by defining viewing position (in plan), height and point to be viewed. By limiting its range, whilst including features such as fast shadow creation and a 'walk-through' tool, a very comfortable, accessible and useful package for prototyping buildings (in particular) has developed.

MINICAD+ is a very comprehensive 2-D and 3-D CAD package. It meets all professional standards and includes tools particularly relevant to architecture/building. Rendering is limited to basic shading and animation is not included, although 'walk-throughs' allow the model to be 'explored'. For such a complex package it remains very accessible and it has been in existence long enough for any rough edges to have been smoothed out. Although easy to build straightforward models, it would be wasted on 'casual' modelling and is very much a tool for the serious modeller. Useful links exist between the drawing and an integral database/spreadsheet, whilst a programming facility allows customisation. An accompanying tape offers a good overview.

AUTOCAD is a massive and long-established 2-D and 3-D modeller that has effectively become an industry yardstick. It is a comprehensive, professional tool that requires time to learn thoroughly, and has been tailored to more than 600 specialist applications. Its functionality is enhanced by extensions which add solid modelling, rendering and animation facilities. Not designed for casual play.

VIRTUS WALKTHROUGH has relatively limited modelling and rendering tools since its main function is to animate interactively a path through the model. Objects can be imported from elsewhere but the speed at which a scene can be navigated is determined by the power of the host computer and the complexity of the object. Simple, intuitive and effective, this is a useful tool for exploring a scene (and perhaps explaining it to a client). Windows and holes are quickly created in an unusual model-building environment and walk-throughs can be recorded and replayed. A library of architectural elements is included, which suggests what the most likely use of the package might be, though any object can usefully be viewed.

ADD DEPTH extrudes 2-D artwork into 3-D objects and is not a full-blown modeller, artwork being either imported or created within the application and surface treatments applied. It has some neat tools for aligning and orientating objects and is a useful addition to a graphic designer's arsenal, particularly since it is a vector based package.

ADOBE DIMENSIONS is another limited modeller for the attention of 2-D designers. With spin, extrude and primitives available, it can make 3-D objects, but its strength lies in its mapping ability which has some particularly versatile features. An obvious application of this package would be for package design and it is complemented by a notably clear and concise manual.

MACROMIND THREE-D has limited model-making ability as it is primarily intended for rendering and for animating imported objects. It does these jobs very comprehensively and easily, having a particularly rich range of surface treatments. Central to its operation is a 'score', which enhances its efficiency by allowing to be shown all properties of all objects at any moment in time. It has features allowing compositing and other post-production effects, which add to its ability as a production tool.

MACRENDERMAN is solely a renderer and is supported by many modelling applications. It can either stand alone or be accessed from within modellers tailored to work with it. Powerful, and adopted across a wide range of hardware platforms, it comes close to establishing a rendering standard.

LIFEFORMS is intended as a program for animating the human figure. As such it has no modelling and rendering facilities built in, and is included mainly because it could provide a useful resource for someone engaged on building models. The means of articulating and positioning the hierarchical figure(s) are interesting and effective.

TOUCH-3D imports 3-D computer models and 'unwraps' them, producing 2-D plans which can be printed out and folded into real-world 3-D models. It produces files which can subsequently be worked on in painting/drawing programs, and provides an interesting means of realising a 3-D idea.

DEBABELISER is included because of its value as a file conversion utility. As yet working only with picture files, it can convert between all the main file types on a wide range of platforms and allows your Mac-originated material to be used on other machines.

INFINI-D   *v2.0.1*

UK distributors: Gomark   071-731-7930
Specular International

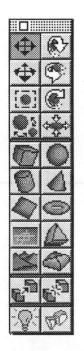

Infini-D, from Specular International, is one of the easiest packages to start using yet has a good range of features. Their claim is for 'powerful technology with a friendly interface' and this package is certainly well on the way to meeting that claim. As with all new software, the ease with which you find you can use it must be dependent on your previous experience, and the conventions in Infini-D match are largely similar to others with which I am familiar, but I know a number of people who comment on rapidly becoming comfortable with and confident in the package. It provided the basis for MacTypical in a previous chapter, though with a few additions and alterations. The manual is good and its cover has some mouth-watering examples of what the package can do (though you will not match them on day one!).

The default screen has top, front, right and camera view windows, the first three having XYZ axis indicators in the lower left corner, and this combination can be reassigned from a choice of six standard view windows plus camera. Each window has a Panels menu built into its top bar, offering control of shading (bounding box, wireframe, shade fast, better or best; anti-aliasing none, low medium and high); navigation (moving point of view or camera, and switching perspective on/off in standard view windows); bookmarks (which list a range of view positions); and options

Above: Main toolbar
Left: ray tracing a selection
Below: Standard window navigation
Bottom: Camera navigation

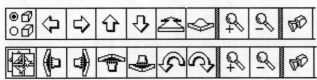

(pre-defined window sizes such as PAL and options of forcing visible wireframes and showing invisible objects). You can choose between having either the active window or all windows updated automatically. Additionally an object floating window is available (interactively displaying name, position, orientation, dimension and scale) as is a surface floating window (interactively displaying surface details). The object floating windows provide a useful means of numerically setting (and optionally, of locking) any of its parameters, whilst the surface floating window gives quick access to the means of setting surface qualities and effects.

Primitives available from the icon bar are cubes, spheres, cylinders, cones, 2-D squares and infinite plane. Facilities to create custom objects can be accessed using the lathe, extrude, freeform and

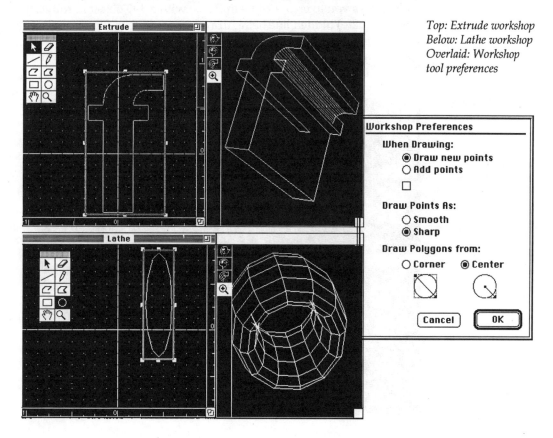

Top: Extrude workshop
Below: Lathe workshop
Overlaid: Workshop
tool preferences

163

terrain tool icons, whilst further icons create lights and cameras. Double clicking on the object creation tools opens a dialogue box with which parameters can be set numerically. Two icons control the axes along which objects can be dragged, three icons control rotation around each axis, a uniform scale tool and a squash and stretch tool re-proportion objects, and two icons create and break links between objects. A local area ray trace icon will ray trace a rubber-banded area.

To create an object the relevant icon is selected and then the cursor clicked in the appropriate window. This is simple and straightforward but provides a rather strange route into the custom object workshops, since you effectively create an unwanted object and then choose to edit it. In these workshops a range of drawing tools allows you to create 2-D templates, with a 3-D object in rough (but adequate) hidden line being drawn immediately. You can also import templates from other packages, which gives you access to spline tools and tracing facilities not included here, and use System 7's subscribe feature. Objects in the lathe and extrude workshops

Freeform workshop

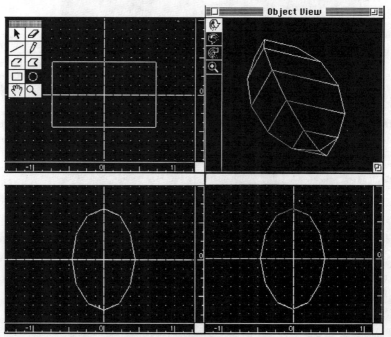

can be converted to freeform for further manipulation in the freeform workshop, and good control is offered of points at the template stage but no low level editing of 3-D objects is available.

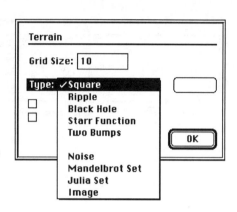

Terrain options

Navigation follows the general paradigm of the Infini-D interface, with the direction of movement or rotation selected first, then the object moved interactively by bounding box. This prevents totally free movement or rotation all at once, a restriction which I find a virtue as it can easily lead to disorientation. The camera movement felt a little less intuitive, but again, the ability to isolate a single direction of movement or rotation made it easy to understand. Locking of objects in a hierarchy (controlling the way children move relative to their parents) is similarly simple, the available options being free lock, pivot lock, position lock and full lock. The ability to switch from standard to perspective view is important for alignment purposes and is conveniently available. The bookmark feature stores separate views for each window, though all are available in the camera window, and is of particular help in constructing animations.

Surface information box

Terrains are rather odd surfaces created from grids that are transformed by mathematical functions and often seem reminiscent of sci-fi landscapes. These functions are pre-defined, which limits the control of surface available, but they are quick and easy to use, and might find a use. Cameras and lights are controlled in the same way as any other object, but have the useful ability to be aimed automatically using the 'Point At' menu item. Both have the usual range of controls.

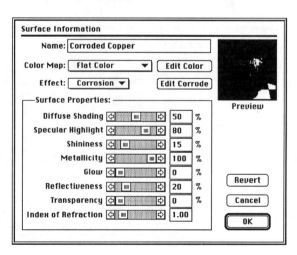

Rendering is efficient and has the usual range available but ray tracing is 500% faster than in the previous version of Infini-D, claimed now to be

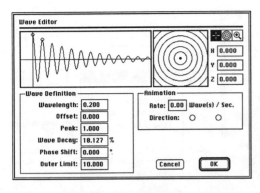

Wave effect editor

Surface composition box

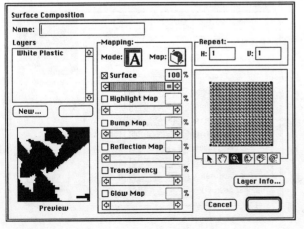

one of the fastest renderers on the Mac. I would, however, prefer rendering to continue in the background rather than for it to tie up the whole screen. Phong will do shadows and anti-aliasing is by super sampling rather than by post-processing. This means that the anti-aliasing is broadcast quality and the anti-aliasing information can be carried in an alpha channel for seamless compositing, which is a very nice detail.

A good basic library of surfaces and textures is included, including procedural surfaces (like wood) and effects (like corrosion), and is fully editable. Maps (such as marble, tile, noise and wave effect) can also be easily edited. Image mapping is well provided, with the ability to combine maps to produce a composite surface; mapping types include highlight, bump, reflection, transparency and glow; and there are the usual map application methods. The environment settings include fog (which does not slow rendering measurably) and environmental mapping.

Animation facilities are efficient and friendly, with features like text morphing a nice touch. Morphing of objects is also possible by editing one object to produce a second and transforming between them. QuickTime movies can be wrapped around objects and there is claimed to be no loss of data if a crash occurs whilst an animation is being created. Luckily, I have not needed to test this feature.

A crash-proof distributed rendering engine named 'Backburner' is available to spread the workload through a network and this can be set for batch processing, and to cut in and render when the machine is idle. It is claimed to be very robust and I have seen it restarted in the middle of a demonstration without any problem.

STRATAVISION 3D v2.6

Strata Incorporated
UK distributors: Gomark   071-731-7930

StrataVision 3D is from The Virtual Studio Company and has
already become established for its fine and very sophisticated
rendering. You are likely to be familiar with an image of pool balls
and pool cue tips on blue-green baize that has been used in publicity
material, featuring beautiful light source reflections and double
shadows. Although these objects are not the most difficult to model
and render, there is an air of sophistication and finish about the
image that leads you to expect a very professional product. Strata
describe their product as a virtual electronic photographic studio(!)
and it has been designed to accept extension tools developed by
either Strata Inc. or a third party. It comes with a fat but well
organised ring binder manual.

On launching, the default screen has the usual menu bar, a single
modelling window, and a palette of tool icons; animation, texture
and lighting palettes are also available. The tool icons stand for:
View move; Object move; View rotate; Object rotate; View
magnification; Object scale; Unlink, Link (establish parent/child
relationships); Camera object (creates new camera); Camera (initiates
rendering; either of full scene or click-drag a box for selective
render); Rounded cube; Cube; Sphere; Cone; Pseudo-primitives (a
sub-menu offers: dodecahedron, frustum, grid, icosahedron,
octahedron, pyramid, rounded cylinder, teapot (!), tetrahedron,
torus; and other objects can be added to provide a customised
set); Cylinder; Rounded rectangle (hollow or filled); Rectangle
(hollow or filled); Regular polygon (hollow or filled, with a
sub-menu to define number of sides); Oval (hollow or filled);
Irregular polygon (hollow or filled); Freehand polygon
(hollow or filled); Polyline; Freehand line; Arc; Text; Spotlight;
and Point light. Modifier keys have familiar Mac functions.

Extra windows can be created and set to any view, so that a
customised selection of views can readily be set up.
Additionally, an unusual feature is that any window can be
split either horizontally or vertically any number of times,

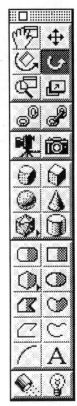

*Above: Main tool bar
Below: Corner of
window showing view
options*

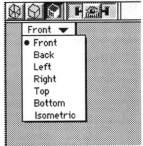

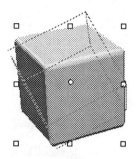

Above: Object with manoeuvre handles
Right: Mouse filter

Extrusion window

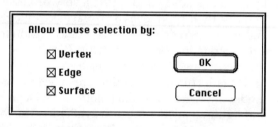

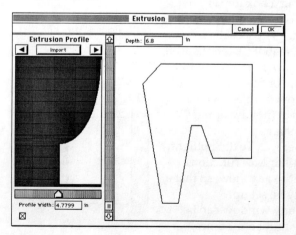

providing that a minimum area of 128x64 pixels is allowed for each window. This provides a quick way of getting several views of an object, whilst a second object can be created in another window (or set of windows). Each window can also be set, by icons in its corner, to wireframe, hidden line or solid view, and to several 'focal lengths'. On creating a new camera, a new window to show that camera's view can be opened and in the margin of that window is a 'slider' for setting the camera's angle of view. Each time the camera tool is used to start a fresh render, a separate window is created in which that rendering is carried out; one advantage being that subsequent renders can then be compared with one another.

The degree of handling control of objects and views doesn't vary greatly between modellers, but some manage to make the process easier than others. StrataVision 3D is, for me, one of the most intuitive to use; the movement of and around objects, matching well the way I think of doing things in the real world. A selected object (or shape) is boxed by a 'view management overlay' which has rotation handles on the sides and corners. Dragging a handle with the single rotation tool rotates the object about an axis (side handles = rotation around vertical axis, top/bottom handles = rotation around horizontal axis, corner handles = rotation in plane of the screen). The centre of rotation is indicated by a circular handle (by default shown at the centre of the object) which can be dragged to any other position. Whilst none of these handling conventions is unique, the combination seems to work particularly smoothly here.

The modelling menu offers 2-D and 3-D functions. '2D Reshape' gives easy control of shape editing with Bezier curves and has a 'Convert to polygon' function. '2D Sculpt' offers a more accurate environment than the modelling window for creating shapes, and includes a 'Bezier extraction' facility. It gives a particularly clear presentation of the shape by using automatic drop-shadows, and toggling from '+' to '-' makes for easy cutting from a shape. 'Extrude' uses a separate window which offers a selection of extrusion profiles (and the ability to import more), having numerical control over extrusion depth and profile width. The presence of profiling is good, but it is worth remembering that the consequence of setting a profile needs to be carefully considered in order to avoid creating confused objects. 'Facet' gives each facet of an object an individual identity so that it can be independently manipulated. 'Lathe' takes a template to its own window where you can set degrees of rotation and the relationship of template to axis of rotation (the latter more clearly than usual). 'Skin' creates objects from a sequence of templates which have been connected using the link tool, whilst 'Unskin' reverses the process. 'Smooth' cleans up models imported from other sources. 'Sweep' looks and works very much like 'Lathe' but allows you to change the template size during the sweep and the number turns. Additional 'StrataExtensions' are available to add functionality, such as with a Fractal terrain modeller.

The rendering seems quick and smooth.

Lathe window

Render options

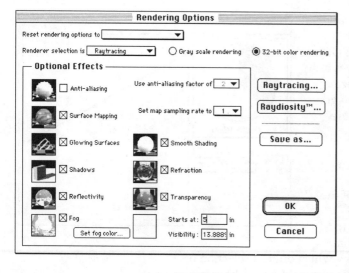

Rendering options

Resolutions can be set for standard Mac screens, HyperCard, Video PAL, video NTSC, 35mm film and custom. Continuous rendering feedback (where the window updates constantly as the render proceeds) can be switched off to improve rendering time and renders can be suspended and restarted or can be queued. 'RenderPro' is available for network rendering. The rendering options are the usual six plus ray tracing and 'Raydiosity'™ (which carries with it a machine health warning about heavy rendering times).

These last two rendering modes can be fine tuned through 'esoterica' windows, which sit one level below the more usual controls, and are typical of the thoughtfulness of the package's design. Optional effects include fog, glowing surfaces, inter-object illumination and soft shadows, in addition to the more standard ones. Features such as texture editing also have two levels of tuning, with a compact range of controls at the top level and an 'Expert' button leading to more sophisticated range of settings. This is a nice touch, which should have added relatively little to the complexity of the algorithms used but offers access to a wide range of the program's variables (though it opens up a level of subtlety which may rarely be needed).

Above: Lighting palette
Below: Texture palette

The global lighting palette (as opposed to the local lighting

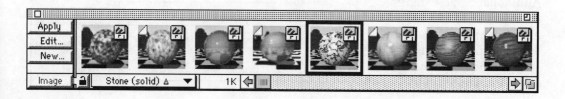

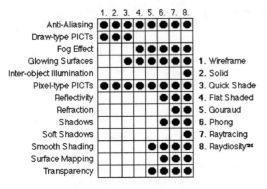

	1.	2.	3.	4.	5.	6.	7.	8.
Anti-Aliasing	●	●	●	●	●	●	●	●
Draw-type PICTs	●	●	●					
Fog Effect				●	●	●	●	●
Glowing Surfaces			●	●	●	●	●	●
Inter-object Illumination								●
Pixel-type PICTs	●	●	●	●	●	●	●	●
Reflectivity						●	●	●
Refraction							●	●
Shadows						●	●	●
Soft Shadows								●
Smooth Shading					●	●	●	●
Surface Mapping						●	●	●
Transparency					●	●	●	●

1. Wireframe
2. Solid
3. Quick Shade
4. Flat Shaded
5. Gouraud
6. Phong
7. Raytracing
8. Raydiosity™

Raydiosity™ Esoterica

☐ Enable stochastic (random) sampling

Maximum Initial Pixel Samples: 1
Maximum Propagation Samples: 1
Maximum Diffuse Lighting Samples: 200
Maximum Diffuse Ray Bounces: 1
Maximum Light/Shadow Samples: 100

OK
Cancel

Raytracing Esoterica

Maximum Reflectivity Recursion: 1
Maximum Transparency Recursion: 6
Maximum Octree Height: 7
Maximum Tracing Block Size: 4
Block Subdivision Threshold: 11

OK
Cancel

provided by the spotlight and point light tools) uses a paradigm for setting light direction which appears on several modellers and with which I find very comfortable. A circle comes to be understood as a sphere when an icon (which looks like a large-headed nail running through the sphere) is moved; the head and shaft of the nail implying surface highlight and direction (although it works intuitively rather than by rational understanding). Additional light sources each contribute an additional 'nail' which is displayed in the colour set for the light it represents. The texture palette displays a good range of supplied textures as thumbnails (including 'invisible'!), and has the usual ability to create and edit textures.

Top left: Rendering options available within each rendering algorithm
Top right: Fine tuning for Raydiosity™
Above: Fine tuning for ray tracing

The whole package has a good, professional feel and a well thought-out interface that takes you through processes in logical, sequential steps. It includes a comprehensive keyframe animation facility which includes the use of spline paths and hierarchical paths, and StrataVision 3D now has Alpha channel support and the ability to import Adobe Illustrator files. Other packages, such as MiniCad+, are able to export files to StrataVision 3D in order to make use of its rendering ability. The setting-up procedure for the program includes a range of caching options to optimise processing for the machine configuration in use (such as an image cache to allow rendering of files bigger than the available RAM).

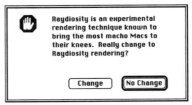

Raydiosity is an experimental rendering technique known to bring the most macho Macs to their knees. Really change to Raydiosity rendering?

Change   No Change

RAY DREAM DESIGNER v2.0.2

Ray Dream Inc.
UK Distributors: Amtech International Ltd. 0202-476977

Ray Dream Designer is described in the preface to its manual as a 3-D illustration tool which suggests a program intended for designers rather than engineers; it does not include an animation facility. The package comprises two applications: LightForge, in which objects are built; and SceneBuilder, in which the objects are brought together in a scene. Although untypical, this configuration is less cluttered than most, the object building stage being clear of scene considerations, and the scene building stage uninvolved with object creation. This paradigm matches more closely the way things are likely to happen in the real world, and might also help to create greater clear-sightedness at each stage. The manual is clear and concise.

On entering LightForge you are confronted by either cross-section and elevation windows (if you are in extrude mode) or profile and lathe specification windows (if you are in lathe mode), in both cases accompanied by a preview window. As you develop an object using the tools available in the first two windows, a smooth shaded view is automatically drawn in the preview window. It might sound as though this constant redrawing will delay the modelling work, but a good, fast algorithm is being used, and the redrawing only continues when no work is being done elsewhere; also it can be switched off if the

Above: Main tool icons.
Below: Main screen

scene gets too complex to redraw fast. A surface parameter window also allows adjustment of the complexity of the rendered object; a simpler model rendering faster. The object in the preview window can be interactively rotated, using the cursor to drag a bounding box. This object creation environment is so 'clean' and easy that it immediately invites experiment and fine tuning, where a more crowded environment might be less welcoming to changes.

There is no library of primitives available but simple shapes can be created very quickly, and a personalised library could be readily compiled. At this stage there is no numerical sizing of objects, that can come later in SceneBuilder, LightForge builds by eye (though template can be imported from applications which might permit accurate proportioning).

Details at this stage include: the usual ability to set the lathe rotation angle and to determine whether the lathing is polygonal or smooth; a neat method of scaling cross sections in the extrusion mode using sliding pointers (though you can't use scale factors to effect backward portions of an elevation that bends back on itself); the ability to define the way in which cross-sections are interpolated; and spline and Bezier tools included in all creation windows. Whilst a text tool is available, it is also possible to autotrace contours from an imported PICT file, which offers a useful alternative for creating logos.

The shaded preview object can be set up with the usual lighting and surface parameters, including reflection, refraction, transparency, colour and highlights, and a standard sphere shows immediate effects of changes. I liked being able to definehighlights by brightness and size, rather than by changing the light source and surface type; it is an intuitive method which might be appreciated by the package's intended user. Anti-aliasing is not necessary at this stage and is not, therefore, an option.

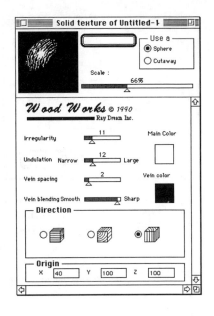

Editors for wood and marble solid textures

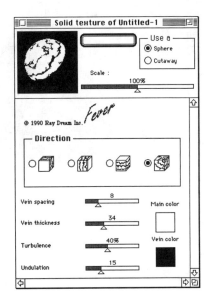

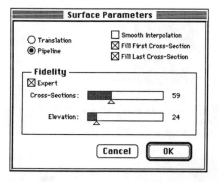

Above: Surface parameter box
Below: Perspective window

Texture mapping has the normal controls for alignment and wrapping/projection method; white can be defined as transparent, and tiling is included. As with other controls, the mapping is as easily set as in any package. The manual tells you not to bother with environment maps as reflections are automatically generated in the final render. Solid texture is selected from a comprehensive library, which can be edited. The editors arecustomised for the texture type and are user friendly. As well as the usual marble, wood and checkers editors, there are wires editors and a 'Basic magic' editor for simulating stones, clouds and such like, in which bump size and amplitude and spot size and blending can be set.

Having created your object(s) in LightForge, you then take them to SceneBuilder in order to construct your scene. The main window in SceneBuilder is the perspective window, in which the scene is represented by a cube. Objects in the scene are shown in free space but also in relationship to the backwalls and floor of the cube by projection of their bounding boxes onto these surfaces. This gives a clear understanding of their relative position(s). The objects are orientated by dragging, rotating and scaling the 'shadow' projections, which might sound counter-intuitive but works well. The projections which are to be shown can be selected in order to keep the amount of graphic information displayed to a minimum (which seems to be a consistent and eminently sensible part of the Ray Dream Designer philosophy).

The Hierarchy window displays a hierarchical description of the elements of the scene, being described as a symbolic text and icon-based counterpart to the graphic-based perspective view. The tree hierarchy expresses spatial proximity of elements and interconnection of multiple-part objects. Elements can be added to the tree from the objects window (which displays icons of all available objects) or duplicated, additional lights can be created and their properties set in the light source parameters dialogue box.

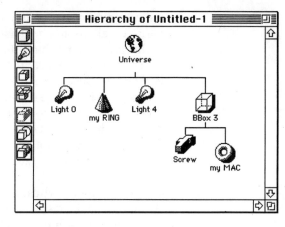

Scene hierarchy

Elements of the hierarchy can be grouped into containers called (somewhat confusingly?) bounding boxes, which function like folders in the Macintosh file hierarchy, and which have useful parallels with the way things are grouped in the real world and, perhaps, with OOPS (object orientated programming systems). A 'phantom' icon hides objects, which simplifies the scene and speeds rendering, and bounding box or shaded display for separate items can be selected with further icons.

The usual constraints can be set on object movement and 'nudges' provide a simple incremental

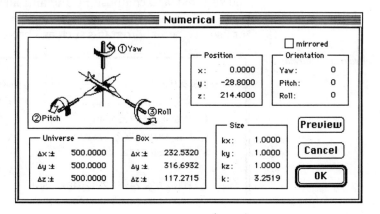

Numerical input box

way of achieving movements. Four kinds of automatic constraint are possible: alignments on the universe (makes the selection parallel to the universe walls); relative alignments (for multiple selections you can align along an axis, distribute along an axis, and bring bounding boxes into contact); numerical placements (numerical control of position, orientation and size); and symmetries (allows transformation into a mirrored position). A convenient variant realigns an object as it was when first dragged into the scene. Lights and cameras have the usual controls.

The menu item 'Production formats' immediately confirms that Ray Dream Designer is built with production environments in mind, offering a wide range of video and print formats for the final image. The manual, at this point, gives a worthwhile explanation of some of the issues involved in displaying and outputting images, showing that the output resolution and colour depth is not dependent on your computer's display capability. Proof image quality can be chosen prior to a full resolution render, the draft being produced with a two-pass Z-buffer whilst the final image is ray traced (currently claimed to be the fastest ray tracing on the Mac, all Ray Dream Designer's rendering algorithms seem good). A batch queue can be set up to render listed images in sequence and DreamNet allows networked machines to share the computing load (DreamNet is a system extension that adds distributed computing capability to the Apple system software). The rendering process can be interrupted and restored, and compositing and anti-aliasing are available as post-production facilities and a background mask can be generated for use in external programs such as Photoshop.

Production formats

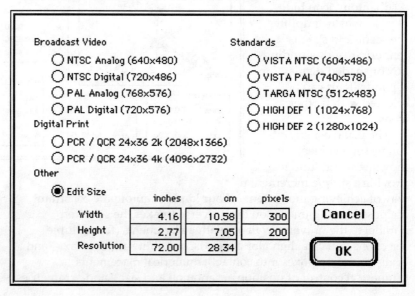

176

SWIVEL 3D PROFESSIONAL v 2.0.11

MacroMind/Paracomp
UK distributors: Computers Unlimited 081-200-8282

Swivel 3D has been long established on the Macintosh and has
played no small part in the Mac being taken seriously as a modeller.
This is reflected in the fact that many applications can export models
in Swivel 3D format. It is described as the best-selling 3-D
application on the Macintosh. Its great strength in the early days
was in its innovative hierarchical linking, which allowed models to
have constrained articulation and which led it to be particularly
associated with animation; its name presumably derives from this
function. It is interesting to note that this seminal program was
developed by VPL Research Inc. who were later at the heart of
Virtual Reality research, developing the DataGlove and DataSuit as
part of their VR system. The package includes Swivelizer, which
converts file types such as DXF and Type 1 fonts into Swivel 3D
format, and QuickPICS, and animation utility. It is also marketed as
SwivelMan when bundled with MacRenderMan (which is also
described in this chapter).

    Swivel 3D Pro launches with a single World window, the
standard menu bar and a column of 15 tool icons. Double-clicking
on an object in the World window (or selecting 'Redesign Object'
from the Menu) takes you to an Object window divided into top,
side, cross-section and object view quadrants, with five tool icons.
The World View tools are: XY arrow (movement in X & Y planes);
XZ arrow (movement in X & Z planes); Yaw arrow (rotate around Y
axis); Pitch arrow (rotate around X axis); Roll arrow (rotate around Z
axis); Scale tool; Lathed object, extruded object; free link (makes
child/parent links); lock link; ball joint link; unlink tool; zoom in;
zoom out; and palette tool. The Design Objects tools are: double
arrow (edits upper and/or lower contours of section views), single
arrow (edits single contour of section views); oval tool (with
selectable number of points); and rectangle tool.

    Basic objects are created by using either the lathed or extruded
object tools, a click in the World window producing either a lathed,
cube or an extruded triangle which can then be edited in the Object

*Above: World view
tools
Below: Design object
tools*

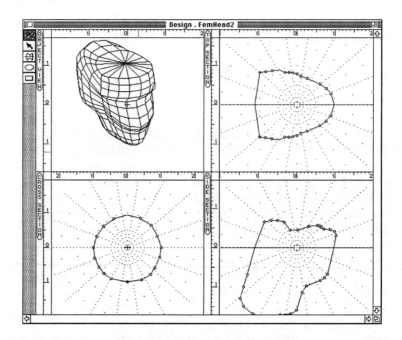

Sample head and Object Window showing polar grid and rulers

Render options

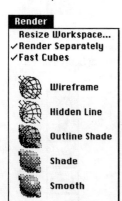

windows to produce the required object. Additionally, skinned objects can be made from a sequence of sections. In the object window rulers can be switched on and off, and, unusually, the grid can be switched from rectangular to polar. A nice feature is the ability to paste a PICT image in one of the Object view quadrants, in order to trace from it; one existing object can be also used as a template for creating another. Returning to the World window the objects can be positioned, scaled, linked and rendered (either using five basic rendering models within Swivel 3D or setting more sophisticated properties which can be rendered within MacRenderMan). It is worth noting that the Wireframe rendering mode removes backfaces, though a full hidden line mode is available, and that objects can be rendered separately using different rendering modes (which is untypical but often useful). 'Fast Cubes' is another rendering option, which creates and shades bounding boxes for the sake of speed – helpful in a complex model. Rectangular or triangular facets can be chosen for an object. The range of both tools and menubar commands is kept compact and the manual is clear and concise.

Objects can be dragged into position in the usual manner or a dialogue box can be used to enter numerically the position (relative either to the centre of the world or the centre of the object's parent) and scale, together with permitted limits of movement along each axis. The object can also be locked in its position and a similar dialogue box controls the object's attitude and constraints using yaw, roll and pitch. Objects are linked by dragging a line from 'child' to 'parent', and thereafter the child's position is shown in the dialogue boxes relative to the parent, rather than to the world. Similarly, its freedom of movement can be constrained relative to its parent and scaling operations on the parent apply also to the child. Three tools permit free linking, locked linking (with which relative position and attitude are fixed) and unlinking; a fourth tool sets ball-joint links, in which position only is locked. This system of setting and adjusting links is simple and effective. A nice detail which helps to confirm position in a hierarchical tree is the use of the cursor keys (or the 'Find' dialogue box) to navigate up, down and across the tree to discover parents/children and siblings. Particularly in the early days of experimenting with linkage, it is easy to forget in which order objects have been linked.

In the same way that objects can be positioned and orientated, so the world itself (which is a finite sized cube) can be moved and angled. The direction from which the world is viewed can be set (or selected from six predefined views) and the viewing angle set from 'very wide' to 'narrow' or 'orthogonal'. As well as being able to close in or pull back from the view in the World window, 'Size to fit' will size the model to fit the window comfortably; this is convenient for tracking down 'lost' objects (though the Find dialogue box offers an alternative method). Zoom tools work in a standard fashion.

The palette tool offers a range of colours for the background if clicked in the World window away from any object, and, if clicked on an object brings up the material palette. This palette leads to the material editor dialogue box where direct and specular reflectance can be set, environment maps added, and 'Material Shaders' set. This allows a choice from RenderMan shader options (which will only be visible in RenderMan, not in Swivel 3D) and the option of editing material values. New materials can be created and added to the palette. The number of colours to be used can affect the smoothness of shading (since more gradations of each colour are

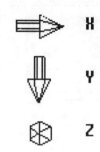

X

Y

Z

Position and orientation symbols

 Yaw

 Pitch

 Roll

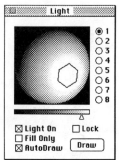

Light panel

available if the number of colours is reduced) and the number of object colours can be set in the 'Palette Options' dialogue box, as can the darkness of shadows cast. Swivel 3D uses an optimised 8-bit colour palette in the World window and dithers 32-bit environment maps to fit; information is retained as 32-bit for export, however.

Eight light sources are available, their direction being established by dragging a hexagon over the surface of a sphere in the light panel. Lights can be directional (creating highlights and shadows) or 'fill' lights, and their position can be locked to that of the world or left relative to the viewpoint. An effects menu offers a range of rendering options: shadows cast; anti-aliasing; projection mapping across the whole world or onto the side of any object (in this case, a wireframe image of the object can be exported to a graphics package and used as a template for the mapping image); object outlining (which can improve visual clarity); and depth edging (which changes line weight according to depth).

A simple but effective keyframe animation facility is included, and objects can, of course, be exported for animation elsewhere. Output styles are good, including draw or paint types and .rib files for RenderMan, and the half-tone facility included is intended for printing colour separations on a black and white PostScript device. A Script Command Set is also available, providing a set of text commands to control Swivel 3D, and whilst this is not to everyone's choice it is a feature I always like in a package, adding another level of control; its language is particularly straight forward.

Left: Half-tone dialogue box
Right: Output dialogue box

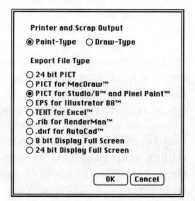

MACROMODEL v1.0

MacroMind/Paracomp
UK distributors: Computers Unlimited   081-200-8282

In the introduction to the manual,
MacroModel is described as providing
solutions for modelling needs ranging from
prototype design to light CAD. This
suggests a modeller for the designer rather
than the engineer and its *forte* proves to be
the speedy production of general models. A
compact tutorial booklet takes the user
smoothly through the basic functions and
the main manual is quite efficient in
explaining the full functionality, though I
had to reread some sections before fully
understanding the functions they described.
I found that the main manual required that
certain simple operations had been learnt
from the tutorial, but this led to a slightly
more streamlined reference, which is
preferable once you start to become familiar
with the application.

There is a single view window, in which
a working plane is described by a grid, and
this can be moved and rotated to match any
desired view. Automatic alignment of the
working plane is optional, and it can be used
in conjunction with the construction axis tool
to align planes as a foundation for object creation. Objects are
created by the operations of extrude, lathe, sweep and skin on 2-D
templates created and modified with a set of largely familiar
drawing tools, and a range of 'snapping' options lead to convenient
alignment of template elements. The action of commands selected
by icons is modified by the usual Mac keys (for instance the 'hand'
icon is selected in order to move the working plane; with the
Command key held down it moves the view, dragging rotates the

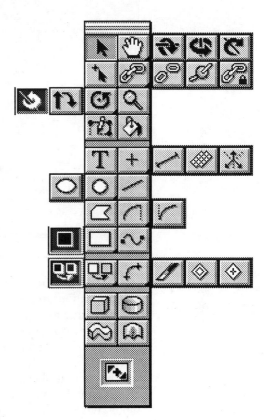

*Main tool bar
(showing hidden
options)*

Right: Light Browser
Left: Surface Browser

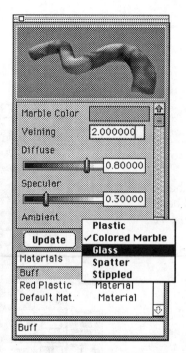

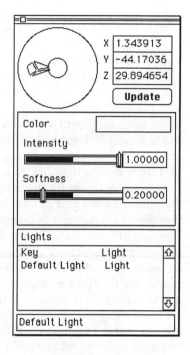

view; with the Control key held down the view is zoomed). As with all applications, the use of a number of mouse+key combinations means a little more learning at the outset but swifter working once learnt, providing that the package is in regular use. If it is only used occasionally then you either need a better memory than mine or reference back to the manual.

View browser

The main tool icons are grouped in blocks and selected by clicking, with several icons revealing sub-menus of further icons when they are clicked and held. Once selected, the sub-menu icon becomes the one shown in the main tool bar, which keeps the

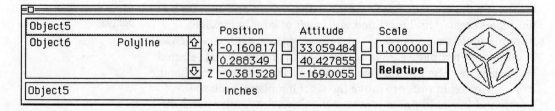

number of icons on display at any one time to a manageable 23. The
top block of icons controls movement and editing functions
(selection, movement and rotation of objects; addition of control
points; movement, rotation and scaling of view; exact rotation and
placement of objects; linking; zooming; specification of position and
attitude of working plane; 'painting' with current material). The
second icon block controls 2-D drawing tools (text; lines; circles and
ovals; squares and rectangles; segmented lines and
polygons; arcs; spline curves). The third icon block has
modifiers of 2-D and 3-D objects (fillets; trims; offsets;
movement of object centres) and mirroring. The fourth
icon block is for 3-D object creation from 2-D templates
(extrude; lathe; sweep; skin). The final icon toggles
between edge and centre as starting point for circles,
rectangles, etc. After using any tool the system returns
to a default selection, and a nice detail is that any tool
can be set as the default by selecting it with the Option
key held down. The usual Undo function is
supplemented by the ability to undo (or redo) the last
five operations.

Surface options
Top: low
Centre: medium
Bottom: high

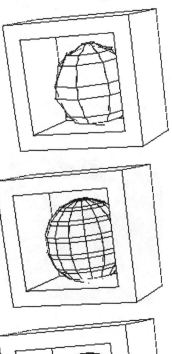

The methods of object creation are fairly
predictable once you know the tools available, with
several key combinations available to constrain
movement, etc. and an editable numerical
specification appearing in a bar at the bottom of the
window during construction. I found both the
method of object rotation using the proxy object in the
view browser and the means of repositioning the light
source using the diagramatic representation in the
light browser particularly quick and intuitive. Lights
can be easily set and altered and simulation of camera
lens focal lengths is clear and matched to view
distance, so that the effect is of changing perspective
(which is often less straight forward to achieve).
Concentric templates can be used to make objects with
holes (or pipes, etc. with wall thickness) and objects
can be mirrored.

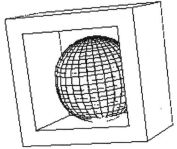

The ability to create versatile splines as a basis for
object creation is one of MacroModel's strong points,

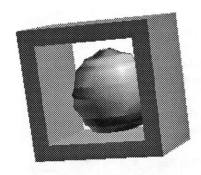

*Smooth shading
Above: no anti-
aliasing, no shadows,
low surface option
Below: high anti-
aliasing, shadows &
high surface option*

the splines defining either 2-D templates or paths for swept objects. The splines can be edited and fresh points added for a high level of control. Objects can be edited by returning to the component geometry shown in the object browser and operations such as filleting and trimming can be carried out if needed. The vertices of the mesh geometry can be dragged to provide another level of editing and skinned surfaces can be edited at both spline and vertex level. Duplicated objects preserve the properties of the source object and linked object heirarchies can be readily created with several link types and with easy parent/child alignment. Objects can be numerically positioned using absolute or relative values or with 'Delta' values (in which case the value represents the amount of the required change). The program has been written to allow outside developers to build specialised functions which can be 'plugged in', tailoring it, for instance, as an architectural modeller.

Rendering within MacroModel is kept simple and you are required to export the object to a higher level renderer for more sophisticated effects. A very small library of surfaces, such as glass and 'splatter' is available (and more can be created) to be assigned within the modeller, but these can not be seen until the object is exported, which seems odd. Images can be imported as backgrounds but not mapped onto objects. Properties such as colour, reflectance (direct and specular) and roughness can be set and viewed directly, however. Levels of anti-aliasing and surface smoothness can also be set, together with the options to show shadows and to draw a line around an object's edges. The latter is an unusual feature, but one which can be useful in clarifying the appearance of an object, particularly if it is to be exported as a picture. The program does not include an animation facility but models can be exported, typically to MacroMind 3D (a program with excellent animation facilities from the same company).

ALIAS SKETCH! *v1.0.2*

Alias Research Inc.
Aptech 071-627-1000

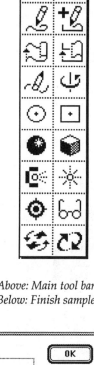

Alias Sketch! is a new product for the Macintosh from Alias Research Inc., a firm well known for its software at the top-end of the computer graphics market where their products are used by many major production houses. The reputation of the package goes before it as a 3-D 'ideas' tool and its provenance earns it a thorough inspection. It is aimed particularly at 'illustrators, graphic designers, product and package designers, and other creative professionals who work in the productive world of 3-D design' and goes some way towards making creation and manipulation in three dimensions as intuitive as working with two dimensions can be in a paint or drawing package. It has received strangely mixed reviews; including extreme enthusiasm from the design world and reservation from the computer press. This, in itself, is interesting, as it suggests a unique product perhaps geared to specific demands.

Although it proves far easier to produce subtly curved and sinuous 3-D surfaces and shapes in this freeform environment than in many modelling packages, it can be difficult to edit surfaces comprehensively. One reason is that all points which can be edited have an effect on the splines which determine the surface, and the

Above: Main tool bar
Below: Finish samples

movement of a point therefore modifies much of its surroundings. This is fine for articulating smooth changes in shapes but is more problematic when you want a local change which is discontinuous with the splines that mould it. You can change lines and surfaces this way but not resite individual points, although a facility permits

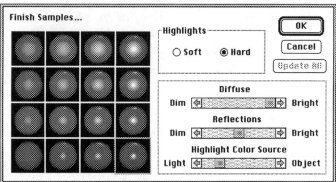

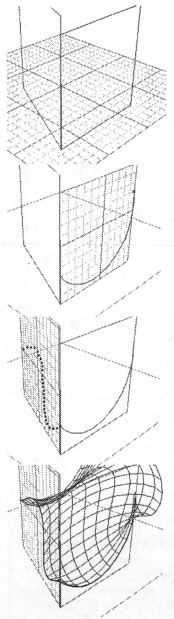

you to create cusps (sharp points) in lines which may suffice. It would be interesting to find a vertex level editor which allowed you to operate without reference to the original spline control points, i.e. to use all the super splining to create a form which could then forget its history and be manipulated from scratch. This is unlikely to be a trivial change to implement and would forfeit its great strength, the ability to manipulate the splines again. The way to get the best of both worlds is, perhaps, to create in Sketch! and then export to a second application for low-level editing. Whether or not these reservation are valid depends very much on how you will use the package, and I would certainly recommend that you experience its original approach to manipulating and orientating in 3-D space if you get the chance. If I had several modellers provided for teaching, I would certainly want this package to be one of those available for my art and design students.

The opening screen displays the ground plane of a 3-D world, a perspective grid, rather than the more usual three separate views of the object space, and you can already sense a fresh spatial paradigm. Further grids can be created orthogonal to the floor plan or to one another, and angled and rotated into any chosen position. These then provide the reference planes for laying down templates that can be swept into surfaces. This interface encourages you to build models 'in the round', although you still have access to the normal plan/elevation/etc. views when, and if, required. An interesting detail is that during rotation, for instance, reference lines relating the position of the selected object to the floor plane are shown to aid orientation, together with a numerical presentation of height and rotation angle.

The main tools icons are: Move; Rotate; Putty (change shape of object); Handle (change size, angle or position of

Top picture: Two planes created, orthogonal to floor plane
Second picture: Curve drawn on first (selected) vertical plane
Third picture: Freehand line drawn on second (selected) vertical plane
Bottom picture: Freeform object created by extrusion

objects); Pick & Place (place an object exactly on another); Plane (create sketching plane); Pencil (draw freehand curves); Curve-o-matic (create precise curves and lines), Extrude (sweep curve along a freehand path); Extrude-o-matic (sweep curve along a precise path); Erase (erase part of curve); Revolve (sweep curve for a lathed shape); Circle; Square; Sphere; Cube; Spot Light (create spotlight); Point Light (create point light); Match Backdrop (match live surface to backdrop perspective); View (create a new view); ZPR (zoom, pan & roll view); and Navigate (change viewpoint). Many of the tool functions are modified to different degrees by key combinations, and this requires that the sheet summarising the tools is left open on your desk until they are learnt. Unlike a number of programs, where key changes to tools offer minor modifications, in Sketch! some of these modifications are fundamental to the use of the program and must be used from the outset. The manual has the

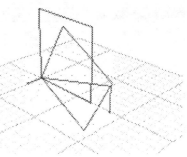

Above: Reference lines during rotation
Below: Materials catalogue

usual mixture of tutorials and reference section and seems to tell you everything you need to know, but I sometimes found it unclear on first reading and had to use trial and error to clarify a few details.

On starting you are presented with a perspective 'floor' grid, the tool icons and the usual menu bar. Unless you just want a sphere or cube, you create objects by drawing templates on this plane (or new planes, which you select to make 'live') and either extruding them along paths drawn on further planes, or by spinning them around adjustable axes. Objects can be given a fairly typical range of

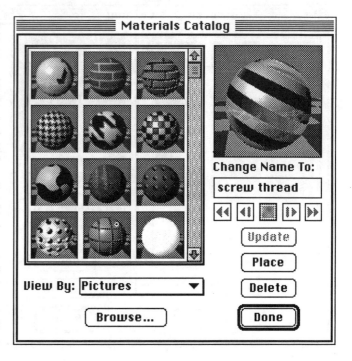

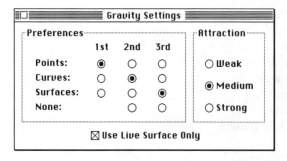

surface properties and textures, materials and backgrounds being selectable from their catalogues by name or picture. 'Gravity' settings assign priorities for snapping to points, curves and surfaces, and also the distance at which snapping becomes effective. Curves can be interactively modified with the putty tool which also allows the setting of "cusps" to make points act as sharp corners (rather than to be part of a smooth curve). Objects can be grouped and a list of assembly hierarchies displayed.

Above: Gravity settings
Below: Backdrops catalogue

A number of view options are available so that the common Front/Side/Top/etc. views can be toggled between as well as the 'Home' perspective view and custom views. 'Birds-eye' offers a distant view of the whole scene, and 'Fit to view' closes in on the

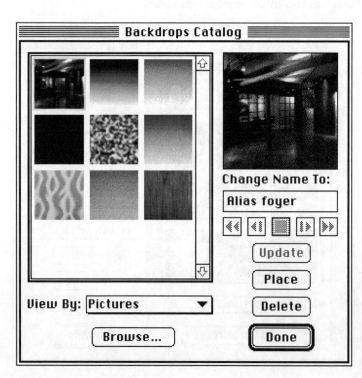

selected object(s). Once an object is built the 'Render' command produces a rendered image in a separate (default) 320x240 window, and each subsequent render creates a new window, which allows several versions to be easily compared. The rendering continues while the main window is being used. Five render qualities are available, from 'Preview' to 'Photo-Realistic', with options to tune edge smoothness, reflections and refractions, and altering the render window size.

Positioning of images on objects or on the background is dealt with in greater depth than is often the case, and a particularly interesting feature is the ability to match the lighting and perspective of an object to that of its photographic background. The floor plane of your scene is manipulated to match the size, position and perspective required in the composition, and even allows the simulation of shadows being cast 'in' the environment of the backdrop image. The backdrop can also be 'Dimmed'. These features are obviously intended for the designer wanting to show a new product in a realistic environment; the tutorial on this plants a chair (made earlier in the tutorial) in the middle of the Alias foyer.

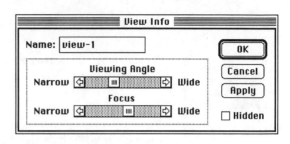

Above: View settings
Below: Materials setting

At the moment hole boring is not supported and so you need to export a template and modify it elsewhere, and, like many programs, there are no cutting planes or Boolean type operations. It is not at its best producing typical CAD geometry but it produces fluid, tuneable, curved forms very easily and its operation could well feel closer to the real world of hand modelled shapes than most CAD packages. It also has the valuable compositing with a background feature. For a designer new to modelling this could feel like a very friendly package and this suggests it is intended not as an all-purpose modeller but as a powerful tool for a modeller with particular needs.

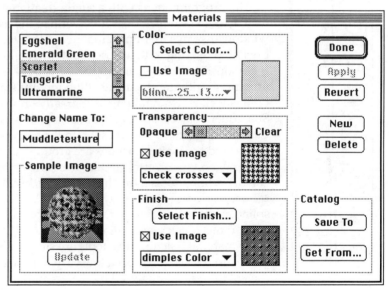

MacTOPAS   v1.0

AT&T Graphics Software Labs
UK Distributors: Techex Ltd. 0628-777800

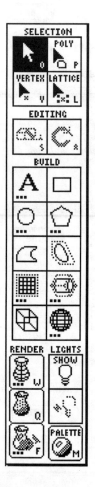

MacTOPAS is mainly aimed at the 3-D animation production market. It is a relatively expensive package, though the price is due to drop, but has features which would justify its price in a production environment. The manual is particularly clear and unpretentious, dealing with potentially complex issues in a straightforward way. The whole program has a good, sensible feel to it and seems both efficient and modest.

The program opens with a single creation window and a compact display of tools which does not overload the user. A small, floating window displays real-time cursor coordinates, and a second offers brief help relating to the chosen tool (pre-balloon help). A nice touch is obvious immediately an object is created – it is shown in wireframe with depth cueing; although this feature can be switched off it is well worth retaining as it greatly improves object readability. Subsequent objects are created in a sequence of default colours. Camera and zoom icons are set into the corners of the main window frame, and the main tool icons are grouped into: selection tools (general, polygon, vertex and lattice, each with its own marked cursor), editing tools (stretch and rotate), building tools (text, rectangle, circle, regular polygon, irregular polygon, spline polygon, spline mesh, spline cylinder, cube and sphere) and render/lights (wireframe, quick view, full render, show lights, add lights and show material palette). The tools are simple and efficient

The four selection tools allow easy modification of an object at each of the levels suggested by their names and the selection of each tool causes small adjustments to the environment which are relevant to the chosen use. For example, irrelevant icons are greyed out and the menu bar selections are modified. Selection of the rotate icon overlays an XYZ axis indicator, and selection of an axis label determines the axis of rotation, the object then being rotated by dragging the mouse. This works well and there is a

Above: Main tool bar
Below: Camera & zoom icons

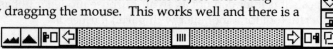

neat cursor arrow for choosing between
overlapping objects. When stretching an object,
the percentage stretch is shown in a numeric
display. Letters created with the text tool can be
treated either as a group or as individual objects.
The irregular polygon icon brings up sub-icons
for the selection of line, tangent arc, centred arc,
spline and to close the polygon. The spline
polygon icon brings up two sub-icons, allowing
for an open or closed spline polygon. Details of
splines, arcs and meshes can be set numerically.

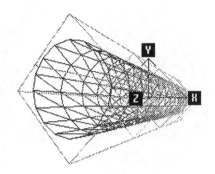

XYZ rotation tabs

Objects are created by default in wireform
within a lattice bounding box; Quick View offers
a faceted, solid rendering : Full Render provides a default smooth,
shadowed rendering (with options to set the precision, accuracy,
highlights, shadow, flare, fog and texture details). There is no ray
tracing, and this seemed surprising at first. In a production
environment, however, time is of the essence and the ability of the
system to provide shadows, reflections, fog and so on without
resorting to a slow ray trace means it is unlikely to be missed. (It
also proved something of a relief not to feel obliged to sit through a
ray trace periodically as a matter of habit; if the feature is there it is
hard to resist using it, whether it is needed or not.) It is good to be
able to tune the quality of shadows, using map resolution, graininess
and edge width to influence the softness and smoothness of
shadows, whilst an offset value helps to improve realism. There is
no facility to render a selected part of a scene but objects can be
hidden prior to rendering. On moving or deleting an object, traces of
its position are left behind until you redraw the screen. Other

Left: Palette window
Right: Flares

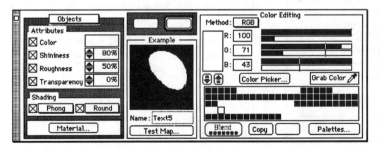

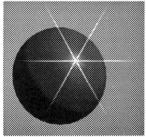

Drill function

features include an alpha channel to carry information on transparency mapping, fog density setting and flare setting. This last setting produces customisable flares ('stars' of lines reaching out from highlights) which are effective in an animation.

The material palette has fairly standard functions, but a Grab Color facility is included and the colour blending function works well; the Macintosh colour picker can be accessed. Selection of material is by filename rather than by sample; Set Highlight lets you work backwards from the effect you want to achieve, rather than having to guess-and-move lights; a standard range of mapping and wrapping abilities is present and reflection mapping can be by environment or buffer (this is a choice between having the scene, or an external picture, reflected in objects – or both). The amount of distortion occurring when a scene is reflected can be set numerically.

Objects can be aligned by centres or by matching a selected point on one object to a point on another, and the Bring command aligns a selected polygon of an object to the drawing plane. The Object menu includes extrusion, bevelling and drilling (with which holes can be simply and quickly cut in objects by use of polygonal templates). It allows for deletion of selected polygons, for duplication of objects (which are presented in mobile bounding boxes for easy placement) and for mirroring. The Spline Objects function includes bending (folding a spline mesh or cylinder around a special axis), twisting (spinning the control points of a spline mesh or cylinder around the object's principal axis), tapering (expanding or contracting an object around its principal axis), the control of spline settings, and access to an object hierarchy tree. When the polygon tool is selected the Object menu is replaced by the Polygon menu which allows extrusion of individual polygons on an

Spline settings

Spline Settings

Tension:	Bias:
○ Very Tight	○ Far Under
○ Tight	○ Under
⦿ Medium	⦿ Medium
○ Loose	○ Over
○ Very loose	○ Way over

Polygon Subdivisions per Lattice Pt: 4

[Cancel]   [OK]

object; the bevelling of a selected polygon; lathing; creation of spiral objects; lofting (with or without splines); and connection, cutting, trimming and subdivision of polygons. Other interesting functions are a repair function to correct incorrectly rendering polygons; Page Turn which flips over, or rolls up, a polygon (particularly useful for animation); and an add/delete point function.

Camera controls are referred to by real-world labels such as pan, tilt and zoom; each control is separate and works well, bringing a bounding box view of the scene under mouse dragging control. Perspective can be toggled on/off, degree of perspective controlled and drawing plane moved.

Above: Sun sttings
Below: Hi-Res settings

Natural lighting can be simulated by defining time, place and weather conditions, and fog boundaries can be set by dragging far and near boundary lines in a top view of the scene. Images can be digitised directly into the program (with a supported board fitted) and the image incrementally softened if required. Auto-trace is also included, to produce a polygon from an image. Hi-res and batch rendering are available.

The animation facilities are very promising and obviously designed as a serious production tool. They include a quick, useful storyboard feature; a flipbook providing a neat preview device; timelines and timegraphs as good visual editing models; motion blur and motion trails available amongst the record options; and an animation script available in text form for easy editing.

form•Z   v2.1.5.1

Auto•des•sys Inc.
UK Distributors: Gomark 071-731-7930

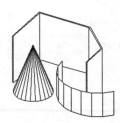

3-D enclosure(angular wall), solid object (cone) and surface solid(curved surface)

form•Z is a general purpose solid and surface modeller with drafting and rendering capability which is 'particularly responsive to the needs of the conceptual and preliminary stages of design as it is able to treat the elements of the composition as "soft" and easily changeable entities'. The introduction to the user's manual describes the design philosophy behind the applicatio, and gives a very positive feeling ; its designers have analysed how the 3-D design process works and have created a practical tool to deal with the tasks that arise. The product is dongled and comes with three manuals. These are clear but necessarily contain a lot of information and are not to be breezed through lightly; the tutorial manual, however, offers a straightforward entry to the world of form•Z.

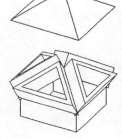

Source pyramid and derivative 3-D enclosure

The program opens with a single view window showing a 'floor plane' grid with XYZ axes indicated, viewed from Z = +30°, X=30°. The 'Tile Windows' menu item creates four windows with standard views. Modelling tool icons are to the left of the main window (but can be toggled from vertical to horizontal orientation); window tool icons at the bottom, together with memory status; co-ordinate, views, layers, colours and prompts windows overlay the main window; the Apple menu bar is as normal. When drafting mode is selected the tool palettes change accordingly. Nearly all the icons offer up a further row of icons when selected and these pop-up palettes can be 'torn off' and dragged to any chosen screen location. The window tool palettes pop-up vertically but can be toggled to a horizontal format. Both individual tools and rows of tools can be switched off from within the help window and will then disappear from view until recalled. A good help system can be called up, presenting all the relevant icons, menus or key combinations and offering an explanation of each as selected. The prompt window instructs on the action required to be taken at any point in the modelling/drafting process, and a 'query' icon calls up an information dialogue box which explains any system 'beep'. An historical undo/redo facility resides in the 'Edit' menu.

The modelling tool icon groups are: object generation and insertions (2-D surface object, 2-D enclosure, 3-D extruded solid, 3-D converged solid, 3-D enclosure; insertion of ..point/segment, ..outline, ..face/volume, hole, ..opening); polygons and circles/ellipses (rectangle, 3 point rectangle, polygons, circle ..by centre and radius, ..by diameter, ..by diameter); lines, curves, streams and arcs (vector lines, smooth lines, stream lines, clockwise arcs, anticlockwise arcs); topological levels (point, segment, outline, face, object, group, hole/volume); selection pointer; derivative objects (extrusion, convergence, 3-D enclosure, object of revolution, sweep along path, section of solid, terrain model, projection

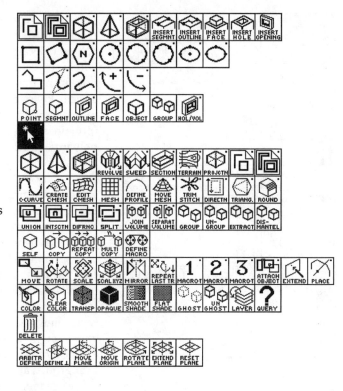

Modelling tool palette

of solid, 2-D surface object, 2-D enclosure); curves and meshes (controlled curve, create controlled mesh, edit controlled mesh, mesh, define profile, move mesh, trim and stitch, directions, triangulate, round); Booleans, joining and grouping (union, intersection, difference, split, join volumes, separate volumes, group, ungroup, extract, dismantle); self/copy modifiers (self, copy, repeat copy, multi-copy, record macro translation); geometric transformations (translate, rotate, independent scale, uniform scale, mirror, repeat last transformation, 3 micro transformations, attach, extend segment, place on line); attributes (colour, clear and colour, make transparent, make opaque, make smooth, make flat, ghost, unghost, set layer, query); delete; and reference planes (define arbitrary plane, define perpendicular plane, move plane, move plane origin, rotate plane, extend plane grid, reset plane). The drafting tool icon groups are: polylines, arcs and modifiers (polylines and arcs, area generation);

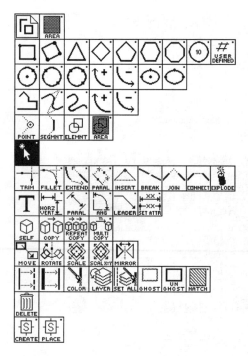

Above: Drafting tool palette
Below: Window tool palette

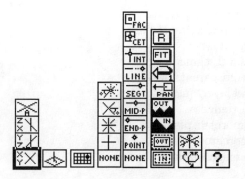

polygons; circles/ellipses (rectangle, 3 point rectangle, triangle, diamond, pentagon, hexagon, octagon, decagon, N-sided polygon); lines/arcs (circle ..by centre and radius, ..by diameter, ..by 3 points on circumference, ..clockwise arc, anticlockwise arc, ellipse ..by major and minor radius, ..by diameter and radius); polylines (polylines, polycurves, polystreams, clockwise polyarcs, anticlockwise polyarcs); topological levels (point, segment, element, area pick); selection pointer; line editing (trim, fit fillet, extend line/arc, parallel offset, insert point, break line, join, connect, explode); text/ dimensions (text, horizontal/vertical dimension, parallel dimension, angular dimension, leader line, set dimension/lead line attributes); self/ copy (self, copy, repeat copy, multi-copy); transformations (translate, rotate, independent scale, uniform scale, mirror); attributes (set ..line type, ..line weight, ..colour, ..layer, ..all attributes, ghost, unghost, hatch); delete; and symbols (create symbol, place symbol). The window tool icon groups are: reference planes (XY ref. plane, YZ ref. plane, ZX ref. plane, arbitrary ref. plane); perpendicular switch; grid snap switch; direction snaps (no directional snap, ortho snap, ortho + diagonal snap, snap to angle/slope, radial snap); object snaps (no object snap, snap ..to point, ..to endpoint, ..to midpoint, ..to segment, ..to line, ..to intersection, ..centre of face, ..to face); zoom and pan (zoom ..in by frame, ..out by frame, ..in incrementally, ..out incrementally, pan, go back one, fit all, reset); view (set view, rotate view); and beep query. A number of these functions are supplemented by dialogue boxes through which to select further options or give numerical values to parameters.

It must be clear from this litany of tools that form•Z has a high level of functionality, and this is further enhanced by an equally comprehensive range of menu bar commands. The art, however, is to keep this wealth of functions under control, and this is successfully done with a logical and hierarchical interface, assisted by the prompt box reminders and backed by the inbuilt help. The 'feel' of form•Z is a little different from other modellers that I have used, and the visual style of the interface is not 'classical Mac', but all is sufficiently similar for one to be quickly at home. Being a solid modeller amongst many surface modellers it has a number of distinctive features that are not found in MacTypical, and it is instructive to weight a description of this application towards its differences rather than its similarities. form•Z offers limited rendering (just enough to make models understandable) and no animation, concentrating on pure, versatile modelling, models being exported as DXF files to other applications.

Terrain models:
Plan and sections
Mesh terrain
Stepped terrain
Triangulated contour
terrain

Objects can be created in two dimensions with open or closed surfaces, and in three dimensions as solid objects, surface objects or 3-D enclosures. Mesh objects can be one sided (surface objects), double sided (surface solids) or solid meshes (solid objects). Enclosures are created with walls of predefined thickness and one of their obvious uses is architectural. Sweep, revolve and section tools are available to build objects from 2-D templates, which can be created using a good range of tools. To give an idea of its functionality, note that extrusion with convergence (i.e. to make a pyramid or cone) is one of the tools, and derivative extrusion another (generating derivative objects from all faces of an object). A terrain model is a derivative object generated from contour lines which can be either mesh, stepped, triangulated or a mixture of all three, and can additionally be generated on the faces of solids. The 'Modelling options' menu item leads to a range of dialogue boxes for entering parameters relevant to each type of modelling operation. There are no predefined primitives.

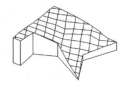

A range of alignments between objects and surfaces are offered with attachments (defined for points, segments or faces). Whilst present in most modellers, the range and flexibility of alignments options available in this package is extensive and seems to cater for all foreseeable contingencies. One feature allows the extension of segments to meet surfaces and the tutorial example of flashing one roof to another and lining up a chimney gives a practical example. Another function places 2-D shapes on a line (perpendicular to the placement line), the tutorial example leading to a mesh object.

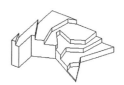

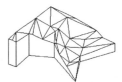

Layering and grouping assist organisation.

Some of the most interesting features of form•Z regard its ability to modify objects, the range of modifications available being determined by the type of object created. Available modifiers include Boolean functions, trimming and stitching(using objects or lines), mesh editors, and rounding for edges and corners. When modelling it is often necessary to decide what you want to happen to an object and then to compromise with the features available in order to arrive at something that looks similar. In form•Z I found that my mental picture of what I wanted to happen was usually matched by a tool to do exactly the job I had in mind, and this (for me) made the move from idea to object much smoother. A good example is the editing facility of 'Insertion' (mirrored by 'Deletion') with which segments, outlines, faces, volumes, holes and openings can be added to an object. One tutorial example bisects the top of a cuboid with a line parallel to an edge, and then lifts this line to create a 'house' shape; easy to do in any package but particularly elegant here.

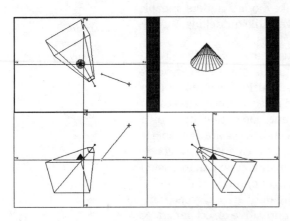

Editable cone of vision

Other useful details are: the clear 'Topological levels' icons with which to select whether you are operating on a point, segment , face, etc. ; the numerically defined transformations facility , which deals with repeated operations well; the ability to define macros of sequences (graphically or numerically) of transformations for subsequent application as a tool; and the 'Profiles' palette for storing dimensionless custom profiles. There are the standard controls for viewing the model, but unusual is the editable 'cone of vision' which graphically represents all the parameters affecting the viewing of the modelling environment.

This is a serious modeller with a high level of efficient functionality. Although I quickly discovered that you can use it immediately to build simple models, it is best to spend time with it and come to appreciate and capitalise on its power. It is a package I would like to get to know better.

MODELSHOP II v 1.2

MacroMind/Paracomp
UK distributors: Computers Unlimited 081-200-8282

ModelShop is one of the longer established modellers on the
Macintosh, the early version having been updated into ModelShop ll
to add features that more recent modellers were offering. Its name is
subtitled with the legend 'Desktop Architecture and Design for the
Macintosh', which points to its intended area of application, and it
has always been the first package shown at introductions (that I have
attended) of computer modelling to architects. An obvious reason
for this choice is that ModelShop II has a very logical and
uncluttered interface and goes from the creation of a familiar, plan-
view drawing to an extruded wireframe 'building' to a shaded
model as quickly and simply and any modeller. The application
concentrates on being able to build models from relatively simple
elements with great ease, so that it does not require a dedicated
computer expert to operate, but is accessible to anyone in the office.
Two versions of ModelShop II are supplied, one for 68020 machines
(or better), and one for all other Macs; this is an interesting point as
many modellers are too sophisticated to work with low end
machines. The comprehensive manual has a particularly well
pitched chapter explaining ModelShop basics before carrying on
with the usual tutorials and reference section, and the package
includes QuickPICS to allow animations to be played back without
the need for a designated animation program. A library of objects
such as domestic and office furniture and trees comes on the discs.

    The program opens with an icon palette, the standard Apple
menu bar and a single modelling window. At the bottom of this
window, real world coordinates update to show the current cursor
position or dimensions as they are drawn, whilst at the top of the
window a prompt bar responds to the process in hand. Additional
windows can be opened, their contents being updated only when
that window is live. The toolbox icons fall into three groups:
creation, modification and viewing, with a further pair to toggle
between 2-D and 3-D. There are no other icons hidden away but
several reveal a dialogue box choice on double clicking.

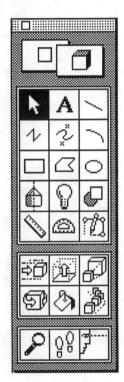

Main tool palette

The creation tools are: Selection; Text; Line/Wall; Poly-line/Linked wall; Bezier/Curved wall; Arc/ Arced wall/Solid arc (fence, wedge, wall, chord); Rectangle/Cuboid; Polygon/Polyhedron; Ellipse/ Cylinder; Objects of revolution; Point light source; Primitive; Linear measurement; Angular measurement; and Working plane. The modification tools are: Move; Extrude; Scale; Rotate; Paint object; and Duplicate. The view tools are: Zoom; Walk tool; and User defined perspective.

The creation tools are used in the expected way to make 2-D shapes, and to make 2-D templates for 3-D objects. If working in 3-D, then once the template has been drawn in plan view (with or without a grid), the cursor is dragged a distance which corresponds to the required extrusion height. This felt slightly odd on the first occasion, since the direction in which the mouse is dragged is irrelevant, but the line it draws is reminiscent of a projection from the base. No change is observed in plan view, but switching to elevation will now show a side view of the object and switching to axonometric will show a 3-D projection. (Axonometric projections are non-perspectival but give a good sense of three dimensions whilst maintaining scale.) It is possible to draw on the ground plan whilst in the axonometric view, in which case the object appears extruded immediately. The perspective tool creates a perspective view from positions selected by the user with the cursor (and sequentially requested by the prompt bar), in the order: standpoint position, standpoint height, view position and view height. Standpoint and position can also be changed from the menu selections. Numerical selection is always available as an alternative to selection by cursor. In all views the Arrow keys can be used to 'nudge' the viewing position in 5º units (or 15º with the Option key held down), in azimuth or elevation. The Fly tool works in perspective view to allow the user to 'walk through' the model interactively by dragging the cursor up (forward), down (backwards), left (left) and right (right). It works in all rendering modes, but is obviously less responsive the more calculation it is required to do for each step.

Objects can be created by spinning and extruding in fairly standard fashion (the extrusion tool also alters existing extrusion heights) and objects can be broken down into individual points for vertex level manipulation. Wall thickness can be defined in a dialogue box and set to left, right or centre. Movement, rotation and scaling are achieved by setting an origin with the cursor, and then setting the required offset, angle or scaling factors (respectively). Objects can be duplicated with the option of specifying the number of duplications and amount of offset and rotation of the duplicates. This is a useful facility, for instance in the creation of a spiral staircase. Holes are possible within certain limitations and objects can be stored as primitives, in which case their geometry is fixed (though breaking it down into points with 'Clear geometry' removes its 'primitive' status and allows it to be altered). Layers are available and have an obvious relevance for architectural models, and special provision is made for creating topologies from contour maps. Objects and light sources can be given colours and objects can be automatically tagged with volume and area labels.

The rendering modes are kept simple but the model can be exported elsewhere for more sophisticated treatment. Included is: wireframe and 'hidden surface' which is a quick, shaded (presumably cosine) model; in this mode object edges can be specified to be drawn or not, and shadows cast or not. Shadows are quickly generated, with edges softening (by dithering) the further they are from the object casting them; if an object is added, removed or altered within the scene the rendering automatically adjusts. This is a small point but makes the operation much more 'worldly', the environment changing 'naturally'

Previous two pages:
shadows moving across
a model as time passes

rather than being forced to update. Geographical location can be specified, and if the site is known to the program, it will set the correct longitude, latitude and GMT correction. Time of day can also be set, so if the sun is defined as the light source then the shadows cast will correspond to those of the named place. It is informative to use the simple animation facility within the program to see shadows moving through the day as the frames on the previous two pages show. The print dialogue window allows the image to be tiled over a number of sheets and can be set to ignore blank sheets.

By the standards of some current modellers, ModelShop II might seem fairly unsophisticated, but its simplicity makes it extremely easy to use, and if a package is easy to use it is likely to get used more often. It also has the ability to capitalise on the features of other packages by exporting its own models. The economical range of tools and functions makes keyboard shortcuts quicker to learn and once familiar with them, then you can work very fast and can comfortably handle even complex models.

Left: Standpoint
window
Far left: Tool settings
window
Below: Print setting
window

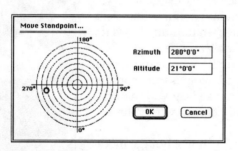

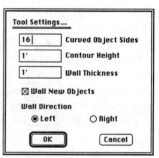

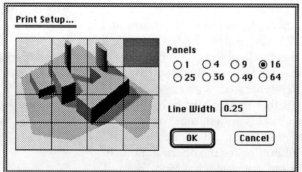

MINICAD+ 4.0v2

Graphsoft Inc.
UK distributors: Gomark 071-731-7930

MiniCad+ is a comprehensive 2-D/3-D CAD package which has regularly won awards over a number of years. It is widely used by professionals for the production of designs from concept stage through to detailed drawings and specifications, and includes an integral database and spreadsheet. It comes with tutorial manual, comprehensive user manual, programming manual and an explanatory video tape lasting nearly an hour. The description here of MiniCad+ is much more a list of functions than is the case with other packages in this chapter; this seems to be the best way of giving a useful account of its breadth and insight into its potential application areas.

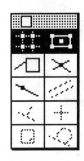

Above: 2-D constraints palette
Below: 2-D tool palette and pop-out selections

For someone like myself, who rarely uses drafting systems, MiniCad+ provides a very accessible environment, opening with a grided work plane (centred on 0,0 but with the origin customisable), icon-based tool palettes and mode bar, an attribute palette and a standard menu bar. The selected tool always has a text description shown in the mode bar at the top of the screen, and the SmartCursor™ automatically identifies relevant points and relationships as you move it across the drawing. It supports dimensioning standards such as ANSI, DIN, ISO, JIS, BSI and SIA, imports DXF, ESPF, PICT, PICT as picture, Text Format and Worksheet, and exports Database, DXF, EPSF, PICT, StrataVision, Text Format and Worksheet.

A quick (pre-manual) exploration reveals a wealth of

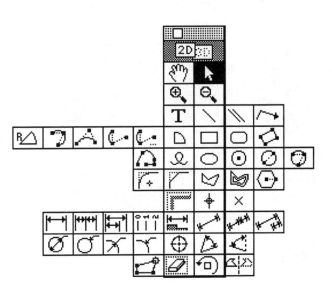

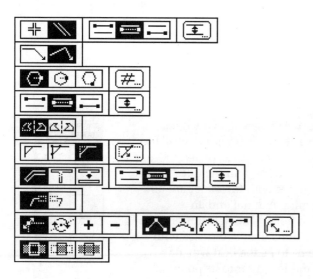

Mode bar choices
Above: 2-D
Below: 3-D

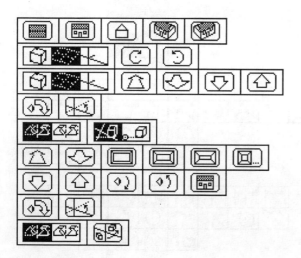

inter-related, and mainly understandable, tool selection icons, most of which seem to function intuitively – a property which usually indicates a friendly application. The video tape, although claiming not to be a manual, takes you smoothly through all the functions, and when I finally opened the manual I already felt comfortable with the package. The main tool palette can be toggled between its 2-D and 3-D functions, and selection of most of the 2-D tool icons offers a further 'pop-out' selection of related icons. When a tool is selected the mode bar can display further icons with which to specify more precisely the tool's function, and a text message gives a compact description of the function of the selected tool. A second palette of icons offers constraints relevant to the selected tool (whether in 2-D or 3-D), such as snapping to line or surface, or creating parallel lines. The cursor takes one of 33 forms according to its current function, and can offer screen hints (in graphical and/or text form) to indicate when it is snapped to a point or at a horizontal vector from a point, for example. Automated Roof, Wall and Floor tools speed up specialised tasks and, together with the architectural examples in the tutorial, give a clear indication of one of the intended uses of

MiniCad+. A data display bar shows data either as a reference or as a field that can be edited, and a customisable symbol library operates in both 2-D and 3-D. An attributes palette allows setting of factors such as line type and weight, arrowhead style, fill and pen colour, and fill pattern. Multiple layers are available.

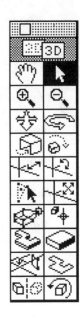

The basic tools in the 2-D palette, with additional pop-up menu items in brackets, are: Pan; Selection Arrow; Zoom In; Zoom Out; Line (Single, Double, Leader); Arc (By radius, By three points, Tangent to line, By two points & centre, By two points and specified radius, Quarter arc); Rectangle (Rounded, Proportional, Rotated); Polyline & Freehand (Arc vertex, Cubic vertex, Bezier vertex, Corner vertex); Circle/Ellipse (By radius, By diameter, By three points); Fillet & Chamfer; Polygon (Single line, Double line, Regular); Wall; Symbol & Locus; Constrained & Ordinate Dimension (Horizontal or Vertical - Chain, Baseline, Ordinate, Auto); Diagonal Dimension (Chain, Baseline); Diametral & Radial Dimension (Internal, External, Centre mark); Angular Dimension; Reshape & Clipping; Rotation & Mirror.

3-D tool palette

Two examples of the many further options available in the mode bar are: 1) with Fillet selected (Normal, Split, Trimmed, Fillet radius - entered numerically into dialogue box); 2) with Walls selected (Create wall, Join wall, Remove wall breaks/caps, Top alignment, Middle alignment, Bottom alignment, and Wall preferences: Separation - entered numerically; Caps - none, start, end, both; Type - flat, rounded; Cavity lines and/or fills; Offset).

The basic 3D tools are: Pan, Selection Arrow, Zoom In; Zoom Out; 3D Translate; View Rotate; Walkthrough; Flyover; Translate Along Working Plane Normal; Rotate About Working Plane Normal; Set Working Plane; Translate Working Plane; 3-D Reshape; 3-D Symbol Insert; 3-D Extrude; 3-D Slab; 3-D Align Face; 3-D Polygon; 3-D Mirror; Object Rotate.

3-D constraints palette

Further functions are added by the Command Menus which, of course, include the usual Mac File and Edit commands. As with the icon-based tools there are too many functions to describe all of them, but some of obvious interest are listed. Smoothing (None, Bezier, Spline, Cubic Spline, Arc) will apply to polygons, polylines and freehand lines. Alignment to grid or to objects is comprehensive; Rotate is by degrees, minutes or seconds (the 3-D rotation box uses a simple model effectively to clarify orientation); hatch patterns can be

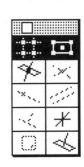

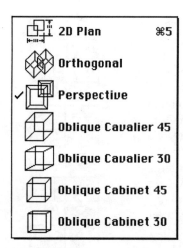

Projection choices

3-D rotation box

created and allocated to materials (e.g. brick, glass, ceramic tile); Trace Bitmap converts PICT images to vector objects; Tool Trim removes excess lines; Add Surface will remove overlaps and can be used to cut holes; Combine into Surface combines several objects into one.

Organisation of elements can be achieved by layers, grouping and classes. Because MiniCad+ is a 3-D CAD program, layers do not merely indicate stacking order but have a spatial relationship (a Z dimension). Symbols, hatching, dimensioning and text all help improve legibility and understanding.

Extrude and Sweep commands are present, and Multiple Extrude creates objects from sequential templates in a 'step ladder' fashion, enabling the easy building of pyramids, etc. Convert to Mesh makes individual vertices of an object available for editing; Convert to 3D Polygon takes a 2D object into 3D space. Several commands offer specific assistance with roof and floor construction. 2D slices can be cut from 3D objects and sections can be cut through 3D objects.

Objects and views can be moved freely or with constraints, and different projections and perspectives chosen. Walk-throughs and fly-overs enable the model to be 'explored' intuitively. Rendering is limited to wireframe, hidden line, solid, shaded solid and shaded without lines, but the model can be exported for sophisticated rendering (and/or animation) in another package. StrataVision is specifically supported but DXF files are accepted by most applications these days.

Links between the drawing and a database/spreadsheet facility make for a total, integrated, professional tool, and the programming ability (using the Pascal language) enables the user to customise the program and automate many functions. It includes over 300 subroutines and is a feature I would welcome in all applications.

In all, MiniCad+ confirms its reputation as a thorough, high precision tool with a friendly

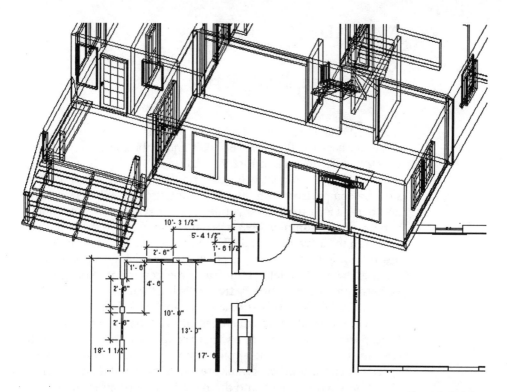

Above: 2-D plan with 3-D projection
Below: Integrated database/spreadsheet

interface, providing on screen help enabling you to learn as you go. Although I have said that I will not list prices because they are subject to dramatic changes, I cannot resist commenting that the current (1993) price for MiniCad+ is far less than the wealth of features might lead you to expect.

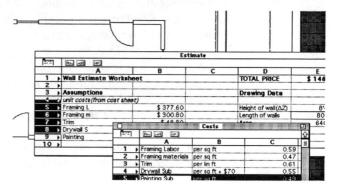

	A	B	C	D	E
1	Wall Estimate Worksheet			TOTAL PRICE	$ 146
2					
3	Assumptions			Drawing Data	
4	unit costs (from cost sheet)				
5	Framing L	$ 377.60		Height of wall (ΔZ)	8'
6	Framing m	$ 300.80		Length of walls	80
7	Trim				640
8	Drywall S				
9	Painting				
10					

Costs

	A	B	C
1	Framing Labor	per sq ft	0.59
2	Framing materials	per sq ft	0.47
3	Trim	per lin ft	0.61
4	Drywall Sub	per sq ft + $70	0.55
5	Painting Sub	per sq ft	0.49

AutoCAD

AutoDesk
UK Distributor: Datech 081-308-1800

AutoCAD is a long established name in CAD software with a
customer base totalling over 600,000, and is the source of what has
effectively become the industry standard file – DXF. It made the
move to Macintosh relatively late, and early Mac versions were very
slow by comparison with their PC counterparts (MSDOS versions
also being faster than those running under Windows). The Mac
version due in summer 1993 is promised to improve the situation,
although the advantage of a GUI (on either the Mac or Windows) is
always going to carry a speed penalty. It is too big an application for
it to be reviewed in detail here, but is too important to be ignored. It
is therefore described briefly from existing material.

AutoCAD offers a comprehensive range of 2-D and 3-D tools, and
has an open architecture which has allowed the development of
third-party applications for a variety of specialist needs; this built in
customisation making the application very flexible. More than 600
specialist application programs are available to tailor AutoCAD to
almost any requirement, and there is a built in programming
language called AutoLISP (and a new development system based on
the C-language). There are also a number of extensions from
AutoDesk which extend the range of AutoCAD's functionality.
These include Advanced Modelling Extension (AME) which allows
the integration of sophisticated solid modelling and AutoShade and
Autodesk Renderman for high quality rendering. AutoDesk 3D
Studio is a high quality modelling, rendering and animation program
designed for use in video production and 3-D animation. The big user
base means that training and back-up are well catered for.

The application supports a full range of entities and utilities for
constructing and editing designs in both 2-D and 3-D space, as well
as a comprehensive set of inquiry tools for interrogating existing
drawings and models. AutoCAD also provides efficient tools for
associating a number of drawings with a single 3-D model and there
is a HyperCard style on-line help.

The great depth of AutoCAD's resources means that it is not a modeller to be learnt quickly and used occasionally but is one that requires proper training to make best use of its performance and facilities. It is far more accessible to casual use now that it runs on machines with friendly GUIs, like the Macintosh, but is still a modeller for the serious, industrial user. As at version 11, a dedicated user might well prefer the speed of MSDOS to the features we all like on a Mac, but new versions will close the gap.

VIRTUS WALKTHROUGH v1.1.3

Virtus Corporation
UK distributors: Gomark 071-731-7930

Although Virtus WalkThrough is a modeller, it is distinguished from other modellers, as suggested by its name, by its ability to allow you to 'walk around' your model in real time. As you might expect (and as is made clear in the manual) the speed of your machine and the complexity of your model determine how close to real time you can actually get. The program comes with a straightforward manual and the usual quick reference card, plus a 'Quick Start' card. If you are as impatient as everyone else to get started with a new program, you will welcome this card, as it tells you everything about loading the program in one short page; in five sentences it shows you how to build a model and walk through it; and it covers memory allocation in a final page. It also lists the '5 Virtus Rules', these being:

1. Do not overlap objects
2. Non-convex objects are not allowed
3. Speed and detail are inversely proportional
4. Transparent and translucent objects and surfaces drain processing power
5. You cannot draw a line. All objects drawn have depth.

Following these instructions, I had, in less than 30 seconds, built a 'two box' environment and was walking around in it. The card works! The manual then takes you through the usual tutorial projects and, as a nice detail, tells you how long each should take. This introduction, plus the simple screen interface, immediately suggests a very user-friendly product (despite being the first manual I have read which contains a quotation from Albert Einstein).

Although it is not immediately apparent, the nature of the product requires a reconsideration of the nature of objects and the space they occupy. It is perfectly possible to carry on without this rethink, but a clearer understanding of the way your intentions are translated into models is bound to improve the way you use the modeller. In the context of this book, it is also interesting to consider fresh paradigms and I quote directly from the short section in the manual on 'Volumetricity: Space Modelling and Containment'.

Walk View tools

"When you create an object it may appear to be solid. But every object – whether a room or a table leg – has an interior: it is volumetric. Volumetricity has three consequences you should consider as you build models with Virtus WalkThrough.

The first consequence is *space modelling*, that is, you are able to use Virtus WalkThrough to model space itself. Consider a space to be defined by a skin wrapped around it. To redefine the space just stretch the skin. Try to think in terms of space defining an environment rather than in terms of environment defining space.

A second consequence of Volumetricity is *containment*. Every object in Virtus WalkThrough knows what objects it contains and what object contains it. Containment provides you with some important benefits. For example, if you move a container all objects contained within it also move. In Virtus WalkThrough, containment is an all-or-none state...objects cannot overlap.

The third consequence of Volumetricity is that *each object surface has an inside and an outside*. In Virtus WalkThrough, you can edit the inside or outside of any surface to create object surface features...,used to represent doorways, windows, holes and other items."

The operation of Virtus WalkThrough is very straightforward, and largely intuitive. On opening the package you are confronted by the modelling tool palette on the left of the screen, next to the 'design view' window, with the 'walk view' window to the right. The windows can be sized in the usual way and clicking in the 'walk view' window replaces the tool palette with one relevant to navigation. Creation tools draw 2-D plans which are 'inflated' into objects. (Inflation is superficially similar to extrusion but the object has other properties than one which was a simple

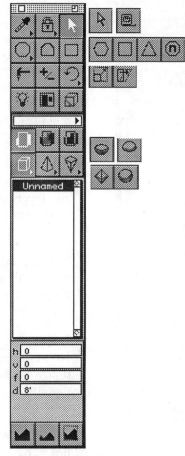

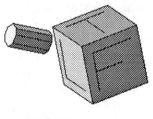

Above: Design tools palette
Left: Lighting editor window with motion constraint icons

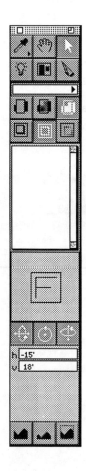

_Above: Tumble editor
tool palette
Right: Inflation tool_

extrusion.) The object can be viewed in plan view from any direction and 'handles' (similar to vertices) can be added, removed and moved. The inflation process can be modified to create sides perpendicular to the base, sides inflated to a point (up, down or both ways) or sides inflated in a hemisphere (up, down or both ways – the latter being a sphere). A depth window controls the depth and position of inflation. Objects can be sliced with a cutting plane in the 'tumble editor' (where the object can be rotated in 3-D view), scaled and skewed. This offers a fairly economical range of modelling tools but with ingenuity it can used to represent a good range of objects and layering is available. Objects created in other modellers can be imported, but the tools within Virtus WalkThrough are designed to keep objects simple so that they can be 'flown through' at a reasonable speed. Bringing in a complex model from elsewhere would necessarily slow down the animation stage, though this might still be acceptable in order to benefit from this application's original viewing mode.

A number of tools are unique to the Virtus WalkThrough environment, since it has very particular requirements. It is quick and simple to create windows, doorways and holes in walls and to modify their placement as being on the front or back of the surface or through the surface. Surfaces can be defined as opaque, transparent or translucent, and can be coloured from the palette. To create, for example, two rectangular rooms linked by a doorway, you: 1) draw two touching rectangles with the 'square object' tool; 2) define the connecting walls as being shared by clicking on them with the 'connect surfaces' tool; and 3) create a doorway by clicking on the joining wall with the 'surface editor' tool (which takes you to a surface editing window) and drawing a rectangle to represent the opening using the 'square object' tool. As you build your object, so the view of it in the 'walk view' window is updated, and by moving to that window you can immediately navigate the scene at any time. You can also record and playback your walkthrough using the buttons 'record path', 'stop recording' and 'play path'. This records the route taken but not the model itself, so that subsequent changes to the model are shown in future playbacks; a walkthrough can be saved as a PICS or QuickTime file.

Navigation is simple, with mouse movement forwards, backwards, left and right (relative to a cross hair in the centre of the window) corresponding to movements through the scene in those directions; speed of movement increases as the mouse moves away from the centre. Use of the 'shift' and 'option' keys with the mouse enables movement or tilting up and down, or rolling or panning left and right, and a 'focal length' tool sets an angle of view. When you are moving through the scene in the navigation window, a representation of the viewer (a circle with a directional line) moves in the design window to indicate orientation and position. This representation can be moved in the design window in order to change the view in the navigation window – another simple device which works well.

A library of furniture, staircases, etc. is supplied, and the whole is clearly geared towards use in an architectural context; perhaps looking at a kitchen, viewing a house or roaming an estate or town. There is no reason why the application should not be used for other jobs but an architectural application is, perhaps, the most obvious, and a number of companies are using it for just that. The necessary compromise between detail and speed leads one towards a relatively simple model (on current hardware, at least), but the ability to move about the scene lends itself to exploring space, however, and this does not require detail.

Design view window with tools (live) and walk view window

Virtus WalkThrough stands alone on the Mac, as far as I am aware, in offering immediate, interactive navigation of user-created models and could provide a valuable tool in a modeller's armoury, particularly at the overview stage and, perhaps, in discussion with a client. A companion program, 'Virtus Voyager', creates stand-alone walkthrough models which can be used on any Mac.

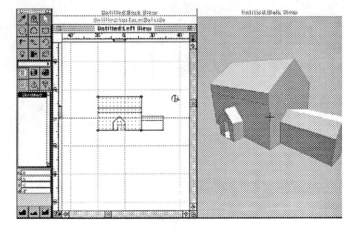

213

addDepth v1.0

Ray Dream Inc.
Amtech International Ltd. 0202-476977

The name of this application explains better than most what it is designed to do; it adds depth to 2-D artwork by simple extrusion. The source artwork can be created within addDepth or imported and the package is particularly configured to deal with text. As such, this does not try to be a complete modeller but is aimed at designers wishing to add a dimension to their work easily and without recourse to a full-blown modelling application. The feel of the addDepth interface is close to that of 2-D drawing applications, with the obvious intention that this application is for the 2-D designer. The tool bar contains the following tools: 3-D Selection/Moving/Sizing tool; Virtual Trackball; Perspective Box; 3-D Box tool; Zoom in/out; Text tool; Hand tool; 2-D Selection/Moving tool; Pen tool (for drawing 2-D paths); Convert Point, Delete Point/Path segment, Add Point; 2-D primitives.

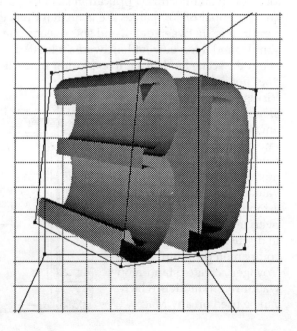

Text can be entered directly within the program, having the usual modifications available as well as a range of controls over scaling, kerning, leading, spacing and so on. Once entered, the text is given depth and can then be freely manipulated in three dimensions

Above: Tool bar
Right: Text in perspective window

using 'virtual trackball' (where the mouse controls rotation around all axes) and movement tools (including 'Nudge') as well as the diagrammatic numerical dialogue box. Bevel can be set at the time of extrusion and objects grouped for easier control. A good alignment dialogue box offers Align, Distribute and Contact as controls for relative positioning, and updates a display of representations of the objects concerned. Rectangular boxes can be made and sized within addDepth. Dragging 'handles' on the back wall of a perspective box encompassing the text/object provides an interesting control over perspective distortion, and a working plane can be displayed to assist with orientation and transformation. Imported artwork is extruded on the working plane, which can be positioned before the import.

Eight 'styles' are provided for application to the object and more can be created. These differ from usual modeller surfaces in that the treatments carry forward 2-D design concepts, including variables like 'stroke and fill' and gradation, and the choice of RGB or CMYK colour models. The supplied styles are: Basic; Bricks; Metallic; Imported; Pastels; Tubular; Grey Scale; Primaries. 'Decals' provides the opportunity to add images and textures to surfaces (each surface and bevel can be treated differently) but using non-bit

Above: Numerical positioning
Left: Alignment dialogue box
Below: Bevel setting

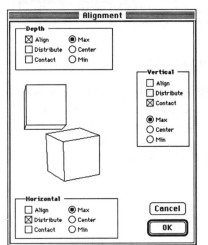

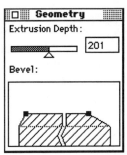

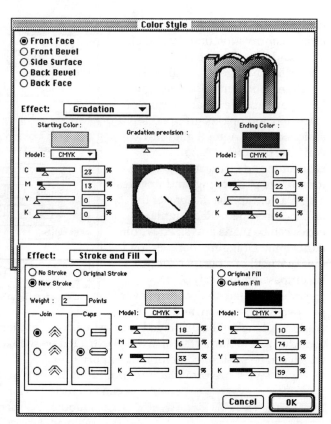

*Right: Colour Style
settings (two
examples)
Below: Style selector*

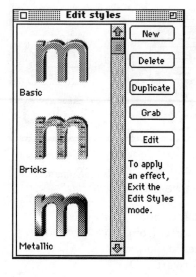

mapped images since this is a vector package. The single light source position is simply set.

addDepth does its job simply and clearly and provides a useful tool for 2-D designers wanting a 3-D element in their work. The application can be expected to be used in conjunction with a standard vector drawing package, such as Adobe Illustrator or Aldus Freehand, but is complete as a stand-alone.

ADOBE DIMENSIONS *v 1.0*

Adobe Systems
UK Distributor: Letraset 071-928-3411

The proliferation of 3-D modelling has created new demands from the graphic designers for tools that enable them to integrate limited modelling facilities with their normal 2-D software. The designer of a label for a wine bottle, for example, could make good use of a program's ability to do image mapping (wrapping the new label around a 3-D bottle in order better to view the effect) but would probably not want to have to come to terms with a full strength modeller. Similarly, a designer working with logos or typography might welcome the opportunity to extrude the images into 3-D forms and light them but again, without the need for a full modeller. At its simplest, the program might be used to add perspective to a piece of 2-D artwork, by rotating it around a 3-D axis. Several applications are now available that do this job and Adobe Dimensions is distinct in that it produces PostScript files rather than pixel and polygon based data. This allows the user not only to import vector based templates created with Bezier curves, for example (from Postscript drawing programs such as Adobe Illustrator and Aldus Freehand), but to export files back to those same programs for subsequent manipulation and editing like any PostScript artwork.

The interface of Adobe Dimensions is kept simple and uses conventions similar to those in the applications familiar to 2-D designers. The manual is clear and brief; less than 100 pages on using the program, plus a 13 page 'Gallery' of first class examples of what the program can do (with a short account of how they were done). The application allows the creation of 3-D objects by extrusion and spinning and includes four primitives (cube, sphere, cone and cylinder). The objects can be manipulated in 3-D and viewpoint, perspective and lighting can be set. Surface properties can be attributed and PostScript images mapped to surfaces. Shading is flat, Gouraud or Phong; reflectance options are ambient, highlight and shininess; viewing is wireframe, filled or shaded.

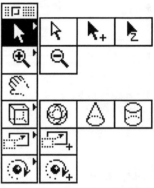

Tool bar with pop-up icons showing

Blend set at 5 (top)
25 (centre)
& 256 (bottom)

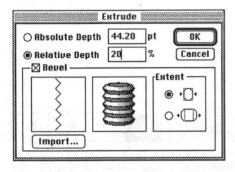

Extrude with bevel

Below: Rotation of cylinder using numerical sliders
Right: Surface property window

The number of blends used in a gradation can be set to achieve a balance between smoothness and file size; this feature is not usually found in a 3D application as it relates specifically to PostScript files. A sequence of images can be generated (between two end frames) for export to drawing or animation programs.

On starting the application, a single window is open with XYZ axis guide in the centre; a status bar above the window reminds us of the current settings and shows the current cursor co-ordinates; the simple tool palette is present (selection modes and z-translation; zoom in/out; move view of worksheet; primitives; scale with/without dialogue; trackball/rotate dialogue); and the standard Apple menu bar sits at the top of the screen. Creation of objects is as expected given the tools available. Of the manipulation tools, the 'rotation with dialogue' seems particularly effective, offering numerical accuracy around each axis combined with interactive movement. Objects can be grouped and transformations repeated to assist manipulation. When bevelling an edge, the bevel template is supported by a 3-D view (showing it applied to a cylinder); there is a comprehensive bevel library and new bevels can

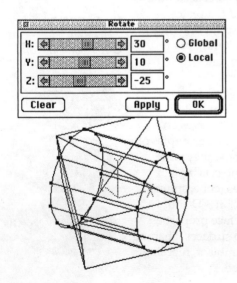

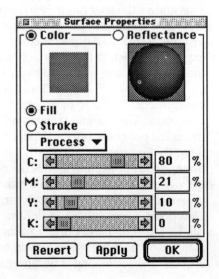

be created and imported. The animated 'rotating cube' cursor, which indicates that a process is being carried out, offers a little novelty but the chime-like 'beep' which announces that a rendering process is finished was soon switched off.

Mapping is a major part of the package's functionality and it works well. The mapping window lets you move through all surfaces in sequence, the currently selected surface being simultaneously indicated on the 3-D model in the work window. The map is imported and tools allow for scaling and placement. It is also made clear which surfaces of the object are visible in its current orientation. In order to create artwork that exactly fits the object, the object's surface (or surfaces) can be exported to a drawing application and used as a guide. When the object is a rectangular box, the artwork can be mapped onto either one surface or all the surfaces at once. The surface orientation can be flipped to map interior surfaces if they are visible.

Adobe Dimensions does not pretend to be a full modelling application but it provides a valuable additional tool for the graphic designer and in a number of situations its vector rendering could offer advantages to some model makers over more standard methods.

Revolve window

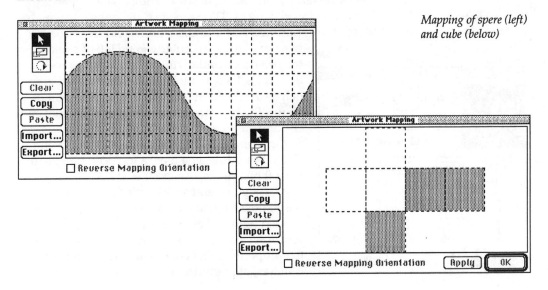

Mapping of spere (left) and cube (below)

MACROMIND THREE-D v1.2

MacroMind/Paracomp
UK distributors: Computers Unlimited 081-200-8282

Lighting type icons

Light information window

The name 'MacroMind Three-D' is potentially misleading since this is not a 3-D modelling program. It probably needn't be described here but it is such an interesting program, and one of general interest to modellers, that it gets a mention. Whilst it does have a set of geometric primitives and can extrude TrueType fonts, it is primarily an animation, rendering and video production tool for the Macintosh. In the context of this book we will mainly consider its function as a renderer of imported models, but if you buy it as a renderer you will also have acquired a very flexible and powerful 3-D animation tool! It includes 'Fireworks', an image processor for digital compositing, and comes with MacroMind Accelerator for viewing smooth animation, and ModelMover for converting several 3-D model formats for use in the application. As well as the necessary manuals, the package has 16 discs and a video tape. The tape is of 'The Three-D Cafe', an animation showing off the application's versatility, and ten of the discs comprise a HyperCard tutorial based on the making of 'The Three-D Cafe', which leaves two discs for the application and four discs for its textures. The manual does a particularly good job of explaining the principles underlying its functions as well as describing its operation, and within the program, help is available either from the Apple menu or by turning the cursor into a help-seeking tool and clicking on the subject of the query.

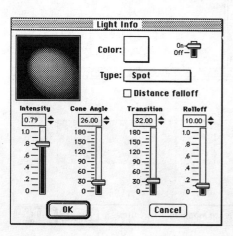

On opening 3DWorks, the main MacroMind Three-D module, you have a tool icon palette to the left of a single, camera view window, a playback panel and a score window, as well as the standard menu bar. More windows can be opened (with usual views) and four views or full screen selected from the menu. The score shows the properties of all objects (including lights and cameras) at points in time along a horizontal track. Since we are ignoring animation here, we can ignore the playback palette and also the time-based element of the script, though this window still has a useful function to play. It can be used to display comprehensive information (position, orientation, shading, etc.) about any object in the scene, including lights and cameras, and provides a convenient central control for accessing many functions and dialogue boxes. (If you are including the time element, a neat detail is that colour changes can be displayed as an harmonic progression between keyframe colours.)

Differing ambient light levels can be set for different objects, and unlimited light sources can be added to the scene. Light sources can be distant lights (shining from an infinite distance), point lights, spot lights or shadowspot lights, the latter being the only one to cast a shadow. A lighting dialogue box has sliders to set intensity, cone angle, transition and rolloff; selectors for light type, colour and falloff (intensity diminishing with distance); and an on/off toggle switch. Lights can be visible or hidden and are positioned with the standard object movement tools, the 'Point at' command being available to point a selected light at a chosen object automatically. Selection of 'Shaded view' gives a rough preview of lighting effect and MacRenderMan is supported. Fog is available, attenuating the object's colour with the background colour and, as an alternative method of depth enhancement, 'Depth cue' works similarly but attenuates to black. The density can be adjusted or even animated.

The standard shading information dialogue boxes offer the opportunity to set the usual surface properties for an object, and switching to the texture shading box allows for the setting of texture, bump and reflection maps together with their type, tiling style and percentile influence on the object. A preview button gives a fairly quick update of the effect of the settings on a standard sphere/box scene. The shading models are, unconventionally, known as: 'Polygon' (= Lambert), 'vertex' (= Gouraud) and 'Pixel' (= Phong). A useful extra control is 'Crease at', which enables an object to maintain both smooth and faceted surfaces

Below: Shading information shown in Score

Below left: Positional information shown in Score

All Values	0
position	
◆ Ambient Light	
◇ x position	0
◇ y position	0
◇ z position	0
◆ Camera 1	
◇ x position	0
◇ y position	0
◇ z position	10
◆ Cone 1	●
◇ x position	-3.8892
◇ y position	2.35293
◇ z position	1.65685
◆ Light 1	●
◇ x position	1.80772
◇ y position	1.38293
◇ z position	0.78253

◆ Cone 1	●
◆ color	
◇ red	1
◇ green	1
◇ blue	1
◇ opacity	0.81001
◆ specular color	
◇ red	0.61998
◇ green	1
◇ blue	1
◇ visible	On
◇ ambient	0.83
◇ diffuse	0.6
◇ specular	0.4
◇ roughness	0.31
◆ texture	●
◇ texture amoun	0.86
◇ texture file	Clouds
◇ texture mappir	Spherical
◇ texture tiling	Repeat
◇ texture u offs	0
◇ texture v offs	0
◇ texture u scal	1
◇ texture v scal	1
◆ reflection	●
◇ reflection amo	0.69
◇ reflection file	Brushed
◆ bump	●
◇ bump height	1
◇ bump file	Stone
◇ bump mapping	Spheric
◇ bump tiling	Repeat
◇ bump u offset	0
◇ bump v offset	0
◇ bump u scale	1
◇ bump v scale	1

221

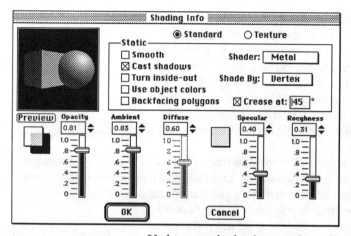

Standard shading information window

Texture information window

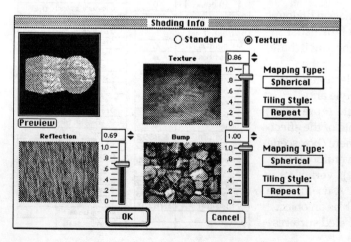

at the same time. Orthogonal, cylindrical, spherical and intrinsic mapping types are available, and three tiling options allow either repeats or for areas outside the map to be black or else for the edge colour of the map to be extended over the rest of the object (the latter being recommended for sticking 'labels' on objects). Animations can be used as maps.

Unfortunately, background rendering is not possible within MacroMind Three-D, although the rendering can continue in the background with other applications running. As a quick preview, it is possible to render a selected part of the image and it is also possible to generate a script from which to render later. The script can be generated in native or RIB form (for MacRenderMan) and by rendering from a script it is possible to open and use the rendering application alone without having MacroMind Three-D open.

Although it does not suit everyone, I like being able to create and/or edit a text script as an alternative way of working. I sometimes find the written form clearer than the subjective tuning that can go on when working interactively on the screen, and like the discipline that it forces on your ideas. Best of all, of course, is to have both options available, as here. When rendering, dithering and anti-aliasing can be toggled on/off.

The 'FireWorks' module of MacroMind Three-D allows post-production effects to be applied to an image or animation, and incorporates the facility of recording to file or to video tape (with the appropriate hardware). Whilst it is a slight distraction from the subject of the book, this functionality has great potential use for some modellers and is therefore briefly described, although its greatest strength is in animation. Compositing (the process of combining separate images into one) is a particularly useful feature for animators, but equally has application for single images. Rendering time is reduced if a background can be composited later rather than included in each rendering calculation (although, if added later, the background image cannot interact with the rest of the scene, such as by being reflected in objects). If a background is to be composited later it is important to be able to preview its relationship to the rest of the scene before that is rendered, and 3DWorks allows for the temporary import of a background image for that reason; this also means that rotascoping is possible (aligning with, or copying from, a sequence of animation background frames).

Blurring in FireWorks

The foreground image (normally) uses an alpha channel to hold transparency information which is used to merge the two images smoothly and the 'blend' function determines the proportion of each of the images in the mix. Boolean operators determine the relationship of the final window to the two images (neither of which need be full window size) and a flexible blurring function can soften images – often useful to give depth to a background. Multiple effects can be used and a script of the instructions for operation(s) undertaken can be saved for application elsewhere. These scripts can also be used by 3DWorks to perform image processing along with rendering.

MacroMind Three-D has strong links with other software in the MacroMind series (such as Director) and any modeller producing animation should consider it seriously.

MAC RENDERMAN *v 1.3*

Pixar
UK distributors: Computers Unlimited 081-200-8282

RenderMan is an important product from Pixar, leaders in computer animation. It was developed through their own use and was used to render (amongst other pieces) 'Tin Toy', which was awarded the first Oscar to be won by a computer animation. It runs on a number of platforms and our version is called MacRenderMan. The value of the application is not just that it is a very good product but that it has been adopted widely as a rendering standard and is supported by many modelling applications. Within Swivel 3D, for instance, there is a direct connection to MacRenderMan which effectively extends Swivel's functionality beyond its own much simpler, built-in rendering capability. Other modellers have the ability to export scene descriptions as RIB (RenderMan Interface Byte-stream) files which can be rendered by RenderMan on any platform supporting it. There are also hardware accelerators available that are tuned to work with RenderMan and give big speed improvements.

The operation of MacRenderMan can be completely invisible to the user but it also offers access at a lower level to anyone prepared to 'get their hands dirty' with a little, gentle programming; this can be either by writing from scratch or, more likely, by editing a file created by a modeller. This is an option that I like to have available so that an application can be entered at several different levels. 'ShowPlace' is also available from Pixar as an easy front-end, allowing the import and arrangement of 3-D objects which are then rendered in RenderMan. This permits the positioning of objects, lights and camera as in a full modelling package, together with the ability to image wrap, using either your own models or 'ClipObjects' from Pixar. (A likely result of the growth of interest in modelling is the development of model libraries, where off-the-shelf models can be used or edited as required.)

MacRenderMan is made up of several components. The RenderMan interface is a language for modellers to communicate with renderers using RIB files; 'PhotoRealistic RenderMan' creates pictures from RIB files (with 'Vector RenderMan' generating wireframes), RenderApp' is for viewing images, managing their display and converting images into standard Macintosh file formats; 'RenderMonitor' renders jobs in the background; and 'ShaderApp' is for creating new 'shaders' (which result in new surface appearances and lighting effects). Dialogue boxes available along the road to creating a final rendered image allow many more parameters to be controlled than on most renderers. You can, for instance, set the sampling rate (effectively – how many separate calculations per pixel), the shading rate (controlling the amount of detail), the bucket size (the size of the area rendered at each step of the process), and the hidden-surface algorithm to be used.

A scene description generated by a modeller will contain precise specification of: the geometry, position and surface appearance of the objects; the position and characteristics of the light sources; and the position, orientation and viewing characteristics of the camera/viewer. Part of the renderer's job of converting this information into an image is that of shading, in which the surface appearance of each object is calculated. In the RenderMan environment 'shaders' are programs written in the RenderMan Shading Language which specify the process used to calculate the appearance of an element in a scene. There are four types of shader: Light source shaders calculate the intensity and colour of light reaching a surface; Surface shaders calculate the light reflected from a surface; Displacement shaders move groups of points on a surface (to create bumps and pits); Atmosphere shaders modify light rays according to atmospheric conditions (such as fog or haze). A library of shaders is provided and this can be supplemented by writing your own or by modifying existing shaders (which can be as simple as changing parameters). The hard-backed manual accompanying the application gives a clear introduction to the structure of shaders, but for serious programming work it is likely that the user will want 'The RenderMan Companion' which is available from book shops or as part of the *MacRenderMan Developers' Stuff* package from Pixar.

RenderMan provides one element of an opportunity to build a modelling, rendering and animating system in parts and gives the creator of a modelling application the option of concentrating on the modeller alone, and outputting files to a very high class renderer. It also provides the possibility of a standard which could be used by bureaux to render files sent to them by the users of modellers.

LIFE FORMS *v1.0*
MacroMind/Paracomp
UK distributors: Computers Unlimited   081-200-8282

Life Forms is not really a modelling package but it is such an intriguing product and of potential interest to so many of those involved in modelling that it is briefly described here. It was developed through the cooperation of people from the disciplines of computing and choreography, and is intended primarily as a program for animating the human figure. It is being used as a design tool by a number of dance companies.

Figure editor

In the context of this book its main interest is that it provides human figures which can be easily manipulated into any position (and animated through any movement) and could be used in conjunction with a model built elsewhere through its links to Swivel 3D or composited with material from other sources. Since many modelling jobs are to create objects which interface with humans (e.g. buildings), it can often be useful to include human figures in presentations of the object, or perhaps even to have figures strolling about in an animated presentation. It might even be possible to use the figure for ergonomic studies relating to the design.

The package provides a standard figure which can be sized and comprehensively animated, and includes a simple figure which can be loaded into Swivel 3D and re-proportioned. It can also provide a control script for figures created in Swivel 3D that follow the joint map of the Life Forms figure; full details of which are given.

Within Life Forms the figure can be shown either as an outline or as a contour figure, and it can be exported to Swivel 3D or MacroMind 3D for full rendering within a scene. Animations can also be exported to MacroMind Director and FilmMaker.

Simple, interactive controls allow the figure to be manipulated very intuitively (like an artist's lay figure) and positioned on the Life Forms stage. Once key positions in a movement cycle have been established, the program creates a smooth animation with full control over timing.

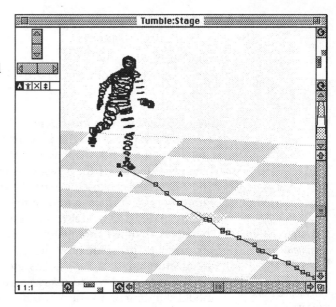

Life Form stage

Clones can be made and separately controlled so that a crowd of autonomous people can soon fill the screen. I suspect that many a designer has avoided including 3-D human figures in his work because of the complexity of dealing with them, but it is possible that this program could, in some cases, provide the answer. The figure and the movement are clearly computer-generated, but it would be interesting to spend some time considering how to make it less symmetrical, and more like the real, lumpy world.

This is a unique program for which many people will have no use whatever but for a few it could give rise to fresh developments (though even if you don't find much practical use for it, it is great fun to use). I, for one, have plans for a project based on Life Forms which only await some spare time.

Animation control panel (top) and timeline

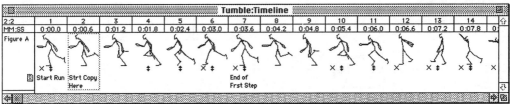

TOUCH-3D

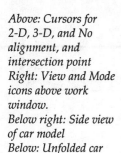

Lundström Design
UK distributors: Gomark 071-731-7930

A new program with great potential for modellers is Touch-3D. It accepts the input of standard 3-D files and allows the model to be 'unfolded' into a flat shape which can be printed out. The print can then be folded along the creases to make a real world 3-D model. The 2-D model can also be exported to programs such as Adobe Photoshop for surface treatment to be added.

The folded 3-D model will necessarily be faceted and can, therefore, obviously not match a smoothly curved surface. This need not present a problem, however, as many objects (such as architectural models, set designs, etc.) are often faceted anyway and the ability to quickly and easily move from a screen image to a model standing on the desk could often prove very valuable. At the time of writing I have only seen a demonstration of the application and have not been able to check its ability to handle complex objects, which would test it to the limit. It is certainly worth looking out for.

Above: Cursors for 2-D, 3-D, and No alignment, and intersection point
Right: View and Mode icons above work window.
Below right: Side view of car model
Below: Unfolded car

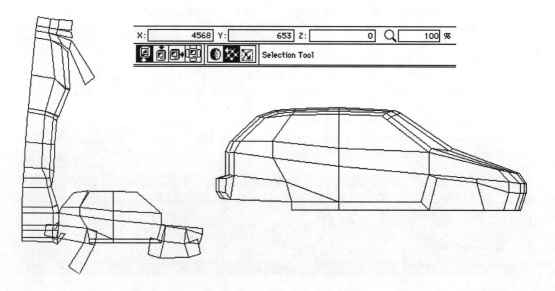

DeBABELIZER v1.4.02

Equilibrium
UK distributor: Letraset 071-928-3411

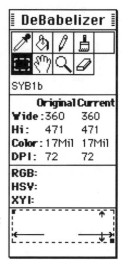

SYB1b

	Original	Current
Wide :	360	360
Hi :	471	471
Color :	17Mil	17Mil
DPI :	72	72
RGB:		
HSV:		
XYI:		

DeBabelizer is a unique piece of software that anyone involved with visual applications on the Macintosh should know about. It is described as a graphics processing toolbox and enables the user to automate many repetitive tasks and to convert a wide range of files between different platforms. In its current form it handles only bit-mapped graphics (except object PICT files) and animation formats but it is rumoured that a future version will also handle 3-D files. Since it does not handle 3-D files yet it might not seem particularly useful to a modeller, but since the end product of a modelling project is often a bit-mapped image or animation, it is well worth looking at now. Although Mac users might like to pretend that other machines are too inferior to bother with, in the real world it can be very important to be able to communicate with the beasts, and DeBabelizer lets you convert both ways between DOS/Windows, Amiga, Atari, Silicon Graphics, Sun Microsystems, X Windows and other general file types (such as Abekas and Raw RGB). You can spread your images throughout the computer world, not merely the Macintosh community.

Above: Tool/info. window
Below: Open/preview window

DeBabelizer can be switched between a 'simple' mode, which deals with file conversion and hides the user from the subtle depths of the program, and an 'advanced' mode which gives the user access to the full power of the

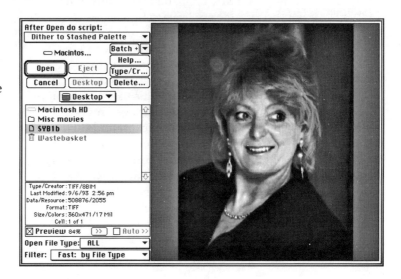

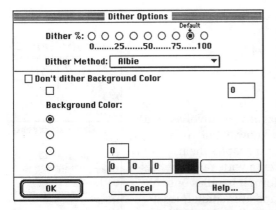

Dither Options

Dither %: ○ ○ ○ ○ ○ ○ ◉ ○
0........25.......50.......75......100

Dither Method: [Albie ▼]

☐ Don't dither Background Color
☐   [0]

Background Color:
◉
○
○   [0]
○   [0] [0] [0] ■ [   ]

[OK]   [Cancel]   [Help...]

Above: Dither options window
Right: File formats handled
Below: Palette options

16 Grays
256 Grays
Apple Icon Colors
Apple][(8 colors)
Apple][DHR (16 colors)
Apple][GS (Super Hi Res)
C64
IBM CGA 1
IBM CGA 2
IBM CGA 3
IBM EGA fixed
IBM EGA flex
Imagewriter II Colors
Mac default 16 colors
✓Mac default 256 colors
Mac old 8
Monochrome
The Stashed Palette
The Super Palette
Windows Paintbrush 16
Windows Paintbrush 256

application. In its full mode it can batch process from scripts, which means that the process (or processes) to be enacted on an image can be defined and then a specified batch of files can be similarly processed without the operator needing to intervene. The script might convert files from Mac to Windows, cropping each image, adding the company name in the bottom right corner of each image, and reducing and optimising their palettes to suit the receiving program. This is, of course, a very useful thing to be able to do with all the frames of an animation. There is a basic tool palette for minor touching up work within the program and DeBabelizer can access Photoshop plug-ins to use on images.

The uses of DeBabelizer will be considered more fully in a Mac animation book, but some idea of its versatility as a production tool can be gauged from the examples given in the booklet accompanying the program. Nineteen commercial users describe the uses to which they put the package, from cleaning out backgrounds of chromakeyed images to palette reduction (e.g. from 24-bit scans to 16 colour computer games pictures) or standardisation (deriving a single palette for a number of images with different palettes), with a clear emphasis on productivity.

Apple][
BMP: Paintbrush
BOB
C64
ANM: IBM DeluxePaint Anim
FLI,FLC: IBM Autodesk
GIF
Dr. Halo CUT: IBM
IMG:IBM GEM
LBM,IFF,HAM,CDI:Amiga,IBM
Lotus PIC: IBM
✓MacPaint
MSP:IBM Microsoft Paint
NEO,Degas,Spectrum:Atari
PCP:IBM
PCX:IBM
Photoshop™
PICT,SCRN,EPSF,PICS,Scrapbook
Pictor:IBM
Pixar
PixelPaint
QDV
QuickTime Movie
Raw Custom
Raw RGB
RIFF
RLE: Compuserve
SGI:Silicon Graphics
SUN
Targa
TIFF
Thunderscan
WPG Word Perfect
X Windows Screen Dump

OTHER RELEVANT SOFTWARE

It was made clear earlier that the software described has been chosen to indicate something of the range available. The choice ,therefore, should not be seen as a recommendation of these applications over those not mentioned. Amongst the modellers not mentioned are a number of specialist products such as 'QuickSurf', a NURBS-based surface modeller which connects to a five-axis milling machine for workshop production; 'MacSurf' for ship and yacht modelling; and 'AVA' a 2-D/3-D package for use by textiles designers which incorporates special fabric draping facilities. Other specialist software can be used in conjunction with modellers, such as 'Tree Pro' by Onyx (Gomark) which creates very effective, parametrically produced 3-D images of trees that an architect might 'plant' on his modelled site.

It is likely that the modeller/renderer will be supported by other software, either as part of the modelling process or as a post-production tool. Applications such as Aldus Freehand and Adobe Illustrator provide sophisticated vector drawing tools for creating 2-D work that can be variously used by modellers as templates for 3-D objects or as PostScript image maps. The applications can also import files from many modellers for subsequent manipulation. Bit-mapped paint packages such as 'Painter' and 'MacPaint' provide the facility to create imagery for mapping and can be used for post-production work on pictures exported from modellers. 'PhotoShop' is a widely-used image manipulation package that tends to become indispensable, particularly at the post-production stage, and incorporates tools that are particularly designed for dealing with photographic images. 'Jag' does sophisticated post-production anti-aliasing which can be substituted for anti-aliasing in the modeller (though not in an alpha channel) and 'Morph' does metamorphic transformations of 2-D images which might provide an alternative to 3-D transformations in the modeller. If the models are to be used in an animation or presentation, then a product like 'MacroMind Director' or the ubiquitous 'HyperCard' might be needed, or perhaps 'Premiere' as a video/QuickTime editor.

There are also a number of programming languages available on the Mac with which you can build your own modeller or renderer! Whilst this might seem daunting, there are a number of books to help you through such an exercise. A basic ray tracer, for instance, is not unduly complicated and I found the designing of a simple, dynamic particle system instructive, useful and fun. Certainly it is worth learning how to use any scripting facilities built into your package, as this offers the opportunity of customising operations for maximum efficiency. Apple has now issued a scripting language called AppleScript which allows you to produce a script either from a series of actions or by simple, written programming. As Mac applications increasingly add support for AppleScript, so it will be possible to create and run scripts which can access facilities from different packages. These can effectively be 'bolted together' to create an application customised for your particular task.

APPENDIX 2

GLOSSARY OF TERMS

1-Dimensional When referring to spatial dimensions: having length but no breadth, such as a straight line.

2-Dimensional (2-D) When referring to spatial dimensions: having two dimensions (length and breadth, or length and height), such as a plane.

2 1/2-Dimensional (2 1/2-D) Usually referring to an animation created in several flat layers to give some of the depth effects of true 3-D.

3-Dimensional (3-D) When referring to spatial dimensions: having three dimensions (length, breadth and height), such as an object.

3-Space Three-dimensional space.

4-Dimensional Usually referring to three spatial dimensions plus the added dimension of time.

AI Artificial Intelligence is involved with building features associated with natural intelligence into machines.

Aliasing (See Spatial aliasing, Temporal aliasing)

Anti-aliasing The removal of aliasing artefacts, most commonly involving the smoothing of jagged edges on output displays.

Artefact Used to describe some part of the image which has been inadvertently created, or is unsatisfactory as a result of deficiencies in the system, and constitutes an error.

ASCII (pronounced 'askey') An internationally agreed set of characters as produced by a standard keyboard.

Axis The line about which an object rotates.

B-rep Boundary Representation method for creating objects by defining a polygonised surface mesh.

Back-face culling A simple, but crude, hidden line removal method.

Bezier Invented a mathematical description of a curve, based on the definition of a few points or use in the car industry. It is widely used in computer graphics, often in a context where the curve is to be 'tuned' interactively, to create 2-D lines, 2-D and 3-D paths and 3-D surfaces.

Bicubic patch A means of describing a curved surface using cubic functions. A surface may be divided into a number of patches with suitable continuity at boundaries.

Bit From 'binary digit'. The basic unit of computer information (which can be represented by either 0 or 1).

Bit map The representation of the screen image in memory, stored as pixel intensities.

Boolean operations Operations based on the logical relationships of AND, OR and NOT (union, difference and intersection). In CSG modelling, for instance, the logical operators can be used to join or cut existing objects into new objects.

Bounding box A simple space frame which can act as a temporary substitute for a more complex object in order to simplify calculations when a quick approximation (of a movement, for example) is needed.

Buffer An area of memory (which may be internal or external) temporarily reserved to hold information which is currently required. A frame buffer, for example, holds the displayed image as a matrix of intensity values.

Bump mapping By perturbing surface normals across a flat surface, suitable rendering algorithms will produce what appears a bumpy surface.

Byte A set of (usually eight) contiguous bits.

Cartesian coordinates Two-dimensional points which can be located by reference to calibrated horizontal (X) and vertical (Y) axes. In three dimensions an additional axis (Z) establishes depth.

Canonical position The expected, default position of an object on creation and before it is moved. Normally centred on the origin and with key facets orthogonal to axes.

Mapping (See Bump mapping, Image mapping, Reflection mapping, Texture mapping.)

Metamorphosis A change of physical form, often easily animated by interpolation between the start and end forms.

MIPS Million Instructions Per Second.

Modelling The construction of objects in a scene prior to rendering (or choreographing movement).

Mouse A common input device which fits in the palm of the hand and is rolled over a flat horizontal surface to control the movement of a screen cursor.

MPEG algorithm Motion Picture Experts Group algorithm for data compression of motion picture images.

Multimedia A term used to describe the mixed use of still and moving visual media, together with sound, normally under the control of a computer.

Multi-tasking The ability of some computers to work on several tasks at the same time. In fact, although things appear to be happening at the same time, the machine is normally avail able CPU time. Not to be confused with parallel computing.

Non-interlaced A raster scan in which each scan line is refreshed on each pass (See Interlaced).

NURB Non-Uniform Rational B-spline. A type of B-spline which is particularly flexible in interactive use.

Normal (See Surface normal)

NTSC Broadcast standard used in USA and Japan.

Object orientated Describes a type of programming language, growing in popularity, in which program elements are considered as separate objects which can communicate with one another. The term is also used to refer to an image which is defined as a number of separate parts and their relationships to one another (as opposed to a raster image).

Object space The 3-D space of the object's world.

Origin The point at the centre of a coordinate system where X,Y and Z all equal zero.

OS Operating System.

Painters' algorithm A simple method of removing hidden surfaces by overpainting.

Paint system An image creation system which simulates traditional materials used for drawing and painting

Clock rate The rate at which operations are carried out by the CPU.

Constraints Limitations applied, particularly to the movement of an object.

Continuity The degree of smoothness with which line and surface sections join.

Convex hull The 'skin' created by enclosing all the extreme points of an object.

Coordinates (See Cartesian coordinates, Polar coordinates and Spherical coordinates.)

Cosine shading (See Lambert shading.)

CPU Central Processing Unit. The heart of the computer.

CSG Constructive Solid Geometry. A modelling method in which primitives, such as cubes and spheres, are combined using Boolean operations.

Data compression The algorithmic reduction in size of data files.

Default state The state in which something will exist until it is consciously changed.

Degrees of freedom of movement The number of singular ways in which an object can move. For example, a particle has three degrees of freedom of movement (along X,Y or Z), a rigid body has six (along X,Y and Z plus rotation around X,Y andZ).

Desktop A visual metaphor used in a WIMP environment whereby the VDU screen is organised as if it were a real desktop.

Digitiser (3-D) A device for acquiring and inputting spatial data about the surface of an object.

Digitising tablet An input device with a flat, sensitive surface which can be drawn on with a stylus in the manner of a pencil and paper. A puck may be used to acquire 2-D coordinates from drawings aligned on the tablet.

Disc drive A secondary storage device in which data are saved on a removable rotating disc (which can be conveniently stored or used to transfer data between computers). The most common storage medium is still magnetic.

Dithering One means of simulating a larger palette of colours than is actually available.

DMA Direct Memory Access.

DRAM Dynamic Random Access Memory.

DTV Desktop Video.

DVI Digital Video Interactive technology.

Dynamics   The branch of mechanics dealing with the way masses move under the influence of forces and torques. In creasingly used to drive animations by the application of physical laws (See Kinematics).

Expert system Provides a means of solving 'significant' problems by applying rules to a data bank of relevant information culled from human experts in the field concerned.

Extrusion A swept surface method of modelling, where a 2-D template is dragged through 3-space along a path, in the simplest case at right angles to the plane of the template.

Facet A planar surface which constitutes one face of a polygonised model.

FFD Free Form Deformation. A method of deforming an object by applying transformations to a cage of control points. Objects can be created by using FFDs on primitives, and the same principles can be used to animate a change of shape.

Firmware The embodiment in hardware of a function normally associated with software. For example, some frequently used rendering algorithms might be built into a chip in order to gain substantial speed increases.

FLOPS FLoating Point Operations per Second.

Fractal A term used to describe the self-similarity of some phenomena when viewed at different levels of detail. The principle is typically used in computer graphics to generate mountains, clouds and such like, from a very small data base.

Frame buffer A piece of specialised memory (which may be internal or external) reserved to hold one or more images for quick access and/or processing.

GUI Graphical User Interface.

Gouraud shading A shading model which improves on Lambert shading by smoothing intensity across surfaces.

Granularity A rough description of the level of detail at which an operation is conducted (e.g. rough-grained = low level of detail, fine-grained = high level of detail).

Hard disc A sealed unit for secondary storage which is costructed internally like tiers of disc drives. It combines larger storage space (typically) and relatively quick access.

Hardcopy Output in permanent form such as on paper or film.

Hardware Refers to the physical components of a computer system i.e. the boxes that sit on your desk.

HCI Human Computer Interface. The boundary between the machine and the user at which they communicate with one another.

Hidden line/surface The removal of lines or surfaces which we would expect to be obscured when viewed from a specified direction.

High level In this context, a high level operation is one in which the operator does not need to involve himself with the details of how the operation is carried out. (See Low level.)

IFS Iterated Function System. Used to derive a simple set of fractal rules from complex data, such as an image, and thus allow potentially extreme data compression.

Image mapping A means of applying a picture to a surface or of wrapping a picture around an object.

Interactive Allowing the user to respond to the running of an application with fresh input while it is in progress.

Interlaced A raster scan in which alternate scan lines are re freshed on each pass. This means that less information needs to be handled at any one moment than in a non-interlaced scan but that the complete image is refreshed less often.

I/O Input/output.

Iteration Repetition, usually of a piece of a computer program   (in which case it is called a loop). Something that computers are particularly good at doing.

Jaggies An informal term for the jagged lines in a pixelated image which it is usually desirable to minimise.

JPEG algorithm Joint Photographic Experts Group algorithm for data compression of still images.

Lambert shading A basic shading model in which each facet is evenly shaded according to the angle at which the light hits it.

Lathe A term sometimes used instead of 'spin'.

Lofting Connecting cross-sections through an object by triangulating a surface between their edges.

Low level A level of operation where the operator is required to become involved with the detail of the machine or process. (See High level.)

Mach banding A phenomenon in which a smoothly shaded surface appears to have dark streaks on it.

PAL Broadcast standard used in much of Europe.

Palette The range of colours available. Dependent on hardware and software constraints, the range can stretch from 2 to more than 16,000,000.

Path The course along which something moves.

Parallel architecture A design of computer in which a number of tasks can be carried out simultaneously, i.e. in parallel'. Some times referred to as 'non-von' since it is a departure from the traditional von Neumann computer architecture.

Parallel processing The simultaneous processing carried out in a parallel computer (See Parallel architecture).

Particle A single point in 3-space. Theoretically infinitely small, but often treated as a small mass limited to three degrees of freedom of movement.

Particle system A system containing a number of particles (typically between ten thousand and a million) which might be used to model 'soft' objects or to animate flow through a medium, for example.

PC Personal Computer. Tends to be used to refer to IBM compatible machines.

PDL Page Description Language, e.g. PostScript.

PHIGS Programmers' Hierarchical Interactive Graphics System. A 3-D graphics standard established by the American National Standards Institute (ANSI).

Physically based modelling The representation of a model in terms of its physical attributes, such as mass, and forces. Such a model can be controlled by the application of the laws of physics and is thus ideal for simulation.

Phong shading A smooth shading method which incorporates specular highlights.

Pixel From 'picture element', the smallest element out of which a screen display is made.

Plotter An output device in which a pen, or selection of pens, is raised and lowered whilst being carried across the surface of a piece of paper. Traditionally associated with engineering and architectural drawing.

Polar co-ordinates A point in two dimensions can be defined by its distance from the origin and the angle between the positive X axis and a line from the origin to the point.

Polygon A planar figure bounded by straight sides.

Precision errors Errors arising from the inability of the computer accurately to store numbers beyond a certain length. If the result of a calculation is a long decimal number the machine might need to truncat it for storage, thus introducing a small error which could become exaggerated in further calculations.

Primitive A simple object (such as a cube or sphere) which is provided as a basic 3-D unit in a modelling system.

Puck A device similar to a mouse but with a cross-hair sight for accurate alignment, used for the input of points (for instance from a drawing). (See Digitising tablet)

Radiosity An effective but ponderous shading method which is particularly good at dealing with diffuse light.

RAM Random Access Memory.

Raster image Often used to describe a pixel based image (in which the image is recorded as a collection of pixel intensities) as opposed to one which is vector based (and can therefore be displayed at the best resolution of the output device).

Raster scan The scanning of a monitor screen by an electronbeam.

Ray tracing A simple, though time-consuming, rendering method which produces 'realistic' shadows and reflections.

Real time A one to one relationship between display time and real-life time.

Reflection mapping A means of applying a picture of an object's surroundings (or imaginary surroundings) to its surface in order to simulate reflection.

Refresh rate The rate at which an image is redrawn on a screen.

Render To make the internal mathematical model of a scene visible. Usually refers to the algorithmic realisation of the effects of lighting, surface colour, texture, and reflection.

Resolution Although a number of factors affect resolution, it is generally taken to describe the apparent level of detail an output device is capable of resolving.

RGB A colour system where all colours are defined as a mixture of red, green and blue (as in a TV).

RISC Reduced Instruction-Set Computing.

ROM Read-Only Memory.

Scanner A 2-D image input device which scans an image (using similar technology to a photocopier).

Screen space The two dimensional space of the screen image. (See Object space)

SECAM Broadcast standard used in France, Russia and elsewhere.

SIGGRAPH ACM (Association of Computing Machinery) Special Interest Group in Graphics.

SIMD Single Instruction Multiple Data. An architecture for parallel processing.

Soft modelling The modelling of non-geometric, often natural, forms.

Software Refers to the programs, expressed in machine readable language, that control the hardware.

Solid texture Texture pattern running right through the volume of the object rather than just on its surface.

Spatial aliasing A problem of discontinuity arising from trying to match correct locations to the nearest available point on an output device. See jaggies.

Spatial occupancy enumeration A volume modelling method in which an object is defined by the presence or absence of voxels.

Spherical coordinates An extension of the polar coordinate system which deals with 3-D by incorporating an extra angular measurement.

Spline A flexible strip of wood used to create smooth curves (originally in shipbuilding), the same result is now achieved mathematically.

Spinning Process of creating a swept surface by rotation of a 2-D template around an axis.

Staircasing (See Jaggies)

Stochastic Random within prescribed limits. Stochastics are often employed to produce variations on a basic theme.

Stylus A pen-like device used in conjunction with a digitising tablet, mainly used for the freehand creation imag creation.

Sub-pixel Theoretical division of a pixel into smaller units for the purpose of calculations.

Super sampling Conducting calculations at a finer resolution than the output device will be able to implement. Used as a means of dealing with aliasing by sampling at a sub-pixel level.

Surface normal A vector orthogonal to a surface. Central to many computer graphics calculations.

Swept surface A 3-D surface created by passing a 2-D template through 3-space.

Temporal aliasing A problem of discontinuity arising from trying to match accurate moments in time to the nearest available time-point on an output device.

Teleological modelling An extension of physically based modelling to include goal-orientation. The attributes of an object include a knowledge of how it should act.

Texture mapping Used to describe both the wrapping of a 2-D representation of texture onto a surface in object space (although this might be better referred to as image mapping) and the transfer of an external bump map to a surface.

Texture space The space inhabited by the 3-D textural information used in solid texturing (where the texture runs through the object like grain through wood).

Texel TEXture ELement. A single unit of texture (which might be compared with a pixel or a voxel).

Transformation The alteration of shapes or objects by applying geometrical rules to their coordinates, e.g. translation (movement in a straight line), scaling and rotation.

Transputer A chip for parallel processing, containing its own memory and processing unit.

Triangulation Division of a surface into triangular facets. The division is often required because a triangular facet is necessarily planar, and non-planar facets would create problems during other calculations.

VDU Visual Display Unit. Normally refers to the monitor screen.

Vector Usually refers to the storage of image data in terms of relative measurements (which can therefore be displayed at the best resolution of the output device) as opposed to storage of an image in terms of pixel intensities. In mathematics a vector is a value having magnitude and direction, and in modelling a point can be represented by a vector and transformed using matrices.

Vertex A point in 2-D or 3-D space which is connected to others in order to build shapes or facets.

Viewing transformation The mathematical conversion of 3-D information so that it can be presented in 2-D, as if viewed from a given point (with perspective).

Virtual Appearing to be something it is not. Hence virtual memory describes the use of secondary storage as if it were main memory and virtual reality describes a simulated situation which aims to be indistinguishable from one of real life.

Visualisation Making complex information (often being large quantities of scientific data) understandable through presentation in a visual form.

Volume visualisation The rendering of 3-D volumes by voxel methods (See Spatial occupancy enumeration).

Von Neumann architecture The traditional computer architecture in which operations are carried out sequentially (as opposed to concurrently).

Voxel From 'volume element'. A cubic unit of 3-D volume defined at a size appropriate to the required resolution, sometimes described as the 3-D equivalent of a pixel.

VR Virtual Reality (See Virtual.)

WIMP Windows, Icons, Menus and Pointers used in an interface.

Wireframe A representation of an object using only the edges of its constituent polygons.

WORM Write Once Read Many. Refers to a storage device from which information can be read but to which it cannot be written.

WYSIWYG What You See Is What You Get. Describes a system where the screen representation exactly represents the hardcopy output. The two are otherwise often not the same since the device resolution determines how accurately images can be shown and this represents a common problem in many graphics situations (such as DTP).

X-axis The horizontal axis in a Cartesian coordinate system.

Y-axis The vertical axis in a Cartesian coordinate system.

Z-axis The axis representing the dimension of depth in a 3-D Cartesian coordinate system. In its most usual presentation the Z-axis can be thought of as going back at right angles to the vertical plane on which the X- and Y-axes exist. (This is a left-handed system. In a right-handed system the Z-axis would come forward from the XY plane.)

Z-buffer An area of memory holding the depth (Z) values of each surface as represented at each pixel location.

Zel Occasionally used to refer to a unit of depth.

BIBLIOGRAPHY

SOME SUGGESTED READING

On the whole field of computer graphics:
Computer Graphics
Vince (Design Council, 92)
Computer Graphics - principles and practice
Foley (Addison-Wesley, 90)

Particularly relevant to 3D:
Fundamentals of Three-dimensional Computer Graphics
Watt (Addison-Wesley, 89)
Principles of Computer-aided Design
Rooney (Pitman Publishing/Open University, 87)
Computational Geometry for Design and Manufacture
Faux (Ellis Horwood, 79)
A Programmer's Geometry
Bowyer (Butterworths, 83)

On animation (particularly 3D):
The Art and Science of Computer Animation
Mealing (Intellect, 92)

On the Macintosh:
The Little Mac Book
Williams (Peachpit Press, 91)
The Big Mac Book
(Salkind (Que Corporation, 92)

For reference:
Que's Computer Users' Dictionary
Pfaffenberger (Que Corporation, 90)
MacIndex (an index of UK dealers/consultants/bureaux/etc.)
(TPD Publishing)
Hardcopy - The Macintosh Book Catalogue
(Computer Generation Ltd.)

Magazines:
MacUser   *Mac specific*
MacWorld   *Mac specific*
CAD/CAM   *computer aided design & manufacture*
XYZ   *creative design & technology*
Byte   *general computing*

INDEX